REAL-TIME UNIX® SYSTEMS
Design and Application Guide

THE KLUWER INTERNATIONAL SERIES
IN ENGINEERING AND COMPUTER SCIENCE

REAL-TIME SYSTEMS

Consulting Editor

John A. Stankovic

REAL-TIME UNIX® SYSTEMS
Design and Application Guide

by

Authors

Borko Furht

Dan Grostick

David Gluch

Guy Rabbat

John Parker

Meg McRoberts

Modular Computer Systems, Inc.

SPRINGER SCIENCE+BUSINESS MEDIA, LLC

Library of Congress Cataloging-in-Publication Data

Real-time UNIX systems : design and application guide / by authors
Borko Furht ... [et al.].
p.cm. — (The Kluwer international series in engineering and
computer science ; SECS 121. Real-time systems)
Includes bibliographical references and index.
ISBN 978-1-4613-6777-2 ISBN 978-1-4615-3978-0 (eBook)
DOI 10.1007/978-1-4615-3978-0
1. UNIX (Computer operating system) 2. Real-time data processing.
I. Furht, Borivoje. II. Series: Kluwer international series in
engineering and computer science ; SECS 121. III. Series: Kluwer
international series in engineering and computer science. Real-time
systems.
QA76.76.063R43 1991
005.4'3—dc20 90-49063
CIP

Originally published by Kluwer Academic Publishers in 1991
Softcover reprint of the hardcover 1st edition 1991

Printed on acid-free paper.

This book is dedicated to the members of the REAL/IX™ development team at Modular Computer Systems, Inc., whose tireless efforts and expertise made the REAL/IX operating system a reality.

REGISTERED TRADEMARK INFORMATION

Table of Contents

List of Figures..xi
List of Tables..xvii
Contributing Authors..xix
Foreword..xxi
Preface..xxiii
Acknowledgements..xxv

Chapter 1 Introduction to Real-Time Computing................1

1.1 Definition and Classification of Real-Time Computer Systems.1
1.2 Computer Requirements for Real-Time Applications...............4
1.3 Systems Issues..12
1.4 Real-Time Measures..21
1.4.1 Rhealstone Metric..21
1.4.2 Process Dispatch Latency Time..26
1.4.3 Tri-Dimensional Measure..27
1.4.4 The Real/Stone Benchmark..30
1.5 Model of an Open Real-Time System..33

Chapter 2 Real-Time Operating Systems........................37

2.1 Requirements for Real-Time Operating Systems...................37
2.2 Real-Time UNIX Operating Systems..40
2.2.1 The UNIX System and Real-Time..40
2.2.2 Real-Time UNIX Standards..41
2.2.3 Real-Time UNIX Implementations..44

Chapter 3 Concept of a Fully Preemptive UNIX Operating System..49

3.1 System Concept..49
3.2 Process Subsystem..55
3.2.1 Process Concept..55
3.2.2 Process Creation and Termination..57
3.2.3 Forking Child Processes..57
3.2.4 Waiting for a Child Process to Terminate.................58

3.2.5 Process States 58
3.3 Memory Management 59
3.3.1 Data Structures 59
3.3.2 Paging 62
3.3.3 Allocating Memory 63
3.3.4 Locking Pages in Memory 64
3.4 Process Scheduling 64
3.4.1 Data Structure Integrity 68
3.4.2 Timers 70
3.5 Interprocess Communication 73
3.5.1 Signal Mechanism 73
3.5.2 Common Event Notification 75
3.5.3 Shared Memory 76
3.5.4 User-Level Semaphores 77
3.6 File Subsystem 77
3.6.1 File Types 77
3.6.2 File Listings 78
3.6.3 File Permissions 79
3.6.4 User View of a File System 80
3.6.5 Accessing Files in Programs 82
3.6.6 File System Structure 87
3.6.7 Accessing Data Storage Blocks 91
3.6.8 Accessing Free Inodes and Data Blocks 95
3.6.9 File System Access Tables 96
3.6.10 Using the File Access Tables 99
3.7 I/O Subsystem 101
3.7.1 Device I/O 101
3.7.2 I/O Transfer Methods 104
3.7.3 Initiating I/O Operations 105
3.7.4 Device Interrupts 107
3.7.5 Drivers for Real-Time Applications 110

Chapter 4 Designing Real-Time Applications 113

4.1 Programming Guidelines 113
4.1.1 Real-Time Program Structure 114
4.1.2 Development Procedure 115
4.1.3 Using System Calls 118
4.1.4 Performance Hints 119
4.2 Scheduling Processes 120
4.2.1 Selecting Process Priorities 122
4.2.2 Setting Real-Time Privileges 123
4.2.3 Changing Process Priority 124
4.2.4 Monitoring the Run Queue 127
4.2.5 Real-Time Timers 128
4.3 Real-Time Memory Allocation 137
4.3.1 Controlling Memory Allocation 138
4.3.2 Locking Pages into Memory 139

4.3.3 Example Program: Preallocating Memory for a Process ... 140
4.3.4 Example Program: Handling Real-Time Memory Violations ... 143
4.4 Interprocess Communications: Pipes, Signals and Events ... 144
4.4.1 Pipes and Named Pipes ... 144
4.4.2 Signals ... 145
4.4.3 Common Event Notification Mechanism ... 146
4.5 Interprocess Communications Using Shared Memory ... 151
4.5.1 Using Shared Memory ... 154
4.5.2 Creating a Shared Memory Segment ... 155
4.5.3 Allocating a Physical Shared Memory Segment ... 157
4.5.4 Controlling Shared Memory ... 162
4.5.5 Attaching and Detaching a Shared Memory Segment ... 168
4.5.6 Getting Physical Shared Memory Segment ... 173
4.5.7 Checking the Status of a Shared Memory Segment ... 176
4.6 Interprocess Communications Using Semaphores ... 177
4.6.1 Creating a Semaphore Structure and Array ... 180
4.6.2 Controlling Semaphores ... 186
4.6.3 Operations on Semaphores ... 196
4.6.4 Using Binary Semaphores ... 201
4.7 Interprocess Communications Using Messages ... 208
4.7.1 Creating Message Queues ... 209
4.7.2 Controlling Message Queues ... 214
4.7.3 Message Operations ... 220
4.8 Using Files ... 229
4.8.1 Fast File System ... 229
4.8.2 Creating Files and File Systems ... 230
4.8.3 Preallocating File Space ... 230
4.8.4 Bypassing the Buffer Cache ... 231
4.8.5 Asynchronous File I/O ... 232
4.8.6 Using Both Synchronous and Asynchronous I/O on a File ... 235
4.8.7 Synchronizing Disk Access ... 235
4.9 Interfacing Devices ... 236
4.9.1 Asynchronous I/O Operations ... 236
4.9.2 Traditional UNIX System Interrupts ... 238
4.9.3 Connected Interrupts ... 239
4.9.4 Direct I/O ... 249
4.10 Writing System Calls ... 251
4.10.1 Overview of System Calls ... 251
4.10.2 Guidelines for Writing System Calls ... 252
4.10.3 Installing System Calls in the Kernel ... 252
4.10.4 Accessing User-Defined System Calls ... 255
4.11 Porting Applications ... 257
4.11.1 Porting SVID-Compatible Applications ... 258
4.11.2 Porting from Proprietary Operating Systems ... 259
4.12 Performance Management ... 261
4.12.1 Creating an Efficient Environment ... 262

4.12.2 Maintaining System Efficiency 265
4.12.3 Solving Performance Problems 266
4.12.4 Measuring Performance 266
4.12.5 Performance Evaluation of the REAL/IX System 269

Chapter 5 Case Studies 273

5.1 The Data Acquisition and Space Shuttle Launch Control System at NASA Kennedy Space Center 273
5.1.1 The Data Acquisition System 275
5.1.2 The Application Processing System 286
5.2 The Communication Processor at Jet Propulsion Laboratory. 292

Bibliography 307
Index 313

List of Figures

Figure 1.1 Response-time requirements for real-time applications 2
Figure 1.2 Fixed priority versus deadline scheduling 3
Figure 1.3 Classification schema for real-time systems 4
Figure 1.4 Typical computer control system for metal industry applications 7
Figure 1.5 Typical computer system configuration for plant monitoring and control of a fossil power plant 8
Figure 1.6 A typical distributed waste water plant monitoring and control system 9
Figure 1.7 A typical centralized HVAC energy management system 10
Figure 1.8 The architecture of the proprietary real-time computer Tri-D 9250 14
Figure 1.9 The architecture of the 98010 CPU 16
Figure 1.10 The open real-time system architecture: Host/target multiprocessor with distributed memory................................17
Figure 1.11 The architecture of the tightly-coupled symmetrical multiprocessor 18
Figure 1.12 The architecture of a high availability real-time system.............20
Figure 1.13 Definition of task switching time 22
Figure 1.14 Definition of interrupt latency time...22
Figure 1.15 Definition of semaphore shuffling time..................................23
Figure 1.16 Deadlock breaking timing diagram 24
Figure 1.17 Datagram throughput measured in kbytes per second.................25
Figure 1.18 Definition of the process dispatch latency time.........................26
Figure 1.19 Two-dimensional representation of computer performance..........27
Figure 1.20 Three-dimensional representation of computer performance 28

Figure 1.21 The Real/Stone program decomposed into a number of processes 31

Figure 1.22 Timing diagram of processes' execution in the Real/Stone 32

Figure 1.23 Model of an open system for real-time applications 34

Figure 2.1 The operating system is the interface between the programmer and the machine 37

Figure 2.2 The main goal of open systems and standards 42

Figure 2.3 Four concepts of scheduling algorithms:
(a) Round-robin scheduler,
(b) Priority-driven scheduler,
(c) Preemptive scheduler with preemption points, and
(d) Fully preemptive scheduler 47

Figure 3.1 Functional overview of REAL/IX - a fully preemptive real-time UNIX operating system 51

Figure 3.2 Layered presentation of the UNIX operating system 52

Figure 3.3 Block diagram of the REAL/IX kernel 54

Figure 3.4 Data segment of executing process 56

Figure 3.5 Diagram of REAL/IX process states 59

Figure 3.6 Memory management data structures 61

Figure 3.7 REAL/IX process priorities 65

Figure 3.8 REAL/IX run queue organization 67

Figure 3.9 Values of kernel semaphores 69

Figure 3.10 REAL/IX spin locks 70

Figure 3.11 Handling events synchronously 75

Figure 3.12 Handling events asynchronously 76

Figure 3.13 A REAL/IX file system 80

Figure 3.14 Adding another file system to root 81

Figure 3.15 REAL/IX file subsystem 83

Figure 3.16 Internal structure of a file system 88

Figure 3.17 Accessing non-contiguous data blocks 93

Figure 3.18 Accessing extents (contiguous data blocks) 94

Figure 3.19 File system tables and their pointers 97

Figure 3.20 Driver entry points 103

Figure 3.21 Three methods of I/O transfer 105

Figure 3.22 Connected interrupt notification 110

Figure 4.1 The structure of a real-time program 115

Figure 4.2 Example of kernel preemption and scheduling 121

Figure 4.3 The example program illustrates the use of the **relinquish** system call 126

Figure 4.4 The example C program which illustrates how to set up a one-shot interval timer using the **incinterval** system call 131

Figure 4.5 The FORTRAN example to set up a one-shot interval timer 133

Figure 4.6 Example: handling real-time memory violations 143

Figure 4.7 Example program: Allocating shared memory by using **shmget** system call 160

Figure 4.8 Example program: Controlling shared memory with **shmctl** system call 165

Figure 4.9 Example program: Attaching and detaching shared memory segment with **shmat** and **shmdt** system calls 171

Figure 4.10 Example program: Allocating physical shared memory with the **shmget** system call 174

Figure 4.11 Data structures for semaphores 178

Figure 4.12 Example program: Creating/getting a semaphore using the **semget** system call 184

Figure 4.13 Example program: Controlling semaphores by using **semctl** system call 192

Figure 4.14 Example program: Operations on semaphores using **semop** system call 199

Figure 4.15 Example 1: Using binary semaphores 203

Figure 4.16 Example 2: Using binary semaphores 206

Figure 4.17 Sending and receiving messages 208

Figure 4.18 Example program: Creating message queue with the **msgget** system call 212

Figure 4.19 Example program: Controlling message queues using the msgctl system call 217

Figure 4.20 Example program: Message operations using the **msgsnd** and **msgrcv** system calls 225

Figure 4.21 System calls and aio 237

Figure 4.22 Example program: Connected interrupt notification using semaphores 241

Figure 4.23 Example program: Connected interrupt notification using the event mechanism 243

Figure 4.24 Example program: Interrupt notification using the polling mechanism 245

Figure 4.25 Example program: Connected interrupts using semaphores with polling 247

Figure 4.26 Example program: Use direct I/O to establish mapping between user/address space and physical address space 249

Figure 4.27 Example program: The user-defined system call **respages** 254

Figure 4.28 Example program: The use of the **respages** system call 256

Figure 4.29 Example program: Accessing **respages** by the *nsyscall* number 257

Figure 4.30 Comparison of process dispatch latency times for four real-time UNIX operating systems 270

Figure 4.31 Graphic results obtained from the Tri-Dimensional analyzer 271

Figure 5.1 The configuration of the NASA core system for data acquisition and launch control 274

Figure 5.2 The functional diagram of the Data Acquisition Processor 276

Figure 5.3 The Data Acquisition Processor (DAP) Model 277

Figure 5.4 Partitioning function of the DAP system into five processing elements: three I/O processors and two CPUs 282

Figure 5.5 The tightly coupled multiprocessor system configured as the Data Acquisition Processor 283

Figure 5.6 Functional diagram of the Application Processor 285

Figure 5.7 Application Processor Model 287

Figure 5.8 Functional partitioning of the AP system into three processing elements: two I/O processors and one CPU 290

Figure 5.9 The tightly coupled multiprocessor system configured as the Application Processor 291

Figure 5.10 System configuration for the JPL demonstration system 293

Figure 5.11 Task 1: Reads data from the IEEE-802.3 and writes to the disk.........296

Figure 5.12 Task 2: Reads data from the IEEE-488 and writes to the disk.........298

Figure 5.13 Task 3: Reads data from the digital I/O (DRIIW) and writes to the disk.........302

List of Tables

Table 1.1a	Real-Time Application Characteristics	5
Table 1.1b	Real-Time Application Characteristics cont'd	6
Table 2.1	Requirements for Real-Time Operating Systems	38
Table 2.2	Open versus Proprietary Systems	41
Table 2.3	POSIX 1003.4 Functions	43
Table 2.4	Classification of Real-Time UNIX Implementations	45
Table 4.1	Real-Time Tasks, System Calls and Commands	117
Table 4.2	System Calls not Recommended for Real-Time Applications	119
Table 4.3	Default Priorities of System Processes	122
Table 4.4	System Calls to Change or Affect Process Priority	124
Table 4.5	System Calls and Structures for System-Wide Timers	128
Table 4.6	System Calls and Structures for Process Interval Timers	129
Table 4.7	System Calls for Allocating Memory	138
Table 4.8	System Calls for Locking Pages into Memory	139
Table 4.9	Valid Values for pid with kill	146
Table 4.10	Event Structure	148
Table 4.11	IPC Flags	153
Table 4.12	Shared Memory System Calls	155
Table 4.13	Shared Memory State Information	177
Table 4.14	System Calls for Semaphores	178
Table 4.15	System Calls for Binary Semaphores	201
Table 4.16	System Calls for Messages	208
Table 4.17	Overview of Performance Problems	267
Table 5.1	Significant Changes Distributed Across Data Types	275

Table 5.2 Processing Power Required by the DAP 281

Table 5.3 Performance Evaluation of the VLAN-E Ethernet Controller 284

Table 5.4 Processing Power Required by the AP 289

Contributing Authors

Dr. Borko Furht is Senior Director of Research and Advanced Development at MODCOMP, a Florida-based high-technology computer company and a division of AEG Frankfurt, West Germany. Prior to MODCOMP, he was an Associate Professor of Electrical and Computer Engineering at the University of Miami, Coral Gables, Florida, and consultant for IBM, RCA, NASA, Cordis, and Honeywell. Furht received BSEE, MSEE, and Ph.D. degrees in Electrical and Computer Engineering from the University of Belgrade, Yugoslavia. He has written 5 books, 4 book chapters, and more than 80 technical and scientific papers. He holds two U.S. patents and has received several technical awards. Dr. Furht is a senior member of the IEEE, a Member of the ACM, an Editor-in-Chief of the International Journal of Mini and Microcomputers, and an Associate Editor of the Journal of Real-Time Systems.

Dan Grostick is Director of Advanced Operating Systems at MODCOMP. He is responsible for the development of the REAL/IX real-time UNIX operating system. During a seventeen year career at MODCOMP, he has held a number of technical and management positions in operating systems, compilers, computer simulation and diagnostics. Prior to joining MODCOMP, he developed real-time applications at Systems Engineering Laboratories. He received a Bachelor of Applied Science degree in Computer Systems at Florida Atlantic University.

Dr. David P. Gluch is a Technical Manager within MODCOMP's R&D organization. For more than twelve years he has been involved in the development of real-time computer systems with a number of high technology corporations including Bendix Aerospace, Schlumberger, and Honeywell. He has filed four corporate patent disclosures and has published more than 20 articles on topics ranging from general purpose open computer systems to the dynamical characteristics of the Space Shuttle flight control computer system. Prior to joining industrial R&D, he held various academic positions. He holds a Ph.D. in physics from Florida State University. Dr. Gluch is a Senior Member of the IEEE and a member of the editorial board of the *International Journal of Mini and Microcomputers*, the IEEE Computer Society, and the American Physical Society.

Dr. Guy Rabbat is President and Chief Executive Officer of Fort Lauderdale-based Modular Computer Systems, Inc. (MODCOMP), a wholly owned subsidiary of AEG and Daimler-Benz of Germany. Prior to joining MODCOMP in 1987,

Dr. Rabbat headed the electrical and electronics engineering department at General Motors in Warren, Michigan. He was Vice President of the Austin operations of the CAE Systems division of Tektronix from 1984 to 1986, and held various positions at IBM Corp. Dr. Rabbat holds a Bachelor's, a Master's and a Doctorate degree from Queens University in England. He taught as an affiliate professor of electrical engineering at Washington University. Citing his significant contributions to computer technologies, Dr. Rabbat was elected Fellow of the Institute of Electrical and Electronics Engineers, Inc., (IEEE) in 1988. Dr. Rabbat has garnered 12 IEEE Invention and Outstanding contribution awards and has published more than 80 scientific technical papers and two books. He has been awarded seven U.S. patents and has held posts as President of the American Automation Association from 1984 to 1986, Editor-in-Chief of the IEEE Circuits and Devices Magazine from 1984 to 1986, Chairman of the International IEEE Conference on Circuits and Computers in 1980 and the International IEEE Conference on Computer Design in 1983.

John Parker is currently the Vice President of Development at MODCOMP, Fort Lauderdale, where he previously held additional technical management positions in compiler and operating systems design. His MODCOMP development department is responsible for the design and implementation of open systems architectures, multitasking, multiprocessor computer systems, associated software and REAL/IX, MODCOMP's real-time UNIX operating system. Additional experience includes positions at McDonnell-Douglas, St. Louis, in real-time, transaction processing and fault tolerant computer systems, and at the North Electric Division of United Telecommunications, Columbus, Ohio in digital process control. He holds a BS in Computer Science from Purdue University, West Lafayette, Indiana, with additional MBA studies at Ohio State University and Washington University, St. Louis.

Meg McRoberts has been a technical writer at MODCOMP for two years. Before that she worked at AT&T, Beatrice Corporation, and was part of the TKAS Research Project at the University of Chicago. She has degrees from the University of Arizona, and additional graduate studies at the University of Chicago.

Foreword

A growing concern of mine has been the unrealistic expectations for new computer-related technologies introduced into all kinds of organizations. Unrealistic expectations lead to disappointment, and a schizophrenic approach to the introduction of new technologies. The UNIX and real-time UNIX operating system technologies are major examples of emerging technologies with great potential benefits but unrealistic expectations.

Users want to use UNIX as a common operating system throughout large segments of their organizations. A common operating system would decrease software costs by helping to provide portability and interoperability between computer systems in today's multivendor environments. Users would be able to more easily purchase new equipment and technologies and cost-effectively reuse their applications. And they could more easily connect heterogeneous equipment in different departments without having to constantly write and rewrite interfaces.

On the other hand, many users in various organizations do not understand the ramifications of general-purpose versus real-time UNIX. Users tend to think of "real-time" as a way to handle exotic heart-monitoring or robotics systems. Then these users use UNIX for transaction processing and office applications and complain about its performance, robustness, and reliability. Unfortunately, the users don't realize that real-time capabilities added to UNIX can provide better performance, robustness and reliability for these non-real-time applications.

Many other vendors and users do realize this, however. There are indications even now that general-purpose UNIX will go away as a separate entity. It will be replaced by a real-time UNIX. General-purpose UNIX will exist only as a subset of real-time UNIX.

In the future, real-time UNIX will touch many people's business lives. It will be used in applications such as communications and networking, factory and industrial plant, military command and control, simulations, telemetry, financial services, transaction processing, office engineering, graphics, medical and scientific imaging, and scientific applications. The new real-time UNIX users will be in organizations and industries such as government agencies, military branches, communications companies, the manufacturing and industrial community, banking houses, insurance companies, airlines, hotels, distributors, and more.

Like anything else, real-time UNIX has its advantages and weaknesses. Real-time UNIX can provide benefits, and make the use of UNIX feasible, in traditional real-time applications, as well as in many areas that people do not think of as real-time. A sure fire way to be disappointed in real-time UNIX is to expect more of it than it can deliver.

This book, "Real-Time UNIX Systems - Design and Application Guide," provides a practical window into real-time UNIX by cogently addressing three important issues:

1. What is real-time?,
2. When is it used?,
3. How is it applied?.

The misconceptions of real-time UNIX are corrected. And, actual case studies of real-time UNIX applications provide understanding of when and how it is used. I recommend this book to anyone who needs a realistic understanding of real-time UNIX.

Wendy Rauch
President
Emerging Technologies Group
Dix Hills, NY 11746

Preface

Since 1974, when the first paper was published on the UNIX operating system [Thom74], many books and papers have covered various topics related to the UNIX system, such as the UNIX programming environment [Kern84], advanced UNIX programming [Roch85], the UNIX kernel [Bach86], and the UNIX system architecture [Andl90].

The UNIX operating system was originally designed for multitasking and time-sharing, and therefore the standard UNIX system does not have an adequate response time nor data throughput needed to support real-time applications. This book is unique, because it represents a design and application guide to real-time UNIX systems.

This book is intended for system designers, engineers, and programmers who are involved in real-time system design and applications. It can also be used as a textbook for senior and graduate students of Computer Science and Engineering by providing a step-by-step procedure in designing time-critical applications with a real-time UNIX operating system. The book includes 15 fully-tested real-time example programs and two case studies of designing real-time systems.

The prerequisites for this book include general knowledge of the UNIX kernel (recommended book: [Bach86]), and programming in the UNIX environment (recommended book: [Roch85]). It also assumes that the reader is familiar with programming in the C language (recommended books: [Moor85] and [Lapi87]).

The book is organized into five chapters. Chapter 1 presents an introduction to the field of real-time computing. It includes a definition and classification of real-time systems, discusses basic issues in real-time system design and presents performance measures used to evaluate real-time systems. Chapter 2 describes the requirements of real-time operating systems, and presents an overview of real-time UNIX operating systems. It also discusses various approaches in implementing real-time UNIX operating systems. Chapter 3 presents the concept of a fully preemptive real-time UNIX operating system by describing the REAL/IX operating system, MODCOMP's real-time implementation of the UNIX System V operating system. The guidelines for designing real-time applications using the REAL/IX system are given in Chapter 4. This Chapter includes a number of example programs. Several case studies of designing modern real-time systems, including programming examples are given in Chapter 5.

Portions of Chapters 1, 2, and 3 are taken from copyrighted documents by permission of Motorola, Inc. and from the following articles:

- [Rabb88b, Furh89a, Carr89, Gluc90] with permission from the IEEE,
- [Rabb88c, Gluc89] with permission from the International Society of Mini and Microcomputers,
- [Gros90] with permission from Elsevier Science Publishers,
- [Rabb88a, Furh89b] with permission from the ACM Special Interest Groups on Operating Systems and Computer Architecture, respectively, and
- [Furh90b, Furh90c] with permission from the International Foundation for Telemetry.

Acknowledgements

This book incorporates the ideas and efforts of many individuals from the MODCOMP R&D Center. Those who contributed significantly to the material presented in the book, and who were actively involved in converting the concepts described here into the REAL/IX operating system include:

Jeff Bernhard
Linda Dunaphant
Nigel Gamble
Geoff Hall
Lars Helgeson
Jim Houston
Jeff Jones
Tom Kapish
Tim Keating
Brett Kennedy
Joe Korty
Wayne McLaren
Charlotte Noll
Hagai Ohel
Ron Papas
Orlando Perdomo
Steve Pietrowicz
Steve Rotolo
Bob Sanford
Ken Shaffer
Andy Tate
Joel Wagner
Carmen Wampole
Mike Zink

We would also like to thank those individuals who were actively involved in testing, evaluating, and benchmarking the REAL/IX operating system and who produced benchmark results published in this book. These individuals are:

Joe Green
Mark Hamzy
Patrick Shironoshita
Ron Stoehr
Ramadass Sureswaran
Teodoro Zuccarelli

A special contribution in this book was made by the individual involved in case studies development. We would especially like to thank *Mr. Robert Luken* from the NASA Kennedy Space Center who provided data for the case study on the data acquisition and space shuttle launch control system.

We would like to thank the Jet Propulsion Laboratory (JPL) for permitting us to publish their case study and also the individuals from MODCOMP who developed the JPL demonstration system. These include:

Mats Hellstrom
Linda Skipper

The credit for typing, formatting, and finalizing the drawings and tables for this manuscript goes to *Ms. Terri Stettner* whose expertise and dedication were invaluable in the completion of this work.

REAL-TIME UNIX® SYSTEMS
Design and Application Guide

CHAPTER 1

Introduction to Real-Time Computing

This chapter introduces the fundamental issues of real-time computing. A definition and classification of real-time computer systems as well as the computer requirements for real-time applications are discussed. Systems issues, such as specifications, analysis and verification, real-time architectures and operating systems, and real-time communications are also presented. Several real-time measures and metrics are discussed and evaluated.

1.1 DEFINITION AND CLASSIFICATION OF REAL-TIME COMPUTER SYSTEMS

A real-time computer system can be defined as a system that performs its functions and responds to external, asynchronous events within a predictable (or deterministic) amount of time.

In addition to sufficient and deterministic computational power to meet processing and timing requirements, real-time computer systems must provide efficient interrupt handling capabilities to handle asynchronous events and high I/O throughput to meet the data handling requirements of time-critical applications.

A real-time computer system, or the controlling system, is typically controlling a process, or a controlled system: (a) by recognizing and responding to discrete events within predictable time intervals, and (b) by processing and storing large amounts of data acquired from the controlled system. Examples of controlled systems are the automated factory floor with robots and assembly stations, rolling mills and furnaces in a steel plant, or power generating units in power utilities.

Response time and data throughput requirements depend on the specific real-time application. For example, in an energy management system, the main function is to monitor and control environmental factors such as temperature and air flow. The computational requirements for this application are modest because of the relatively low sampling rates and slow overall response of the mechanical devices affecting changes within the system. In an electrical power plant, however, data acquisition and calculation become more critical. Plant equipment and system functions must be closely monitored and controlled on a continuous basis to ensure safe operation and prevent costly unscheduled outages and shutdowns. A slight deviation from optimal performance even for a short period of time can significantly impact the cost of electrical energy produced by the plant. Figure 1.1 illustrates various response-time requirements for typical real-time applications.

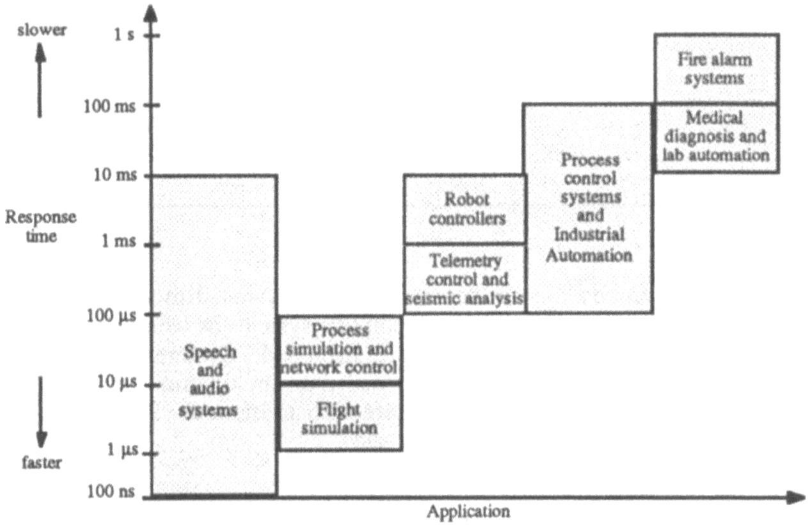

Figure 1.1 - Response-time requirements for real-time applications

There are several classification schemes for real-time systems. From the response-time viewpoint, real-time systems can be divided into: (a) hard real-time (HRT) systems, and (b) soft real-time (SRT) systems.

In HRT systems, the time at which the results are produced should be specified, and the system must schedule the tasks to meet these deadlines. In SRT systems, the level of urgency of tasks is specified in the form of priorities, and the system executes the most urgent task (highest priority) that is ready to execute.

In SRT systems, priority scheduling of tasks is generally used to achieve fast response. However, in HRT systems, it is essential to have a timely response. If the response is very fast, but does not meet deadlines, the system will not operate properly. Thus, while the other aspects remain the same, the main difference between these systems is in task scheduling.

In order to illustrate the difference between SRT and HRT systems, namely the difference between fixed-priority scheduling and deadline scheduling, consider the following example [Falk88]. A real-time system collects and processes data from two sensors, *A* and *B*. The deadline for collecting data from sensor *A* must be met every 20 ms, and the deadline for collecting data from *B* must be met every 50 ms.

It takes 10 ms to process each sample of data from *A*, and 25 ms to process each sample of data from *B*.

Similarly, if a fixed-priority scheduler is used, with *B* having the higher priority, then *A* will clearly miss its deadline, since *A's* deadline will pass during the 25 ms it takes to process the data from *B*, as shown in Figure 1.2a.

If *A* is given the higher priority, *B* will only have 20 ms of computer time by the time its 50 ms deadline is reached, as shown in Figure 1.2b.

By using a nearest-deadline scheduling algorithm, which gives priority to the task with the nearest deadline, all system requirements can be met, as shown in Figure 1.2c. It is assumed that the computer itself can make a scheduling decision every 10 ms.

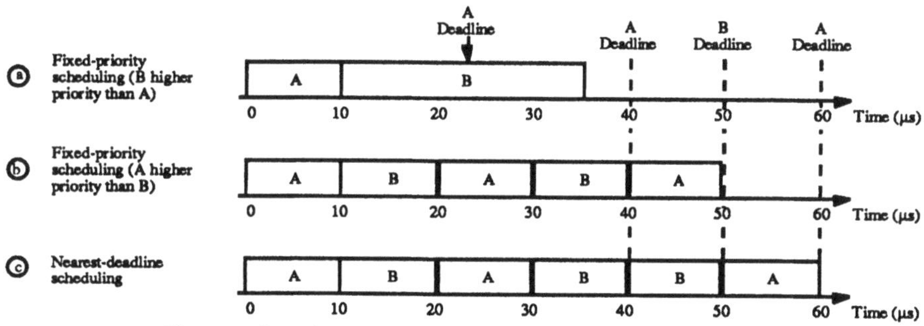

Figure 1.2 - Fixed priority versus deadline scheduling

Another classification scheme groups real-time systems into: (a) proprietary and, (b) open systems. Traditionally, real-time computing has been a realm of proprietary systems. Applications written for these systems in high level languages often require assembly level code and depend on the unique characteristics of the proprietary operating system, hardware architecture and instruction set. With the escalating cost of software development and the massive conversion efforts required for porting real-time applications to state-of-the-art hardware, there is a need for highly portable real-time applications. Therefore, the next generation of real-time systems will be based on open systems, which incorporate industry standards. Open systems reduce system cost and time to market, increase availability of software packages, increase ease-of-use, and facilitate system integration.

Open real-time computer concepts are based on hardware architectures which use off-the-shelf standard microprocessors, standard real-time operating systems, standard communication protocols and standard interface buses.

Another classification of real-time systems uses real-time system architectures as the basis for classification. From this viewpoint, real-time systems can be categorized into: a) centralized, and b) distributed real-time systems.

In a centralized system, processors are located at a single node in the system and the interprocessor communication time is negligible compared to the processor execution time. A multiprocessor system with shared memory is an example of a centralized system.

In a distributed system, processors are distributed at different points in the system and the interprocessor communication time is not negligible compared to the processor execution time. An example of such a system is a local area computer network.

The described classification schema are shown in Figure 1.3.

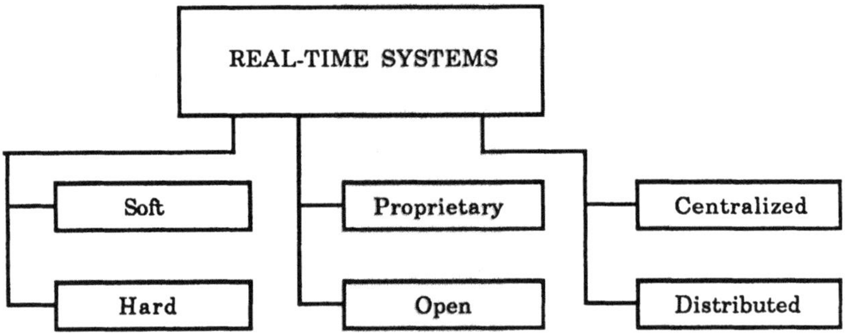

Figure 1.3 - Classification schema for real-time systems

1.2 COMPUTER REQUIREMENTS FOR REAL-TIME APPLICATIONS

In this section, real-time applications are classified into a number of different groups. We used data published by the Emerging Technology Group [Emer89]. The classification is based on various features. These include the response-time required, design and processing complexity, amount of functionality, number of tasks handled, type of human resources, networking capabilities, file system requirements, and type of computer on which the application is typically implemented.

Tables 1.1a and 1.1b present the classification of the real-time applications. A detailed description of these real-time applications is given in [Emer89]. The classification is based on a variety of characteristics including the real-time responsiveness required, the design and processing complexity, amount of functionality, number of tasks handled and/or coordinated, type of human interface, file system requirements, and type of computer on which the application is usually implemented.

In the remaining part of this section we analyze various computer system configurations used in several real-time applications.

Table 1.1a
Real-Time Application Characteristics

Type of application	Response time requirements	Human interface	Design complexity	Functionality	Number of tasks handled	File system required	Dedicated or not?	Machine implementation
Control, Robotic Data acquisition Vision Instrumentation	Low microseconds to 1 millisecond	Simple or none	Simple	Low	Less than 5	No	Usually	Board-level computer, plugged into a bus configuration
Motion control, Robotics, Process control, Testing	Less than one millisecond	Sometimes	Medium	Medium	Medium (more than 10)	No	Addresses a range of applications	Workstation or minicomputer, with custom I/O cards
Scientific data acquisition	Low microseconds to 1 millisecond	Easily usable	High	Large	Many Also handles many processors	Yes	Addresses a range of applications	High-performance minicomputers with local network connections
Medical imaging	Less than 1 second		Medium or greater	Medium	Small to medium (e.g., 10)		Addresses a range of applications	Workstation or minicomputer, with custom I/O cards
Simulation, and Air traffic control	Low microsecond to 1 millisecond	Sophisticated, Bit-mapped graphics, Handles many types of input	High	Large	Many (more than 50), Also handles many processors	Yes	Single application with many components	High-performance minicomputers
Testing, and Machine control	Less than 1 second		Medium	Medium	Medium (e.g., 10-20)	Yes	Addresses a range of applications	Workstation or minicomputer with custom I/O cards
Cell control, Monitoring, Testing, Reporting	200 milliseconds to more than 1 second	Yes, Graphical capabilities a plus	High	Large	Many (e.g., 10-50) Also handles many processors and controllers	Yes	Addresses a range of applications	High-end PC, workstation, or minicomputer, with custom I/O cards

Reprinted by permission of Emerging Technologies Group, Inc. [Emer89]

Table 1.1b
Real-Time Application Characteristics - cont'd

Type of application	Response time requirements	Human interface	Design complexity	Functionality	Number of tasks handled	File system required	Dedicated or not?	Machine implementation
Communications	Less than 100 milliseconds to 500 milliseconds, depending on the application	Yes Usually cryptic character-oriented command line shells; Graphical displays would be a plus	High	Large	Many (e.g., 4-12 for a cell controller, 10-25 for a network server, hundreds for a large PBX); Also handles many processors and controllers	Yes	Usually	Mainframes or large minis to microcomputer-based systems or Risc-based workstations
Factory-wide monitoring, control, and maintenance	500 milliseconds to several seconds	Easily usable; Graphical capabilities a plus	High	Large	Many (e.,g., 10-50) Also handles many processors and controllers	Yes Performs file storage and backup for programmable devices	Addresses a range of applications	General purpose minicomputer or workstation connected to automation gear via a LAN
On-line transaction processing	Emphasis is on high average throughput	Easily usable; For interactrive inputs and displays	High	Large	Many (e.g., thousands of transactions per hour); Usually driven by a fixed small set of inputs; Also handles many processors and terminals	Yes	Addresses a range of applications	Mainframes, large minis, or fault-tolerant computers

Reprinted by permission of Emerging Technologies Group, Inc. [Emer89]

In metal industry applications computers are typically used in casting, hot rolling, cold rolling, finishing, annealing, soaking, and other steel and aluminum processes. These applications require: (a) real-time monitoring and control, (b) high uptime and reliability, (c) redundancy at all levels of the control system, and (d) communications to a broad range of Distributed Control Systems (DCS), Programmable Logic Controllers (PLC), and corporate host computers. A typical real-time computer control system for these applications consists of a dual redundant minicomputer interfaced to PLCs and/or DCS, direct process I/Os, and interfaces, to a higher level of control via a plant wide network. A typical computer system configuration is shown in Figure 1.4.

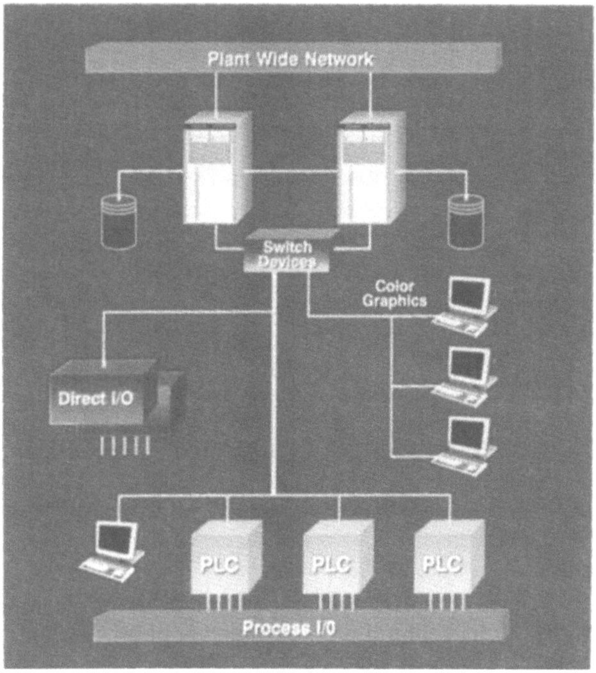

Figure 1.4 - Typical computer control system for metal industry applications

In petrochemical applications, computer systems are used for real-time supervisory control of the production of high-priority commodity chemicals such as ethylene and prophylene. A typical computer control system, besides high performance real-time features, should provide interfaces to regulatory control instrumentation systems, and PLCs.

Batch control applications include food, pharmaceutical, pulp and paper, chemical processes, etc. Batch processes require frequent start-up and shut downs, which means that the computer must be able to handle a variety of conditions, including products that must remain consistent from batch to batch. A typical computer system for batch control applications consists of a single real-time minicomputer, which provides interfaces to distributed control systems and PLCs, and an integrated input/output unit specifically designed for process control systems.

Real-time applications in energy include electric, gas and water utilities, waste water treatment facilities, pipeline companies, architectural/engineering firms, and other energy-related endeavors.

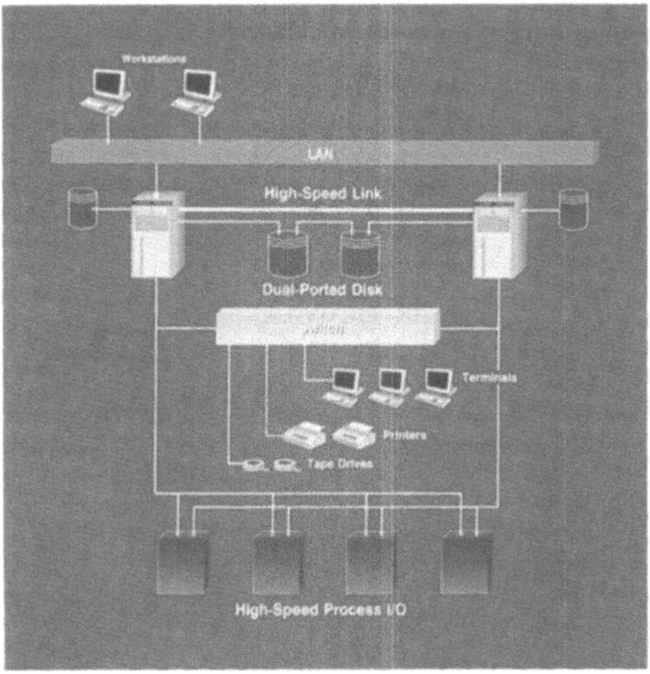

Figure 1.5 - Typical computer system configuration for plant monitoring and control of a fossil power plant

In electric utility monitoring and control applications, computers are used on a continuous basis to monitor and control plant equipment and system functions in order to ensure safe operation and prevent costly unscheduled outages and shutdowns. Furthermore, because of the huge quantities of coal or oil typically consumed by their boilers, slight deviations from optimal efficient performance, even for a short period of time, can seriously impact the cost of electrical energy generated by the plant. For these reasons, plant monitoring systems must be accurate and reliable. A typical computer system for plant monitoring and control of a fossil power plant, shown in Figure 1.5, consists of a dual redundant CPU, dual-ported disk and tape drives, and dual-ported I/O devices.

The computer system typically runs a software package designed to monitor and control real-time processes through the use of basic functions, such as scan, log and alarm, and extensive programming facilities for customized man/machine interfaces.

Energy Management Systems (EMS) for the electric utilities use Supervisory Control and Data Acquisition (SCADA) functions to collect and process raw system data into a real-time database suitable for access by the EMS applications. SCADA systems provide operators with an up-to-the-second status of the network. EMS functions range from basic automatic generation control to the more sophisticated state estimation techniques. Generally in these systems, data acquisition, checking, conversion, logging, and alarming are handled by a front-end machine, while a back-end machine processes computer-intensive applications and handles the man/machine interface functions. A popular approach to large system designs is a dual-redundant configuration. A redundant configuration, that can be switched over in the event of failure, enhances reliability and system availability. Wide area networks are typically used to link energy dispatch centers separated by large distances.

SCADA/EMS systems for the gas utilities differ from electric utility SCADA systems. Typically, gas systems have fewer points to monitor, slower scan rates, and slower response requirements. Furthermore, EMS applications (i.e., gas flow calculations) are fewer in number, less critical, and computationally less intensive. Consequently, gas SCADA systems tend toward simpler configurations utilizing low- and mid-range machines. Gas and oil pipelines present similar requirements.

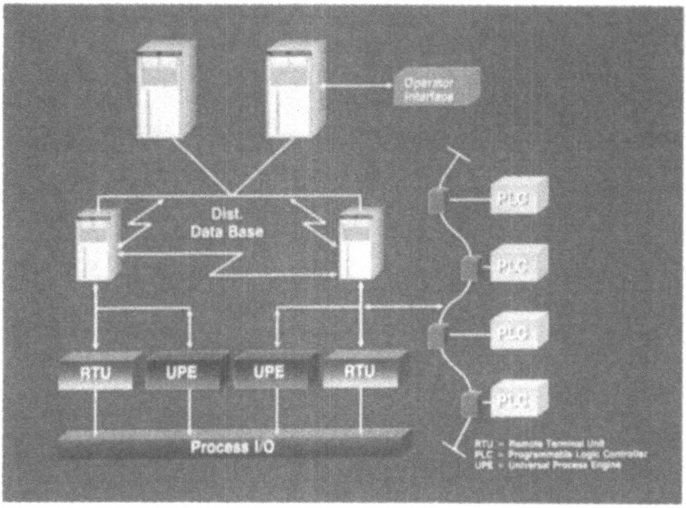

Figure 1.6 - A typical distributed waste water plant monitoring and control system

In medium- and large-scale waste water treatment plants a number of discrete processes are individually supervised and controlled. Typically a dual-redundant master computer controls numerous satellite computers, in a distributed configuration, as illustrated in Figure 1.6.

All computers in the system communicate and exchange data. The distributed operating system enables the host computer to download programs and data which reside in the local databases. Similarly, data that is collected and processed by the satellite computers can be sent to the supervisory computer for further processing. Computers also communicate with PLCs via local area networks. These PLCs provide functions not available within the remote terminal units.

In water plant monitoring and control applications water is pumped from a reservoir and is then transferred to the plant where it undergoes a number of treatment processes such as aeration, chemical injection, flocculation, and filtration through a series of multi-media filters. The transmission system consists of a network of reservoirs and laterals, laced with pumping stations. The water system is typically monitored and controlled by dual redundant computers which serve as hosts to a large number of distributed satellite computers.

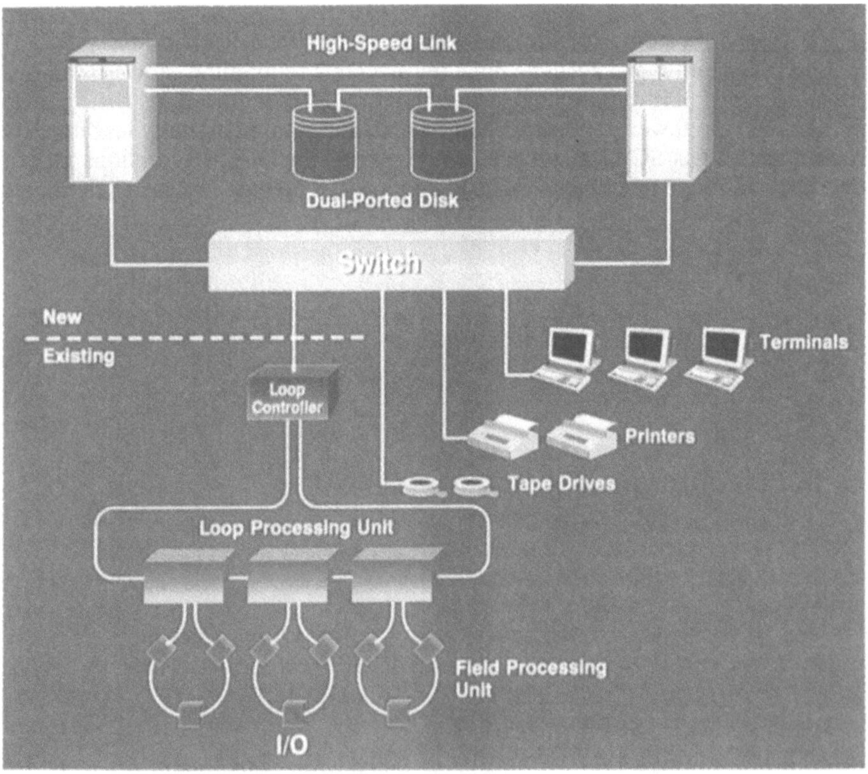

Figure 1.7 - A typical centralized HVAC energy management system

Energy management systems in buildings monitor and control key environmental variables such as temperature and air flows in order to optimize both comfort and operating costs. Expanded systems typically perform security and fire protection functions as well. Computational requirements for these systems are modest because of the relatively low sampling rates and slow overall system response. Consequently, cost-effective lower performance computers are usually adequate. Historically, builders used a single CPU to keep costs down, but current designs may include redundant processors, especially for large buildings where uninterrupted environmental control is important. Another energy management system is the HVAC energy management system, and its typical centralized configuration is shown in Figure 1.7.

Real-time data communication computer applications can be divided into the following categories: Multiple Host Access Systems, Packet Switched Networks, Value Added Reservation Service Systems, Transaction Processing Systems, Information System Access, and Front-end Processing Systems. Two important categories are multiple host access systems and packet switched networks, briefly described below.

Multiple Host Access Systems (MHAS) assume a computer configuration with various host computers from different suppliers. Each host computer usually has its own operating system, command structures, and applications. This environment makes it difficult for a common terminal to communicate with hosts, or for hosts to communicate between themselves. A real-time computer for MHAS applications should provide host-independent terminal switching that transparently manages the protocol, command, and data structure transformations between any terminal and host system.

Packet Switched Networks (PSN) are used for domestic and international data communications to expand network capacity and to better utilize existing resources. A real-time computer can be used as a communication processor providing key features needed on packet switched networks, such as high-speed real-time communications, performance capabilities that can handle both on-line and background tasks concurrently, and extensive line handling for X.25 DTE/DCE circuits.

Real-time computers are used in government and aerospace in a broad range of applications including planetary exploration, national defense, and space transportation systems.

In planetary exploration applications, real-time computer systems gather and analyze data from space exploration missions. In national defense applications, real-time computers are used for the high-volume-data collection in defense systems that track missiles, hostile aircraft, and other objects.

In space transportation systems, real-time computers are used to monitor and control space shuttle missions and to provide structural and aerodynamic testing during the development of the space shuttle vehicles.

In aeronautical engineering, a typical application of real-time computers includes controlling and monitoring of wind tunnels.

Another class of real-time applications includes real-time trainers and simulators. These applications require distributed computer architectures and distributed database management systems.

Real-time computer systems for on-line transaction processing must provide reliable, scheduled transactions, and complex processing capabilities. Typically, mainframe, large mini and fault-tolerant computers are used in these applications.

In instrumentation systems, real-time computers are used for laboratory instrumentation, and medical imaging, such as CAT scanners, x-ray equipment, blood analyzers, and other scientific and medical instruments. Typically, a single workstation or minicomputer with custom I/O is used for these applications.

1.3 SYSTEMS ISSUES

There are several crucial systems issues relating to the design and development of modern real-time computer systems. These issues can be categorized into the following groups:

a. Specification, analysis and verification of real-time systems,
b. Real-time operating systems,
c. Real-time system architectures, and
d. Real-time communications.

The IEEE Tutorial on Hard Real-Time Systems, edited by Stankovic and Ramamrithan [Stan88a], represents an excellent selection of research papers covering these four topics. In this section, we briefly discuss the major problems and challenges related to these issues.

Specification, Analysis and Verification of Real-Time Systems

The major problem in the specification, analysis and verification of real-time systems is how to include timing constraints in specifications, and how to verify that a system meets such a specification.

Methods for the specification and analysis of traditional computers, such as Petri Nets, finite state machines, Hoare/Floyd/Dijakstra logic and others, are not directly applicable to real-time systems. It is not clear how to extend these techniques for real-time constraints. Two strategies have been proposed to solve this problem [Stan88a]:

(1) better specification, analysis and verification techniques to deal with special properties of time-critical applications, and

(2) better software engineering methods based on techniques designed to produce systems that meet real-time requirements.

We would like to suggest two papers for further reading dealing with this problem. Dasarathy examines the timing constraints of real-time systems, proposes constructs for expressing them, and presents methods for validating them [Dasa85]. Coolahan and Roussopoulus modified the augmented Petri Net model by attaching a time variable to each node in the net. They use this model for describing timing requirements for a class of real-time systems [Cool83].

There are a number of excellent references on structured design, specification, and analysis for systems. Structured methodologies and detailed examples for real-time and general systems are published in Hatley and Pirbhai's *Strategies for Real-time System Specification* [Hatl88], and De Marco's *Structured Analysis and System Specification [Dema78]*.

Real-time Operating Systems

Real-time operating systems play a key role in most real-time systems. In real-time systems, the operating system and the application are very tightly coupled, much more than in time-sharing systems. A real-time operating system must be able to respond to some internal and external events in a deterministic timeframe, regardless of the impact on other executing tasks or processes. This is distinguished from a timesharing operating system, which must share system resources (such as the CPU, primary memory, and peripheral devices) equally among a number of executing tasks. In a properly-configured timesharing environment, no task should wait indefinitely for a system resource. In a real-time environment, critical tasks must receive the system resources they need when they need them, without concern for the effect this may have on other executing tasks.

The two crucial topics in real-time operating systems are: real-time scheduling, and real-time kernels.

The function of a scheduling algorithm is to determine, for a given set of tasks, whether a schedule (the sequence and the time periods) for executing the tasks exists such that the timing, precedence, and resource constraints of the tasks are satisfied, and to calculate such a schedule if one exists. A classification and a survey of scheduling algorithms for hard real-time systems is presented by Cheng, Stankovic and Ramamrithan [Chen88].

Another important topic is designing real-time kernels. A real-time kernel should provide features and primitives for efficient interprocess communication and synchronization, guaranteed interrupt response, a fast and reliable file system, and an efficient memory management scheme.

A detailed description of the concepts and characteristics of real-time operating systems is presented in Chapter 2 of this book.

Real-time System Architectures

System architectures to support real-time applications should be designed to provide the following critical features: (a) high computational speed, (b) high-speed interrupt handling, and (c) high I/O throughput. In addition, fault-tolerance features should be incorporated in the architecture to allow continued operation in the event of an abnormal system condition or component failure.

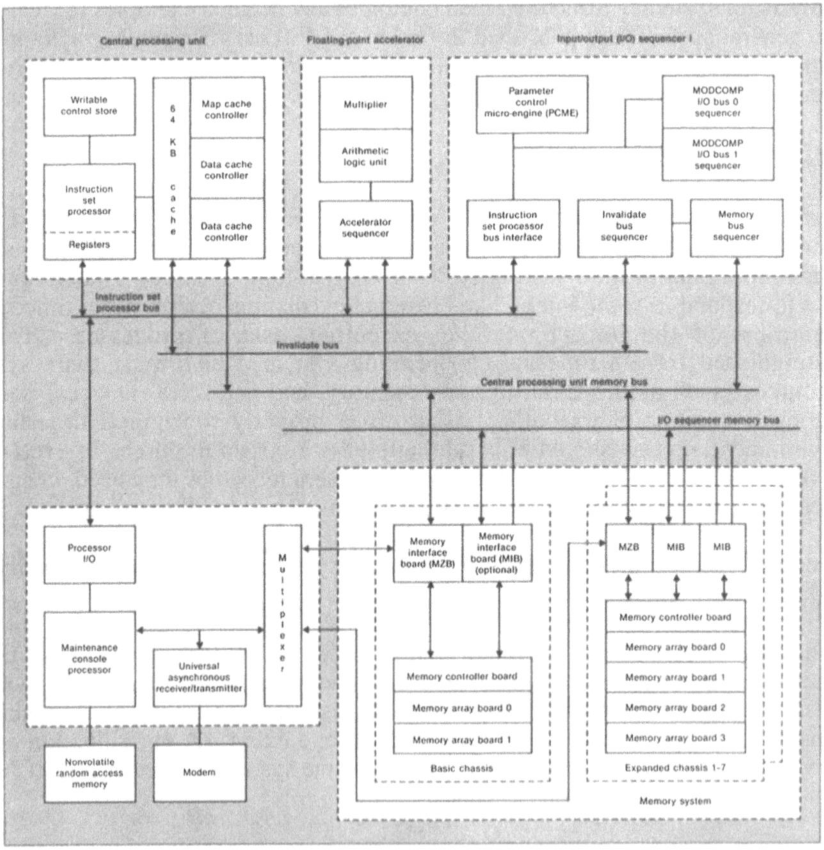

Figure 1.8 - The architecture of the proprietary real-time computer Tri-D 9250

Traditionally, real-time computers have been based on proprietary system architectures, proprietary instruction sets, and proprietary operating systems. These proprietary architectures are well suited for a variety of applications; however, the architecture usually has to change with the change in applications. Proprietary real-time architectures are typically designed with built-in architectural supports for real-time operating systems (such as support for semaphores, caching, memory management, fast task switching and so on), architectural supports for scheduling algorithms and error handling and support for languages and fast communications. In addition, the proprietary architecture typically has multiple buses in order to improve overall throughput of the system.

An example of a proprietary real-time architecture is the MODCOMP® Tri-D® 9250 computer [Carr89]. The 9250 basic architecture is shown in Figure 1.8.

The system includes the following functional units:

1. A single board CPU that contains four ASIC chips, which are:

   - the Instruction Stream Processor (ISP),
   - the Map Cache Controller (MCC), and
   - two Data Cache Controllers (DCC).

   The CPU board also contains a 64 Kbyte data cache, map cache, a context register consisting of 128 sets of 16 registers, and a Writable Control Store (WCS).

2. Up to two Input/Output Sequencer (IOS) boards. Each IOS board supports two proprietary I/O buses and a cache invalidate bus.

3. An Operator/Maintenance Console Controller which provides program execution and monitoring as well as maintenance functions such as a diagnostic tool set.

4. A memory subsystem that is expandable in 8 Mbyte increments from 8 to 240 Mbytes of physical memory.

5. An IEEE 874 floating point accelerator.

The 9250 computer is structured around an internal bus system that is designed specifically to enhance the real-time performance of the system. These buses are the instruction set processor bus, CPU and IOS memory buses and invalidate bus, as shown in Figure 1.9.

At the heart of the system is the 98010 VLSI processor chip which is comprised of approximately 250,000 transistors. The chip has two 32-bit bi-directional data buses and is controlled by an 88-bit Micro Instruction Register bus. It contains the following components: (a) 32-bit ALU, (2) 64-bit barrel shifter, (3) 32x32 multiplier, (4) 16x32-bit register file, (5) 64-bit priority encoder, (6) instruction queue pipeline with on-the-fly decode of 16-bit opcodes, (7) 4-way branch micro address sequencer which generates two 12-bit micro addresses to control separate banks of the external writable control store, (8) 16 level preemptive priority fully nested interrupt structure, and (9) 32/48/64-bit floating point hardware accelerator.

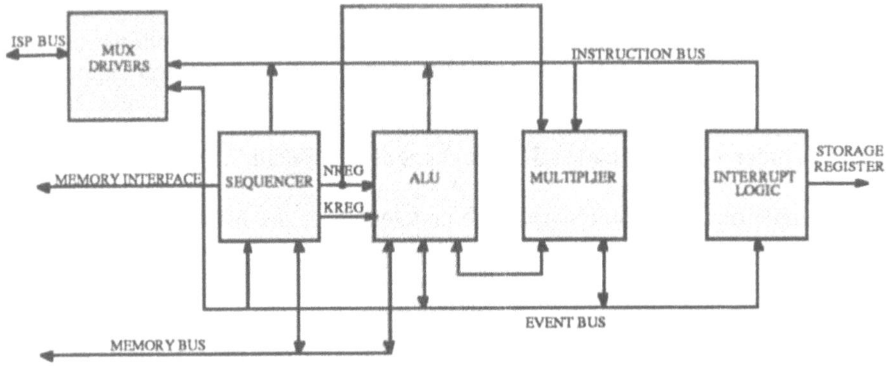

Figure 1.9 - The architecture of the 98010 CPU

The chip is implemented in 1.5 micron CMOS technology using datapath and state machine compilers and chip composer software tools to generate the very large (582x582 mil) standard cell device.

The 9250 computer runs the MAX™ real-time proprietary operating system.

The current trend in real-time architectures, and generally in real-time systems, is toward open architectures based on standard off-the-shelf microprocessors, standard real-time operating systems, such as the UNIX system, and standard interfaces. The standard system architecture provides software portability, because the real-time applications can easily be moved to newer hardware platforms.

Although, the system is open and standard from the user's standpoint, a high performance real-time computer incorporates a special-purpose internal architecture well suited for real-time applications. The system typically consists of one or more processors in a tightly coupled multiprocessor configuration, with built-in fault-tolerance features. It also has multiple buses, and custom-designed ASIC chips to enhance the real-time features of the system.

Two examples of the open system architectures are a host/target multiprocessor with distributed memory, and a tightly coupled multiprocessor system, described next.

The host/target multiprocessor system with a distributed memory is tailored to meet the needs of real-time training and simulation applications. It employs an open system architecture utilizing VME/VSB buses, a real-time UNIX operating system and commercially available single board computers. The system consists of a system host, up to 8 high-performance target computer nodes, standard I/O modules and custom interface modules, as shown in Figure 1.10.

The system can also be configured in a high availability manner by incorporating dual disks, redundant power supplies, and parallel execution of common software modules.

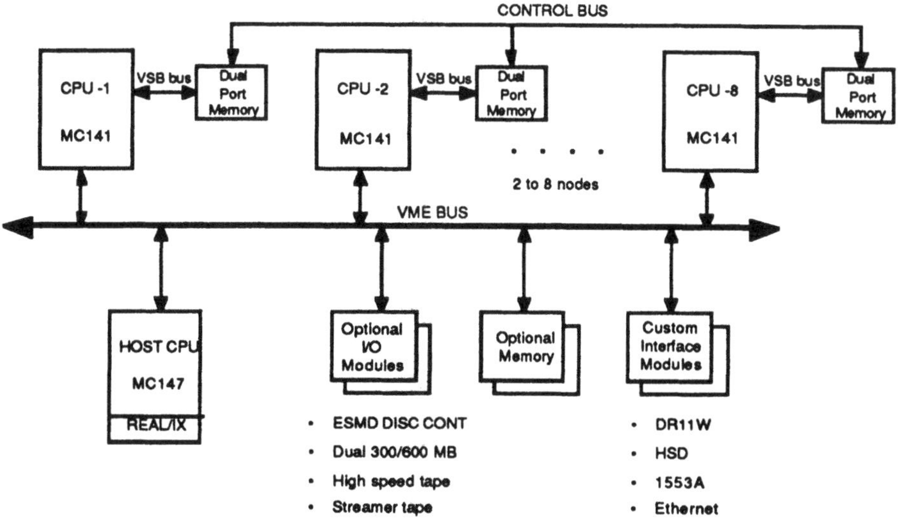

Figure 1.10 - The open real-time system architecture: Host/target multiprocessor with distributed memory

The unique needs of the real-time trainer/simulator market are specifically addressed through the implementation of a mirror memory/distributed database supported by broadcast writes and interrupts in a tightly-coupled host/multiple target architecture.

The tightly-coupled symmetrical multiprocessor system shown in Figure 1.11, consists of 1 to 10 processor subsystems. These processor subsystems can be configured as CPU or I/O units. All of these subsystems share global memory through the high performance Quad Wonder Bus. A single copy of the operating system resides in global memory and provides total operational control over all processing within the system. In addition, there is a Storage Server and a System Support Processor (SSP) which provide diagnostic, maintenance and related system functions.

The CPU is a MC68030 microprocessor. The ASIC chips support high real-time performance and consist of the Event Bus Controller, Cache Controller, and Quad Wonder Bus Controller.

The Quad Wonder Bus (QWB) connects all CPUs, I/O modules, and the SSP to global memory. The QWB is a synchronous bus with non-multiplexed address and data bits, which allows a data transfer rate of 50 MB/sec per bus. The QWB consists of 4 independent 32-bit buses with a clock rate of 12.5 MHz or higher. Each of the four buses operates concurrently with a maximum bandwidth of 200 MB/sec.

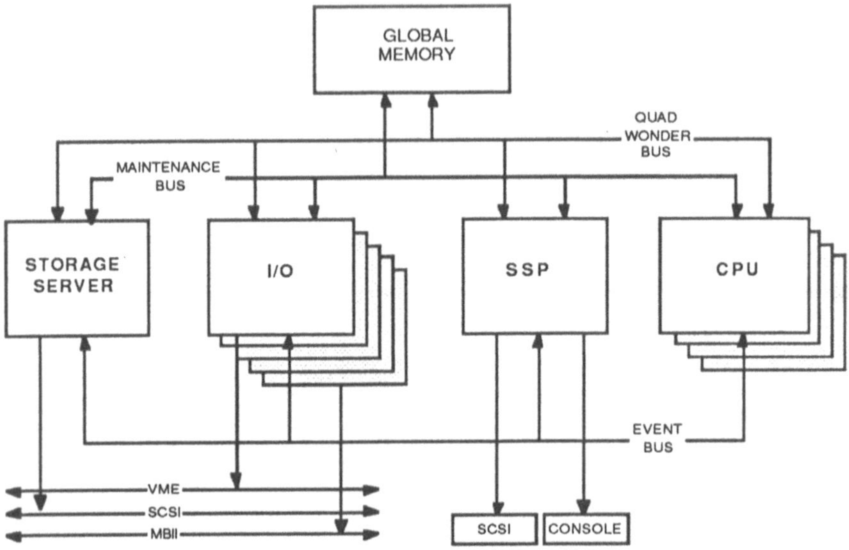

Figure 1.11 - The architecture of the tightly-coupled symmetrical multiprocessor

The Event Bus allows the multiprocessor architecture to handle a large number of interrupts by load balancing the real time interrupts. Modules are interfaced to the event bus via an Interrupt Controller. Event bus timing and control are provided by the Central Event Control. The Central Event Control is the common control element that prioritizes interrupts and generates event bus timing and control signals.

The Cache Memory contains a copy of recently accessed global memory locations. The cache system features include: cache coherence maintained by bus watching, tag RAM and compare circuitry, and write through cache data buffer. The Cache Memory and the corresponding cache controller improves the performance of the system by providing the CPUs with direct access to high speed memories.

Local memory on all CPUs provides storage for operating system instructions. Non-user interrupt service routines utilize private non-shared data. The local memory reduces the CPU access to the QWB and effectively increases the available QWB bandwidth.

High Speed Semaphore Processor functions are implemented in hardware. This significantly reduces semaphore based QWB transactions.

Real-time applications require functionally correct, timely, and reliable computation. To provide enhanced reliability and availability, flexible fault tolerance capabilities should be incorporated into the design of the hardware and software of real-time systems. This flexibility enables the system to adapt to the specific level of availability required by an application without design modifications and results in a comprehensive general purpose high performance real-time system.

Fault tolerant real-time computer systems can be grouped into three qualitative classes [Gluc89]:

- Graceful Degradation Systems,
- High Availability Systems, and
- Continuous Performance Systems.

Inherent in the design of multiprocessor systems is an implicit redundancy that allows for a degradation in performance upon the occurrence of a hardware failure.

Figure 1.12 is an example of a high performance computer system that meets the requirements of the first two fault tolerance classes (Graceful Degradation and High Availability) through a strategy based upon implicit and explicit subsystem redundancy, degraded operational capabilities, and deferred maintenance that collectively provide fault tolerance.

Implicit redundancy is an inherent characteristic of a complex system which consists of multiple hardware subsystems executing the same general function. Coupling the implicit redundancy of the architecture with the ability to restart following the occurrence of a failure results in a graceful degradation system. For example, consider the system shown in Figure 1.12. If a failure occurs within one of the processors, the system can be restarted using only the remaining healthy processor. Thus, the system will continue to function at a reduced performance level (at one-half of the maximum performance) following a failure in one of the processors. In this case repair is deferred until a routine maintenance shutdown where the failed unit is replaced and the system is returned to its full processing power.

As the complexity of the system increases the net effect of a failure is reduced. In the case of a multiprocessor system with n processors, the fraction of system degradation in the maximum values of processing performance is $1/n$ for the first processor subsystem failure.

In the case of the multiple memory modules and I/O subsystems a similar graceful degradation capability is provided. Upon the occurrence of a failure in one of the I/O or memory subsystems the system can be adjusted to operate in a degraded mode. In the degraded I/O mode, performance is reduced by $1/n$ for the first failure in a system with n I/O modules. The effect of memory failures on performance is more subtle and is application dependent.

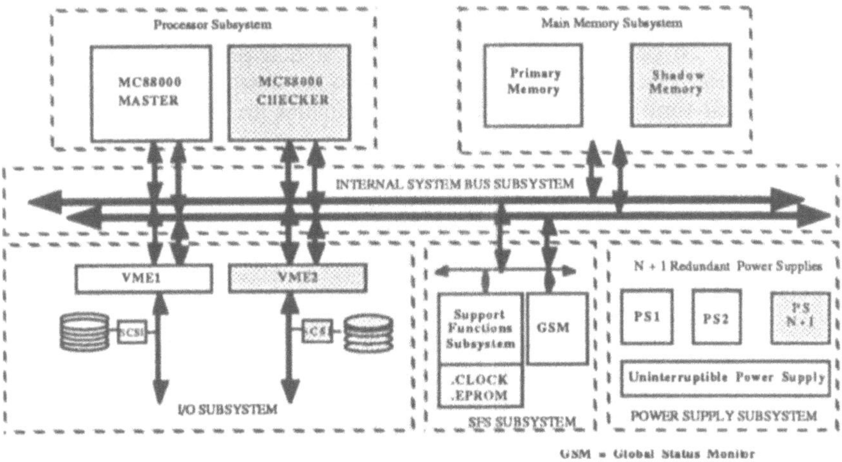

Figure 1.12 - The architecture of a high availability real-time system

For power supplies, an explicit N+1 redundancy strategy is employed. In minimum system configurations, dual supplies are sufficient to provide adequate back-up in the event of a power supply failure. In larger system configurations additional power supplies are used such that upon the failure of any one of the supplies the remaining units provide adequate power to meet operational requirements. The power supply subsystem design enables the on-line replacement of any of the power supply units and provides non-stop performance for single power supply failures. This redundancy in one of the least reliable parts of the system provides enhanced system reliability (through an increase in the system Mean-Time-To-Failure) and improved system availability.

Real-time Communications

In the design of both centralized and distributed real-time systems, there is a need for the use of communication protocols that provide deterministic behavior of the system.

In non-real-time systems, it is sufficient to verify the logical correctness of a communication solution, while in real-time systems, it is also necessary to verify timing correctness. In particular, distributed real-time systems require protocols that result in bounded channel access delays and message communication delays [Stan88a]. Channel access delay is defined as the time interval when a message is placed into the send-queue of a node until it is transmitted through the network. Message communication delay is the time interval from when the message is placed into the send-queue of a node until it is delivered to the recipient node. Therefore, it is the sum of the channel access delay and the transmission time per message.

For further reading, the paper by Kurose, Schwartz and Yemiki is recommended, who provide a comprehensive survey of multiple-access protocols [Kuro84].

1.4 REAL-TIME MEASURES

The performance of general-purpose computers is typically measured in terms of Millions of Instructions per Second (MIPS) or Millions of Floating-Point Operations per Second (MFLOPS).

Standard benchmark programs such as Whetstone, Dhrystone, and Linpack typically measure the CPU speed in a single-task environment. However, a computer may have high CPU performance, but poor real-time capabilities. Therefore, there is a need for performance measures specifically intended for real-time computer systems.

In this section we will present four methodologies and related metrics for objectively measuring real-time performance:

(a) Rhealstone Metric,
(b) Process Dispatch Latency Time,
(c) Tri-Dimensional Measure, and
(d) Real/Stone Benchmark.

1.4.1 Rhealstone Metric

The Rhealstone metric, proposed by Kar and Porter [Kar89], consists of quantitative measurements of six components that influence the performance of real-time systems. These six components, defined below, are: task switching time, preemption time, interrupt latency time, semaphore shuffling time, deadlock breaking time, and datagram throughput time.

<u>Task switching time</u> (t_{TS}) is defined as the average time the system takes to switch between two independent and active tasks of equal priority, as illustrated in Figure 1.13.

In Figure 1.13, all tasks are of equal priority. Task switching occurs because the real-time control software implements a time-slice algorithm for multiplexing equal-priority tasks.

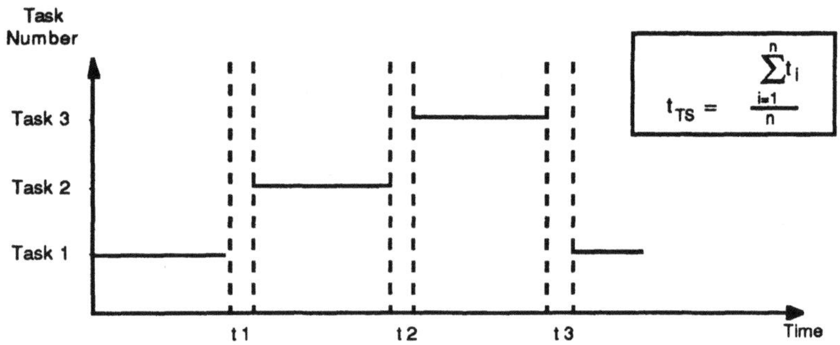

Figure 1.13 - Definition of task switching time

The task switching time is influenced by (a) the efficiency of task control data structures in saving and restoring contexts, (b) the CPU architecture and instruction set.

Preemption time (t_P) is defined as the average time it takes to transfer control from a lower priority to a higher priority task. The concept is similar to task switching (Figure 1.13), however, preemption takes longer. For preemption, the system must first recognize the event causing the activation of the higher priority task, access the relative priorities of both the running and requested tasks, and then perform task switching.

Interrupt latency time (t_{IL}) is the time from when the CPU receives an interrupt request until the execution of the first instruction of the interrupt service routine, as illustrated in Figure 1.14.

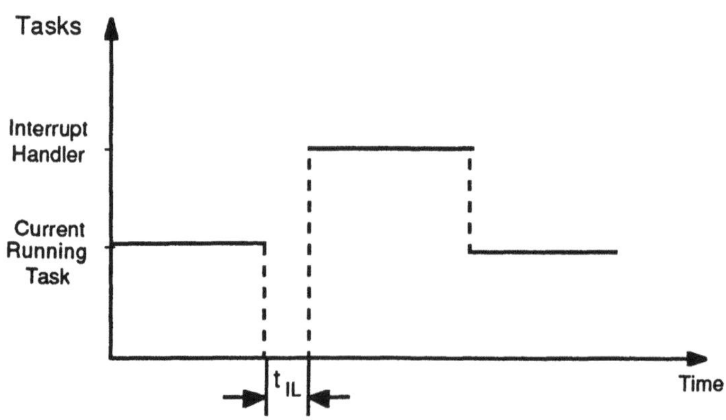

Figure 1.14 - Definition of interrupt latency time

Interrupt latency time depends on the efficiency of both the operating system and the processor architecture in handling external interrupts.

<u>Semaphore shuffling time</u> (t_{SS}) is the time delay between a task's release of a semaphore until the activation of another task waiting for the semaphore. The semaphore shuffling time is an important measure in real-time systems because it represents the overhead associated with mutual exclusion. In real-time systems, multiple tasks usually compete for the same resources. Figure 1.15 presents semaphore shuffling.

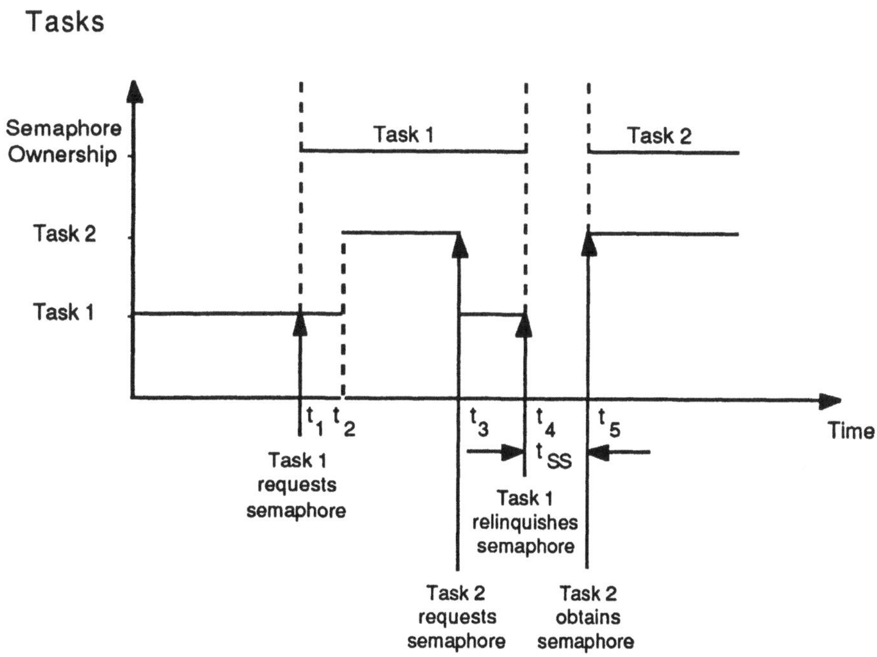

Figure 1.15 - Definition of semaphore shuffling time

In Figure 1.15, Task 1 is a running task and it requests its resource's semaphore at time t_1 to access a common resource. At time t_2 Task 1 gets suspended and Task 2 starts running. At time t_3, Task 2 needs to access the same resource by requesting its semaphore, which is owned by Task 1. Unable to continue, Task 2 gets suspended and Task 1 again awakens. At the end of execution, Task 1 relinquishes the semaphore at time t_4. The scheduler recognizes that the semaphore is now free, and is available for the suspended Task 2. Task 2 will be resumed and will obtain the semaphore. Semaphore shuffling time is the period between when Task 1 releases the semaphore and Task 2 resumes operation by obtaining the semaphore. The semaphore-based mutual exclusion is an efficient technique to assure that only one task has access to a common resource.

Deadlock breaking time (t_{DB}) is the average time it takes the system to resolve the deadlock. The deadlock can occur when a higher priority task suspends a lower-priority task that holds a resource needed by a higher priority task. The deadlock breaking time measures the efficiency of the operating system algorithms in handling deadlocks. Figure 1.16 shows a deadlock breaking timing diagram. Low-priority Task 1 takes ownership of a resource at t_1, and is then preempted by the highest priority Task 3 at t_3. At t_3, Task 3 requests the resource which is still held by the suspended Task 1.

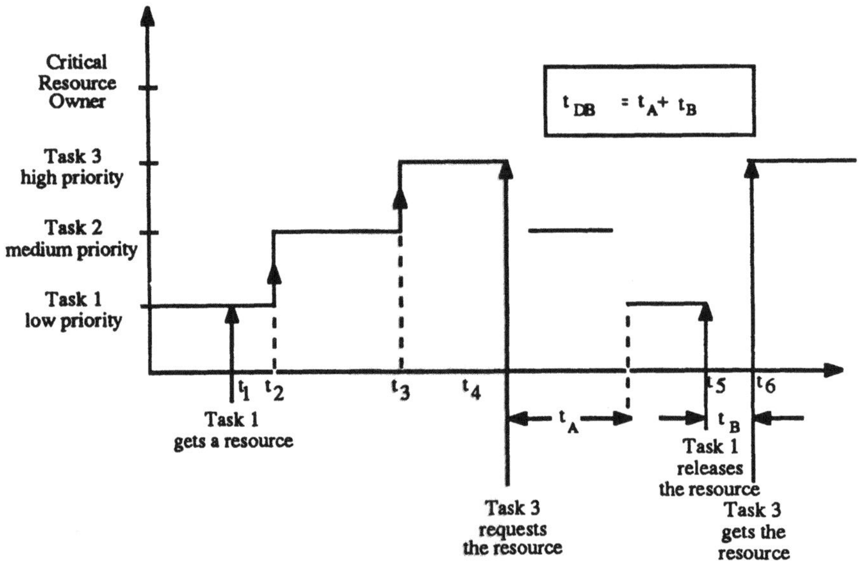

Figure 1.16 - Deadlock breaking timing diagram

The first part of the deadlock breaking time (t_A) then occurs as the system detects the deadlock and then decides how to resolve it. One of the techniques to handle this situation is to raise the priority of Task 1. Through this process Task 1 can run, complete the execution using the critical resource and release that resource. When Task 1 releases the critical resource at t_5, the system suspends Task 1 and enters the second phase of deadlock breaking (time t_B), in which Task 3 resumes and gets control of the resource at t_6.

The deadlock breaking time is then defined as the sum of the times t_A and t_B, which is the time required to resolve the deadlock.

Datagram throughput (t_{DT}) is the number of kilobytes per second one task can send to another via calls to the primitives of the real-time operating system, without using a predefined common message buffer in the system's address space or passing a pointer. The sending task must receive an acknowledgement, as shown in Figure 1.17.

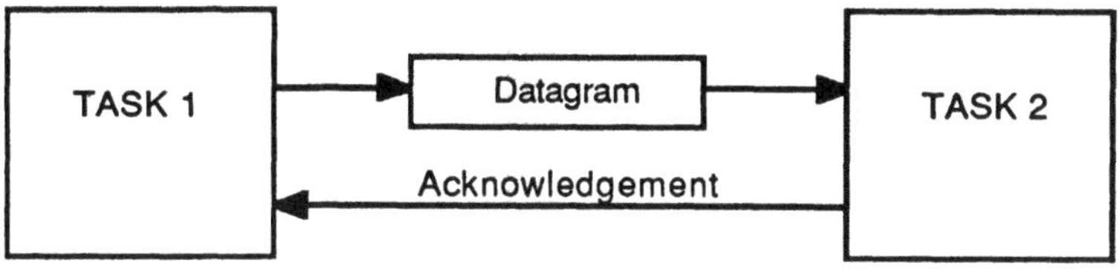

Figure 1.17 - Datagram throughput measured in kbytes per second

The datagram throughput measures the average intertask communication speed. It is important in real-time systems, where one task collects data from the outside world, and sends that data to another task for processing.

Kar and Porter proposed the following procedure in order to calculate the Rhealstone number. The Rhealstone number is determined by first obtaining the five previously described measurements in the microsecond to millisecond range. To combine these measurements into a single value, Kar and Porter proposed that all times be converted to seconds and then their arithmetic inversion (frequency) be calculated. As an example, if one of the measured times is 200 microseconds, it is converted to 0.0002 seconds and the Rhealstone component (frequency) is $f = 1/0.0002 = 5000$ per second. Datagram throughput is already expressed in kbytes per second so no further conversion of this value is required.

A Rhealstone number is then calculated as the sum:

$$R = f_1 + f_2 + f_3 + f_4 + f_5 + f_6$$

where f_1 is the task switching time component converted to a frequency, f_2 is the preemption time converted to a frequency and so on. The larger the value of R - the better the performance of the real-time system.

The Rhealstone metric R is based on the assumption that all six components are equally influential in determining real-time system performance.

To address this constraint, Kar and Porter also proposed a weighted Rhealstone metric (R_w). The weighted Rhealstone metric uses weighting coefficients for each of its component measures. These can be adjusted to reflect the importance of each component in any specific real-time application.

The explicit expression for R_w is:

$$R_w = c_1 \cdot f_1 + c_2 \cdot f_2 + c_3 \cdot f_3 + c_4 \cdot f_4 + c_5 \cdot f_5 + c_6 \cdot f_6$$

In this equation, c_1 to c_6 are the weight coefficients. The values of these coefficients range from zero to a positive value that reflects the relative importance of each Rhealstone component for the specific application.

1.4.2 Process Dispatch Latency Time

The process dispatch latency time (PDLT) is another frequently used measure for the evaluation of real-time systems [Furh89b]. In real-time systems, real-time processes are waiting for some external event to occur in order to be activated. When an interrupt occurs, the currently executing lower-priority process must be quickly switched out and the real-time process switched in. Process dispatch latency time (t_{PDL}) can be defined as the time interval between the time when the system receives an interrupt request until the beginning of the execution of the application task performed by a real-time system. While the interrupt latency and context switching time are the two major components of the process dispatch latency time, there are several other important components which form this measure, as shown in Figure 1.18.

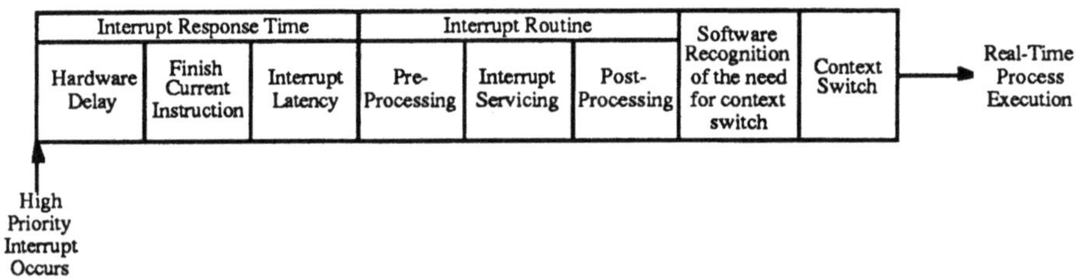

Figure 1.18 - Definition of the process dispatch latency time

As shown in Figure 1.18, the interrupt response time consists of both hardware and software related latencies. The hardware delay is the time required for the hardware to explicitly notify the operating system of the interrupt. Once notified, the operating system must wait until the current instruction has completed execution and then start the interrupt handling functions. During the interrupt latency time these handling functions prepare the system for the execution of the interrupt routine, e.g., save system state variables, etc.

The interrupt routine is executed and services the interrupt request. This processing is partitioned into three sections in Figure 1.18, preprocessing, interrupt servicing, and post processing. There is a further delay from the time of termination of the interrupt routine until the operating system recognizes the need for a context switch. Finally, there is the time required to actually accomplish the context switch such that a new real-time process begins execution.

The process dispatch latency time is an effective performance measure of a real-time operating system.

1.4.3 Tri-Dimensional Measure

The Tri-Dimensional® measure, proposed in [Rabb88a, 88b], includes three most important features of real-time computers: (a) CPU computational speed, measured in Millions of Instructions Per Second (MIPS1), (b) interrupt handling capability, measured in Millions of Interrupts Per Second (MIPS2), (c) I/O throughput, measured in Millions of I/O operations (Mbytes/sec) Per Second.

These three features are not independent and should be analyzed together. For example, if *a* computer has as its maximum features: 5 MIPS1 of CPU speed, 0.1 MIPS2 of interrupt handling capability, and 5 MIPS3 of I/O throughput, it does not mean that these three values can be achieved simultaneously. Generally, increasing one feature will automatically degrade the other two. The extent of the performance degradation in each of these measures, as a function of system loading, is an indication of the effectiveness of the computer system in real-time applications.

To get a sense of the interrelationship between these measures, let's ignore for a moment the I/O throughput, and analyze the interrelation between the CPU speed and the interrupt handling capability of a computer system. This is possible because most modern real-time computers have separate processors to handle I/O operations, and therefore the I/O throughput depends very little on the other two features.

A typical interdependence between the CPU speed and interrupt handling capability for two computers *A* and *B* is shown in Figure 1.19.

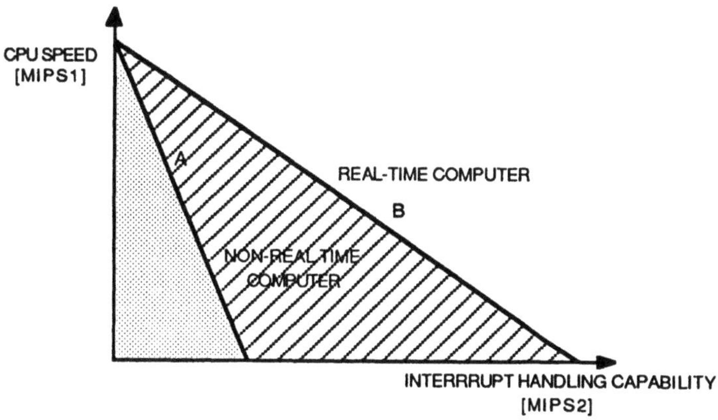

Figure 1.19 - Two-dimensional representation of computer performance

Note that in both cases, when the interrupt loading increases, the CPU power decreases. The major difference is that the performance degrades much faster in the case of computer *A*, while in the case of computer *B* the degradation of performance is much more gradual. This indicates that computer *B* is much more suitable for real-time applications by providing superior interrupt handling capability.

While the detailed features will vary, the performance of a computer system is graphically represented as a surface in a three dimensional Euclidean Space defined by the measures MIPS1, MIPS2 and MIPS3. This performance surface defines the operating points for a computer system as the load on that system changes.

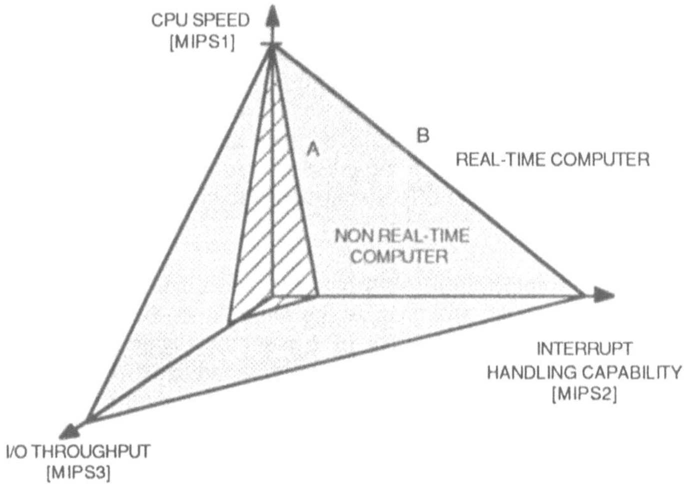

Figure 1.20 - Three-dimensional representation of computer performance

Assuming a conventional computer, in which a single CPU performs both application programs and I/O processing, the three-dimensional presentation can be represented by a plane, as shown in Figure 1.20.

Again, the performance of computer *A* degrades much faster than that of computer *B*, when the interrupt loading and/or the I/O throughput increase.

The three-dimensional representation gives a graphical view of the real-time capabilities of a computer system. In an attempt to combine these parameters into a single performance number, several alternatives can be considered. One based on volume, emerges as the logical choice since it incorporates all three of the measures. The volume of the three-dimensional function can be defined as:

$$Volume = \iint M1\ (M2, M3)\ dM2\ dM3$$

where $M1$, $M2$ and $M3$ correspond to variables along the MIPS1, MIPS2, and MIPS3 axes, respectively; and $M1$ is expressed as a function of $M2$ and $M3$.

In the case where the precise shape of the volume is not known, a more practical indication of real-time performance is simply the volume of the rectangular solid defined by three-dimensional parameters of the computer. This simplistic approximation of the volume is then computed as:

$$Volume = M1 \bullet M2 \bullet M3$$

The tri-dimensional measure (or equivalent $MIPS_e$ of the computer) can then be defined as the cube root of the volume:

$$MIPS_e = \sqrt[3]{Volume}$$

Since the MIPS2 (*M2*) value is typically two orders of magnitude smaller than the MIPS1 and MIPS3 values for a given computer, the MIPS2 value should be normalized by multiplying by 100 prior to calculating the value of $MIPS_e$.

The tri-dimensional measure, $MIPS_e$, demonstrates the overall real-time performance of the system. For example, if a computer has the following maximum values for individual features: MIPS1 = 5, MIPS2 = 0.1, and MIPS3 = 8, then the simplified equivalent $MIPS_e$ value is:

$$MIPS_e = \sqrt[3]{5 \bullet (0.1 \bullet 100) \bullet 8} = \sqrt[3]{400} = 7.4$$

From the two-dimensional representation given in Figure 1.19, two other real-time measures can be derived; these are, Program Overhead and System Overhead.

Program overhead (*P*) is a measure which defines how much time it takes to complete an application program at a specific interrupt loading, compared to the time it takes to complete it at no interrupt loading:

$$P = \frac{tn - to}{to} \bullet 100 \ [\%]$$

where *to* is the execution time under no interrupt loading and *tn* is the execution time at a particular interrupt loading.

Suppose that a benchmark program completes in one second at an interrupt loading zero, and in 1.6 seconds at an interrupt loading of 20,000 interrupts per second. Then the program overhead for this interrupt loading becomes:

$$P_{20,000} = \frac{1.6 - 1}{1} \bullet 100 = 60\%$$

It means, that this benchmark took 60% longer to complete under the specified interrupt loading.

System overhead (S) defines what percentage of the total elapsed time is devoted to handle the interrupts:

$$S = \frac{tn - to}{tn} \bullet 100 \quad [\%]$$

Using the same values as in the previous example, for the interrupt loading equal to 20,000 int/sec, S becomes:

$$S_{20,000} = \frac{1.6 - 1}{1.6} \bullet 100 = 37.5\%$$

The obtained results for S means that 37.5% of time is spent by the interrupt handler servicing interrupts, and the rest of the time is dedicated to the application program.

When measuring the performance of real-time computers, the program and system overhead can be calculated for different interrupt loading. Note that S can not be larger than 100% in which case the saturation point has been reached.

1.4.4 The Real/Stone Benchmark

The Real/Stone benchmark is an artificial, synthetic test designed to simulate a real world environment. It is a pure software benchmark that does not require any test hardware and is easily ported across various computers.

The Real/Stone benchmark is an extension of the Vanada benchmark [Vana84], which has been used by ALCOA in evaluating real-time computer systems. The Vanada benchmark simulates a real-time environment under light task loading. In contrast, the Real/Stone benchmark includes variable loading which is user selectable and ranges from light to heavy.

The Real/Stone benchmark, described in detail in [MODC90], consists of three tests which measure the following features of a real-time system:

1. system responsiveness,
2. system preemptibility, and
3. system I/O throughput.

For the first two tests, the benchmark is partitioned into a set of interactive and real-time processes activated by internal timers, as shown in Figure 1.21.

The TRIANG process generates triangle waves and stores data into the global memory. It is used to simulate an input device which samples data from an external process at a certain activation rate (240 Hz in the Real/Stone case).

Real-time processes are activated by internal timers at various activation rates (240 Hz, 120 Hz, 80 Hz, etc). They are all of the same priority and have identical code. The user can select any number of real-time processes in order to simulate a real world environment. Real-time processes use the current sample from the TRIANG process in order to recreate the triangle wave, and also calculate an error function. The error function indicates how well the recreated triangle wave matches the original function generated by the TRIANG process.

If the system under evaluation is a highly-responsive, predictable real-time system, it is expected that the system can handle a large number of real-time processes before the error becomes high. However, if the system is not highly-responsive and not predictable, it will not be able to handle a large number of real-time processes. In this case the error will increase rapidly with the increase of process loading.

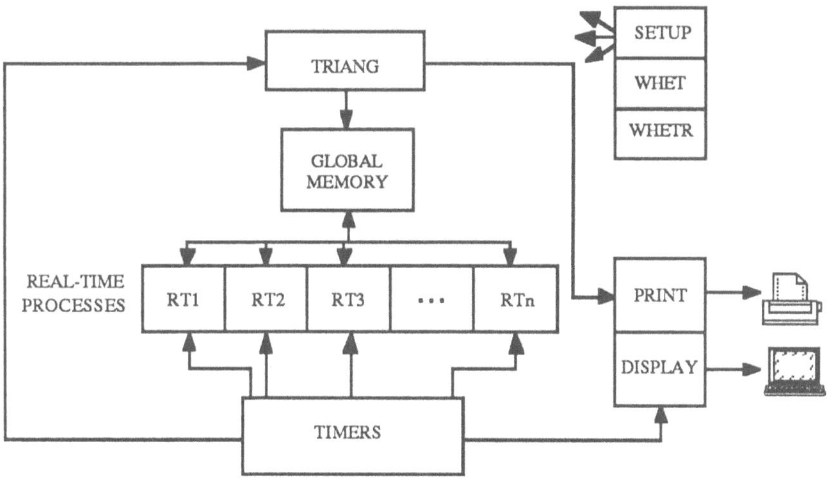

Figure 1.21 - The Real/Stone program decomposed into a number of processes

The DISPLAY process presents how well real-time processes recreate the triangle wave, as well as the error function.

The PRINT process prints the summary of results.

The timing diagram of processes in the Real/Stone benchmark is given in Figure 1.22.

In the first test, the WHETR process runs at a priority lower than other processes and calculates the residual Whetstone MIPS available for application programs or for software development. The WHET process generates the MIPS rating under no loading. On the basis of these values, the percentage of the raw processing power left for application processes is calculated for various process loading. It is defined as the ratio (R):

$$R = \frac{\text{Residual MIPS}}{\text{Raw MIPS}}$$

As the result of the first Real/Stone test, which evaluates the responsiveness of the system under various process loads, the following three graphs are plotted:

- Processing power (Residual MIPS) as a function of the number of real-time processes,
- Percentage of the raw processing power left for application processes (R) as a function of the number of processes, and
- The error as a function of the number of processes.

These three functions present a true picture of the responsiveness of the system under evaluation and indicate system degradation as the load increases.

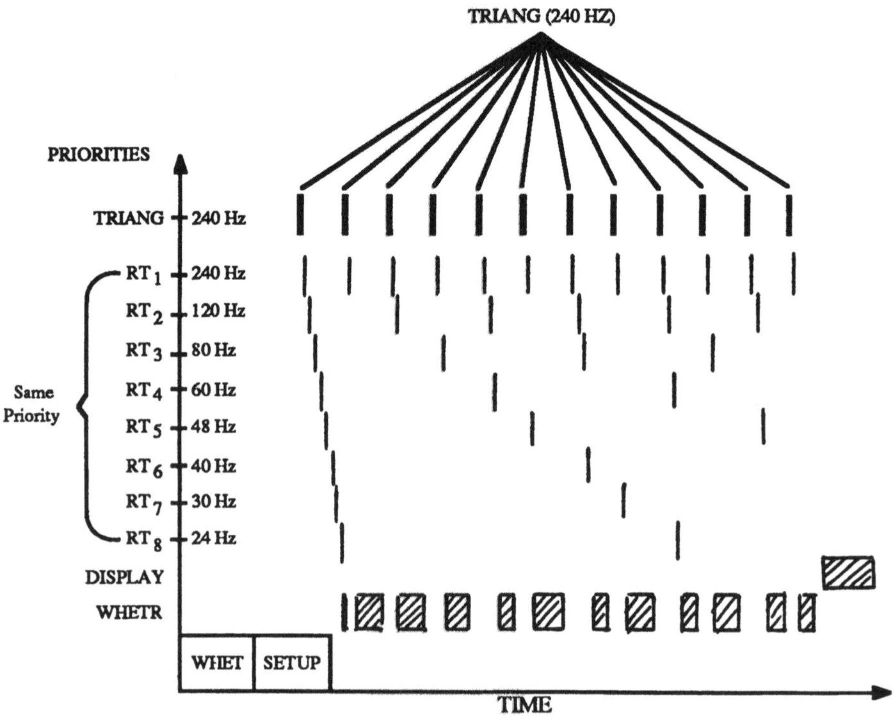

Figure 1.22 - Timing diagram of processes' execution in the Real/Stone

In the second Real/Stone test, which measures system preemptibility, the same program structure, shown in Figure 1.21, is used. The only modification consists of replacing the WHETR process with a SYSCALL process also running at the lowest priority. The SYSCALL process performs long system calls, e.g., *fork* and *exec*.

If the system under evaluation contains a fully preemptive kernel, the following scenario is expected. Whenever a real-time process is ready to run (activated by the timer), the SYSCALL process will be immediately preempted and the control will be transferred to the real-time process. The real-time process will get the current sample from the common memory, and recreate successfully the triangle wave.

If the system under evaluation does not allow full kernel preemption (non-preemptive kernel, or preemption windows), the SYSCALL process will not be immediately preempted. It will run until the currently executing system call is complete or until a preemption point is reached, and then it will be preempted by the real-time process waiting for execution. As a consequence, the real-time process will likely be delayed, will get the wrong sample value, and an error will occur in recreating the triangle wave.

The results of the preemptibility test are presented in the form of a graph which plots the error function as a function of the number of processes.

The third Real/Stone test is used to compare the I/O throughputs of the standard UNIX System V and the system under evaluation. This test is specifically designed for real-time UNIX systems which besides the standard UNIX System V file system, contain a fast file system. As a result of the test, a graph is plotted which compares I/O throughputs of the standard and the fast file system as a function of the size of the block being transferred.

Some results, using the real-time measures presented in this section, are given in Section 4.12.5.

1.5 MODEL OF AN OPEN REAL-TIME SYSTEM

The next generation of real-time systems will be based upon open systems, which incorporate industry standards. Open systems reduce system cost and time to market, increase availability of software packages, increase ease-of-use, and facilitate system integration. The ultimate goal of the open system concept is to provide complete software portability. One version of a real-time application should run on various hardware platforms.

The proposed model of an open real-time computer system, shown in Figure 1.23, is based on the following principles:

1. The operating system is a standard fully-preemptible real-time operating system, preferably a real-time UNIX operating system based on AT&T's

System V. It complies with operating system standards, such as the IEEE POSIX.

2. The system architecture is centralized or distributed, depending on the application. The node architecture in the distributed system, or the architecture of the centralized system, uses a multiprocessor implementation based on off-the-shelf microprocessors. The interconnection topology for processors and I/Os is designed in such a way to provide extensive I/O, high-speed data processing, and efficient interrupt handling.

   ASIC and VLSI technology are used to improve real-time performance by providing architectural supports for operating system scheduling, interrupt handling, fault tolerance, and language features.

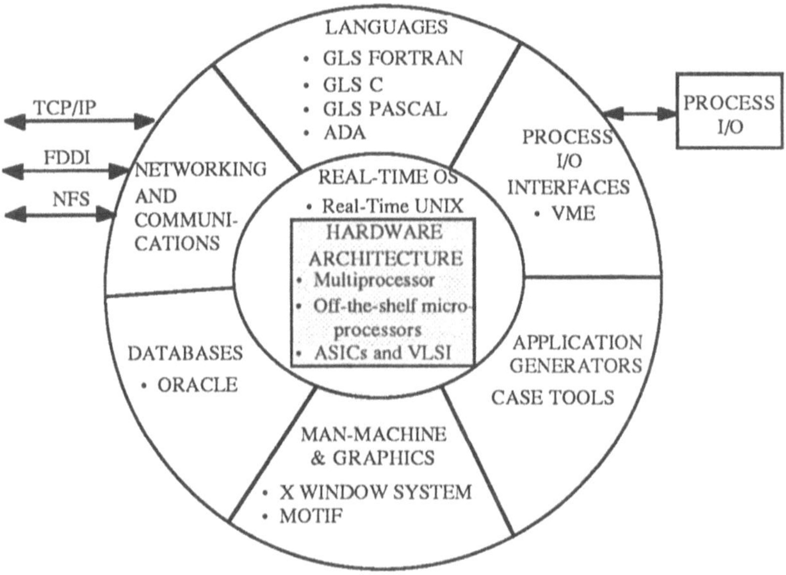

Figure 1.23 - Model of an open system for real-time applications

3. The open system is based upon a General Language System (GLS™) as the standard compiler system. The GLS compiles various high level source languages into a common intermediate language and therefore provides source code portability across different machines. Currently, the programming languages used in real-time computing are standard languages, such as C, Pascal and Fortran; however, as the complexity of real-time systems increases, there will be a demand for the real-time programming languages.

4. The open real-time system includes a user-friendly man-machine interface and graphics user environment based on standards, such as the X-Window System™ and Motif™, which are adapted for real-time use.

5. The open system supports a standard database management system, such as ORACLE®. The next generation of real-time systems will demand distributed real-time databases.

6. The open system provides connectivity through standards. For real-time communications, a standard network protocol such as TCP/IP is used, modified to provide predictable throughput. The communication media used include electrical and fiber optic cable.

   A standard I/O bus such as the VME standard is used for process I/O and peripheral devices. A standard network file server such as NFS® is used for transferring files.

7. Standard Computer Aided Software Engineering (CASE) tools are supported by the system. A set of application generators for various markets is provided.

Collectively, these principles define a comprehensive model for cost-effective high performance real-time computer systems that are founded on industry-wide standards.

Summary

This chapter has presented an overview of the fundamentals of real-time computing and a model for open real-time systems based upon the UNIX operating system and industry standards.

In subsequent chapters, we present in detail a real-time UNIX operating system that represents the foundation for an open real-time computer system.

CHAPTER 2

Real-Time Operating Systems

An introduction to real-time operating systems is the topic of this chapter. General requirements for real-time operating systems are discussed and the standard UNIX System V is analyzed from this standpoint. Real-time UNIX standards as well as existing real-time UNIX implementations are presented. Real-time UNIX implementations are divided into six categories, and these six approaches are described and analyzed.

2.1 REQUIREMENTS FOR REAL-TIME OPERATING SYSTEMS

An operating system can be defined as the set of programs, implemented in either software or firmware, that makes the hardware usable [Deit84].

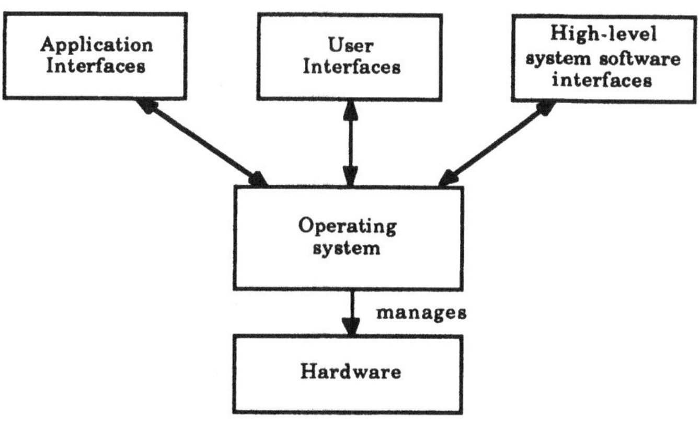

Figure 2.1 - The operating system is the interface between the programmer and the machine

The operating system forms a layer of software between the programmer and the base machine [Emer89], as illustrated in Figure 2.1.

The requirements for real-time operating systems can be summarized as follows (Table 2.1):

Table 2.1
Requirements for Real-Time Operating Systems

- Support for scheduling of real-time processes
- Preemptive scheduling
- Guaranteed interrupt response
- Interprocess communication
- High speed data acquisition
- I/O support
- User control of system resources

1. Support for scheduling of real-time processes

A real-time system should provide support for the creation, deletion, and scheduling of multiple processes, each of which monitors and controls some portion of a total application. Typically, a priority-based scheduling of real-time processes will allow users to define priorities for processes and interrupts to be scheduled. In contrast, in a general-purpose multitasking operating system, only the operating system itself determines the order in which processes execute.

2. Preemptive scheduling

A real-time operating system must ensure that a high-priority process, when ready to execute, preempts a lower priority process. The operating system must be able to recognize the condition (usually through an interrupt), preempt the currently executing process, and perform a fast context switch to allow a higher priority process to execute. A general-purpose operating system, such as UNIX System V operating system, will first complete the execution of a lower priority process currently running in the kernel, and then activate the higher priority process.

3. Guaranteed interrupt response

A real-time system must be able to very quickly recognize the occurrence of an event and take deterministic (well-defined in terms of function and time) action based on the event. A real-time operating system must be able to respond on both hardware and software interrupts. The operating system itself should be interruptible and reentrant. There should be minimal overhead in the operating system, especially when a high-priority real-time process is ready to execute.

4. Interprocess communications

A real-time operating system must be able to support interprocess communications via reliable and fast facilities, such as semaphores, shared memory and message passing. These facilities are used to synchronize and coordinate process execution, as well as for the use and protection of shared data and shared resources.

5. High speed data acquisition

A real-time system must be able to handle very high burst rates in high speed data acquisition applications. Therefore, a real-time operating system must provide a means to optimize data storage on a disk, moving of the disk heads, moving data from system buffers to user buffers, etc. Additional required features include the ability to preallocate contiguous disk files, and provisions for user control over buffering.

6. I/O support

Real-time applications typically include a number of I/O interfaces. A real-time operating system must provide tools for easy incorporation of custom I/O drivers in the system. For standard devices, the standard I/O library should be available. The operating system must also support asynchronous I/O, wherein a process can initiate an I/O operation, and then continue execution while the I/O operation is performed concurrently.

7. User control of system resources

A key characteristic of real-time systems is the ability to provide users with specific control of the system resources including the CPU, memory and I/O resources. Control of the CPU is accomplished by implementing a priority-based scheduling technique in which users can set the priority of user processes. In addition, real-time timers and timer functions are available directly to applications to schedule events and track elapsed time.

A real-time operating system must also provide memory locking facilities to allow the user to lock a program or part of a program in memory for faster context switching when an interrupt occurs. The user should also be able to control and guarantee memory allocation for buffers and enable the locking and unlocking of devices and files.

2.2 REAL-TIME UNIX OPERATING SYSTEMS

The UNIX System V operating system, developed by AT&T Bell Laboratories [Ritch74], has become a standard operating system gaining rapid acceptance because of its superior flexibility, portability, and large number of support tools. However, the UNIX operating system was originally designed for multitasking and time-sharing, and therefore standard UNIX operating system does not have an adequate response time and data throughput needed to support most real-time applications.

2.2.1 The UNIX System and Real-Time

In this section we analyze the requirements for real-time operating systems from a UNIX standpoint.

Scheduling. The UNIX scheduling algorithm is designed to provide equitable access to the CPU and memory. It was designed for timesharing environments, and therefore processes are time sliced. The scheduler periodically recalculates priorities of processes to ensure a fair share of the CPU by each process.

In order to make it suitable for real-time, the scheduler must be modified to allow users to have direct control over process priorities. The priority of real-time processes should be made fixed, not varied by the operating system. Real-time processes of equal priority should be executed in a round-robin fashion, and not be subject to time slicing.

Interrupt handling. In the standard UNIX environment, a process operating in system space (i.e., executing a system call) cannot be preempted. A system call, even one from a low-priority user process, continues executing until it blocks or runs to completion. This can take as long as several seconds for some of the longer UNIX system calls (such as **execute** or **fork** which copy large amounts of data), and therefore the standard UNIX system is unacceptable for time-critical applications.

Interprocess communications. The UNIX System V operating system supports both shared memory and messages as a means for interprocess communications. Both pipes and signals can be used as communication mechanisms. The pipe is a simple and elegant channel for communication between two processes and is one of the innovations of the UNIX operating system. With these functions, a process can send a signal to another process, thereby interrupting the signaled process. The signal handler can either move or respond to the signal.

Data pooling allows large amounts of data to be shared between processes. This can be accomplished by opening a file for access by a number of processes, and also by overlapping the data segments of different processes. The UNIX System V operating system provides the **shmop** primitive to enable data pooling.

File system. In the standard UNIX environment, disk file space is allocated as needed on write operations, and not upon file creation. With this approach, no guarantee is provided that the disk space will be available when it is needed. It also implies that performance on writes will be slower since time must be spent in allocating space during the write operation. Another drawback is the likelihood that the disk file will not be contiguous, resulting in more disk seeking and lower performance. The real-time performance can be improved significantly if the object file is stored contiguously on disk.

I/O support. The standard UNIX operating system does not support asynchronous I/O operations, nor is there a capability for connecting directly to I/O devices. However, the UNIX System V operating system provides for non-blocking reads and for non-blocking writes. Real-time applications usually include the interfacing of custom I/O devices and drivers which will require skeleton drivers provided by UNIX.

User control of system resources. The UNIX System V operating system provides a means of locking a process in memory for fast process dispatching in response to real-time events but does not provide a means of locking a device.

In summary, the UNIX operating system is designed for time-sharing applications, and in its standard form has many deficiencies when implemented in real-time applications. A real-time UNIX operating system can be constructed by combining UNIX functionality and adding real-time features to the system.

2.2.2 Real-Time UNIX Standards

The next generation of real-time systems will use open systems, which incorporate industry standards. Open systems, based on standards, provide a number of advantages for users, as illustrated in Table 2.2

Table 2.2
Open Versus Proprietary Systems

Advantage for Users	Proprietary Systems	Open Systems
Software Portability	Months/Years	Hours/Weeks
Database Conversion	Years	Hours/Days
Programmer Retraining and Availability	Big Issues	Negligible
Flow of Enhancements	Controlled by Computer Manufacturer	Free Market for Major Innovations

The ultimate goal of the open systems concept is to provide complete software portability. One version of an application should run on various hardware platforms, as illustrated in Figure 2.2.

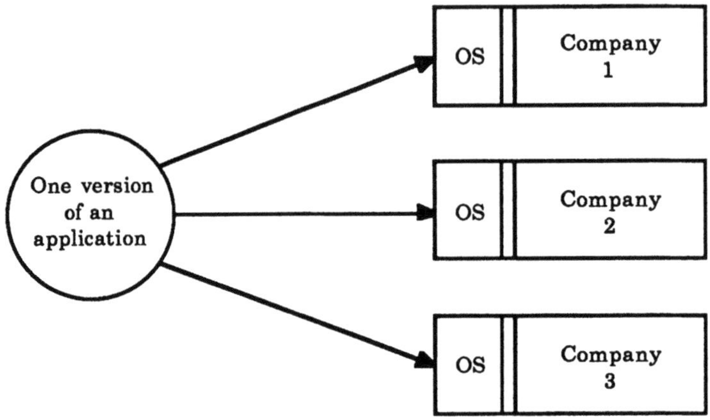

Figure 2.2 - The main goal of open systems and standards

Software standards can be divided into three categories: (a) source standards, (b) object standards, and (c) binary standards.

Source standards provide portability of source code. Examples of source standards are POSIX, OSF™, and ANSI. Source standards provide flexibility between architectures and operating systems, however, software is not protected from unauthorized modification and recompilation and linking are required. Nevertheless, source level standards are essential ingredients for lower level standards.

Object standards provide portability of unlinked objects within a specific processor architecture. Examples of object standards are the 88Open™ OCS and the GKS. Object level standards provide software protection, however, they are bound to a specific hardware architecture. At this level, re-linking of software modules is required.

Binary standards provide portability of executable versions of software across vendors of specific processor-based architectures. Examples of binary standards are ABI and the 88Open BCS. Binary standards provide complete software portability across hardware platforms based upon a common binary language structure.

Over the years, a number of variations of the UNIX operating system have evolved and a number of attempts have been made to standardize the user level interfaces of the operating system. The two major ones are AT&T's System V Interface Definition (SVID) and the ANSI/IEEE committee 1003 (POSIX).

The AT&T SVID includes a Base Interface definition plus a series of extensions. The Base Interface Definition describes the services that all System V operating systems must provide.

The POSIX group is a standardization effort that includes a number of corporations. The IEEE P.1003.1 standard defines an operating system interface acceptable to most vendors. A number of other POSIX standards are under development, which are related to shell and tools (P.1003.2), test methods (P.1003.3), real time (P.1003.4), ADA binding (P.1003.5), security (P.1003.6), system administration (P.1003.7), networking (P.1003.P), and other subjects.

The purpose of the POSIX 1003.4 real-time standard is to develop a set of interfaces that will allow for the portability of applications with real-time requirements. This standard specifies extensions to the POSIX 1003.1 standards. The POSIX 1003.4 draft deals with ten important real-time functions that are summarized in Table 2.3.

Table 2.3
POSIX 1003.4 Functions

FUNCTION	DESCRIPTION
1. Timers	The ability to set and read high resolution internal times
2. Priority Scheduling	A priority-based preemptive scheduling
3. Shared memory	The ability to map common physical space into independent process-specific virtual spaces
4. Real-time files	The ability to create and access files with deterministic performance
5. Semaphores	Efficient synchronization primitives (P and V operations)
6. Interprocess communication	Synchronous and asynchronous message-passing capabilities with facilities for flow and resource control.
7. Asynchronous event notification	A mechanism which provides queuing capabilities, deterministic delivery, and minimal data passing.
8. Process memory locking	The ability to guarantee memory-residence for sections of a process' virtual address space.
9. Asynchronous I/O	The ability to overlap applications processing and I/O operations initiated by the application.
10. I/O Synchronized	The ability to establish assurance of I/O completion at different logical levels of completion.

The POSIX 1003.4 will also identify the real-time performance metrics which will be standardized. The UNIX process dispatch latency time is one of the metrics analyzed by the POSIX 1003.4 committee. They defined the process dispatch latency time as, "the time from which an asynchronous device interrupts the machine causing the highest priority process to execute until that process returns from the system call that caused it to block on that external device" [Unif89]. This metric is expected to be measured and documented for all real-time operating systems conforming to the standard.

2.2.3 Real-Time UNIX Implementations

Many attempts have been made to adapt the UNIX kernel to provide a real-time environment [Falk88, Simp89]. It is very difficult to compare performance among all the versions of real-time UNIX operating systems, because each implementation is dependent on the application code and type of processor.

One classification method [Furh90a], divides real-time UNIX implementations into six categories. These six categories along with the companies taking these approaches, are summarized in Table 2.4.

These six approaches are discussed below.

1. <u>Adding Extensions to Standard UNIX System</u>

This approach in implementing a real-time UNIX system is to add extensions to the core UNIX operating system. The real-time extensions can be implemented in the kernel or outside of the kernel. This is the approach taken by system-level vendors, such as AT&T in its System V.4 UNIX release.

Some examples of adding extensions to create a real-time UNIX system can involve implementing priority-based scheduling in a task scheduler, and implementing real-time timers and priority disk scheduling.

Although this approach provides real-time functionality, it has its drawbacks. The main drawback is that this approach does not allow full preemption in the kernel mode. When an application task makes a system service call, and the task goes into kernel mode, the system has to complete that service call before a higher priority task can gain access to the CPU.

2. <u>Host/Target Approach</u>

The host/target approach toward developing a real-time UNIX environment is to develop an application on a UNIX host and then download it to a proprietary real-time kernel or to a dedicated operating system running on a target system. This approach connects a real-time kernel to a UNIX host via a communications interface.

Table 2.4
Classification of Real-Time UNIX Implementations

TECHNIQUES	OPERATING SYSTEM & COMPANY
1. Adding extensions to standard UNIX	• AT&T System V.4
2. Host-target approach	• VxWorks™ (Wind River Systems) • OS-9® (Microware) • VRTX™ (Ready Systems)
3. Integrated UNIX and real-time executives (or real-time OS)	• MTOS-UX™ (IPI) • RTUX™ (Emerge Systems, Inc.) • CXOS™ (Computer X/Motorola) • D-NIX® (Diab Systems) • REAL/IX (MODCOMP)
4. Proprietary UNIX	• AIX® (IBM®) • LynxOS (Lynx Real Time Systems) • Regulus™ (SBE)
5. Preemption points	• RTU™ (Concurrent/Masscomp) • HP-UX (Hewlett Packard) • VENIX™ (VenturCom)
6. Fully preemptive kernel	• REAL/IX (MODCOMP) • CX/RT (Harris)

The operating systems that use the host/target approach are given in Table 2.4. For example, in the case of the VxWorks operating system, developers use the UNIX host for development. This includes editing, compiling, linking, and storing real-time applications. Then the program is tested, debugged and executed on the target machine running VxWorks. The host and target communicate via sockets and TCP/IP protocol.

The VRTX operating system also allows communications between the target processor running the VRTX real-time kernel and the host computer that runs the UNIX operating system. For communications, a shared-memory implementation is used.

The host/target approach combines the advantages of a UNIX environment with those of proprietary real-time kernel. The response time of the proprietary kernel (under 10 microseconds) is generally faster than the response times of real-time UNIX implementations (from 70 microseconds to a few milliseconds). However, this approach requires two operating systems and as a result, the porting of application software to other platforms is more difficult.

3. Integrated UNIX Environment and Real-time Executive/OS

This approach provides a UNIX interface to a proprietary real-time kernel or a proprietary real-time operating system. Both the UNIX system and the proprietary kernel/OS run on the same machine. The MTOS real-time kernel for example, can log onto a UNIX system. The REAL/IX operating system on the MODCOMP 92XX systems integrates the AT&T System V with MAX 32 real-time operating system. The user can utilize the development tools in the UNIX environment in the development of real-time applications, and then run those applications in the proprietary operating system environment.

This approach, similar to the host/target approach, provides the fast real-time response of the proprietary real-time systems, but requires that programmers understand two operating systems, and the porting of applications is more difficult.

4. Proprietary UNIX Operating System

This approach to real-time UNIX implementation consists of developing the real-time kernel from the ground up while, at the same time, retaining the standard UNIX interfaces. Since a complete rewriting of the software is required, this approach is referred to as being proprietary.

For example, the Lynx operating system, AIX operating system, and Regulus operating system use this approach. Their internal implementations are proprietary, but the interfaces are fully compatible with a standard UNIX operating system such as AT&T's System V operating system. These interfaces are specified with standards such as SVID and IEEE POSIX.

This approach provides relatively high-performance, however porting applications to or from another real-time UNIX implementation often requires rewriting code. Standard UNIX applications will run under these operating systems, but code using the real-time extensions generally must be rewritten.

5. Preemption points

One of the most critical requirements for a true real-time UNIX implementation is kernel preemption. Most non-real time operating systems implement a round-robin scheduler, in which a real-time task is added to the run queue to await its next slice, as illustrated in Figure 2.3(a).

In the standard UNIX environment, a process operating in system space is not preemptible. A system call, even one from a low-priority user process, continues executing until it blocks or runs to completion. This can take as long as several seconds, as shown in Figure 2.3(b).

Another real-time UNIX implementation approach is to insert preemption points, or windows into the operating system kernel. Preemption points are built into the kernel, so that system calls do not have to block or run to completion before

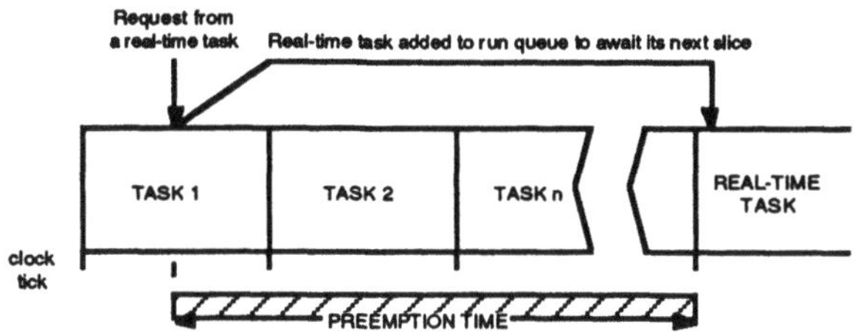

(a) Round-robin scheduler

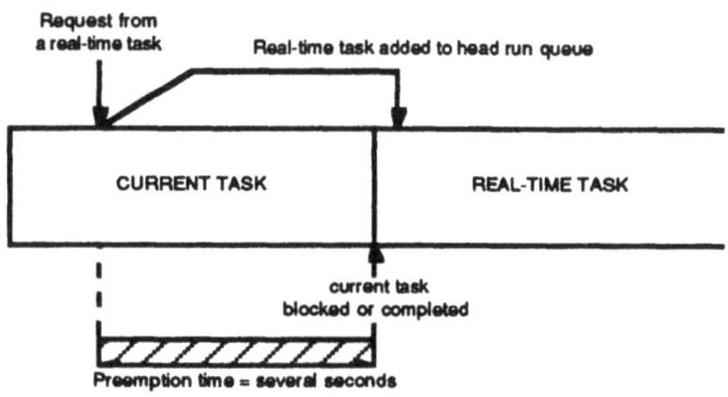

(b) Priority-driven (non-preemptive) scheduler

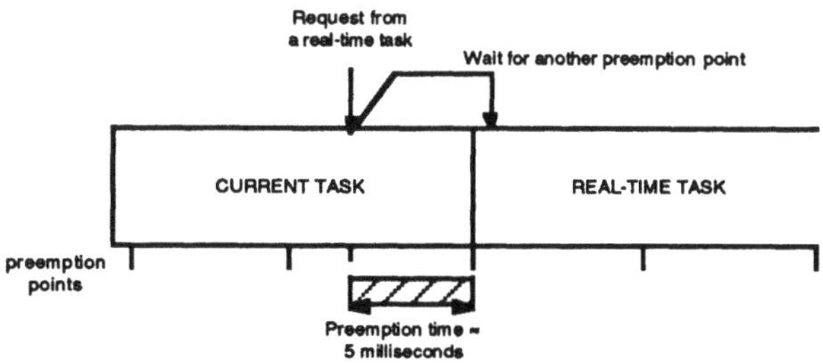

(c) Preemptive scheduler based on preemption points.

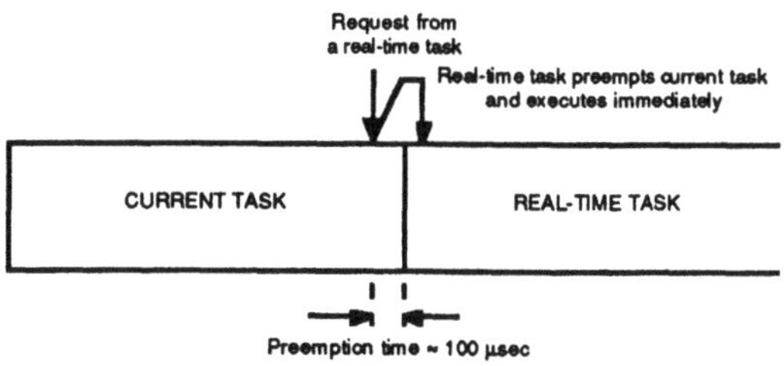

(d) Fully preemptive scheduler.

Figure 2.3 - Four concepts of scheduling algorithms: (a) Round-robin scheduler, (b) Priority-driven scheduler, (c) Preemptive scheduler with preemption points, and (d) Fully preemptive scheduler

giving up control. This can reduce the delay before the higher-priority process can begin or resume execution. However, as an impact of preemption points, there is still a preemption delay which may be as high as several milliseconds, as shown in Figure 2.3(c). This delay corresponds to the longest period of time between preemption points. The preemption points approach is taken by the RTU operating system, HP-UX operating system, and VENIX™ operating system. The RTU operating system includes approximately 100 preemption points and 10 preemptible regions. At the preemption points, the operating system performs a quick check to see if a real-time process is ready to run. At these preemption points a preemption region is initiated in the kernel wherein the scheduler is always enabled.

The preemption points approach provides a high degree of determinism and fast response time, but it is still not a fully preemptive system. The drawback is similar to the drawback of the adding extensions approach previously described.

6. Fully preemptive kernel

This approach provides for full preemption in the UNIX environment, wherein preemption can occur anywhere in the kernel. The preemptible kernel can be built by incorporating synchronization mechanisms, such as semaphores and spin locks, to protect all UNIX global data structures. By implementing a fine granularity of semaphores, the preemption delay can be significantly reduced to no more than approximately 100 microseconds or less, as illustrated in Figure 2.3(d).

A fully preemptive kernel provides the system with the ability to respond immediately to interrupts, to break out of the kernel mode, and to execute a high-priority real-time process. This approach is implemented in the REAL/IX and CX/RT operating systems, while the VENIX and RTU versions of fully preemptive UNIX kernels are under development.

Summary

This chapter presented an introduction to real-time operating systems based upon the UNIX system.

Chapter 3 covers, in detail, the concept of a fully preemptive real-time UNIX system, including a case study of the REAL/IX operating system.

CHAPTER 3

Concept of a Fully Preemptive UNIX Operating System

This chapter provides a detailed description of the concept of a fully preemptive real-time operating system, based on AT&T's UNIX System V. Special emphasis is given to the features added to the UNIX system to provide support for real-time programming needs. The concept and the detailed real-time capabilities described in this chapter were used as the basis for the development of the REAL/IX operating system, MODCOMP's real-time UNIX operating system [Furh89b, Gros90, Furh90a]. Therefore, the name REAL/IX operating system is used for the real-time UNIX operating system throughout this chapter.

3.1 SYSTEM CONCEPT

The major weaknesses of the UNIX System V for real-time applications are the lack of a preemptive kernel and the limited ability to preallocate resources for a process (see Section 2.2.1). The system described in this chapter is a fully preemptive, low-latency real-time UNIX kernel that provides a user environment similar to that of UNIX System V, but with extensions that provide the capabilities required by real-time applications. These real-time improvements are summarized here by the major subsystems of the UNIX operating system: process subsystem, interprocess communications, file subsystem, and I/O subsystem.

<u>Process subsystem</u>

The REAL/IX process subsystem includes the following enhancements required by real-time applications:

- fully-preemptive kernel with synchronization mechanisms to ensure data structure integrity,
- fixed-priority based process scheduler for critical real-time processes,
- real-time timer mechanisms, and

- enhanced memory management facilities that support preallocation of memory resources.

Interprocess communications

The standard UNIX System V interprocess communication mechanisms: signals, shared memory, semaphores, and messages, have been augmented with the following extensions:

- a common event notification mechanism that is more reliable than the signal mechanism (since more than one signal of a given type can be queued at once) allowing signals to be received synchronously as well as asynchronously, and
- a binary semaphore mechanism, which is a faster version of the UNIX System V semaphore mechanism.

File subsystem

The real-time UNIX file subsystem includes the following enhancements to the UNIX System V file subsystem:

- an alternative file system architecture that supports preallocation of space and contiguous files,
- the ability to bypass the buffer cache for file I/O,
- synchronous updates of physical storage devices,
- larger logical block sizes for faster throughput to files, and
- improved locality of reference.

I/O subsystem

The I/O subsystem enhancements to the UNIX System V I/O subsystem include the following capabilities required for real-time computing:

- support for asynchronous I/O operations,
- disk I/O queuing prioritized according to the process priority,
- direct I/O between a user-level program and a device, and
- connected interrupts for notifying a user-level process of a hardware interrupt.

Other enhancements

A number of other modifications have been made to the basic UNIX operating system to provide the control and performance required for real-time computing. Most of these are internal modifications that are completely transparent to users, but some will be visible:

- A number of daemons[1] have been added to the system to provide necessary kernel functionality (such as writing error messages to the console) without degrading system interrupt latency. Many of these daemons and other system processes have tunable parameters that determine their execution priority.

- The SCSI interface simplifies the administrative tasks involved in adding disk and tape devices to the system as well as providing the flexibility of the SCSI interface.

- System calls can be installed into the kernel by entering them into a table and relinking the kernel. On other UNIX operating systems, system calls (which execute with less overhead than library routines) can only be added by customers who have source code and can recompile the entire kernel.

A functional overview of the REAL/IX operating system is shown in Figure 3.1.

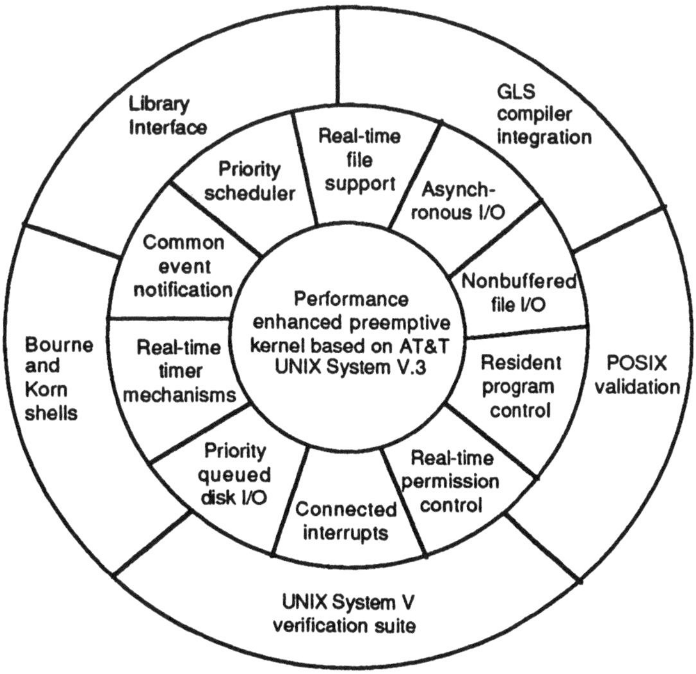

Figure 3.1 - Functional overview of REAL/IX - a fully preemptive real-time UNIX operating system

1 *Daemon* processes run at user-level but do system-wide functions. They are either kernel-resident or spawned by the init process and exist through the lifetime of the system.

The REAL/IX operating system can be viewed as a layered entity, as illustrated in Figure 3.2. Users always interact directly with the *user level*, usually through the shell. From the shell, the user may call utilities and user programs, which in turn may call library routines.

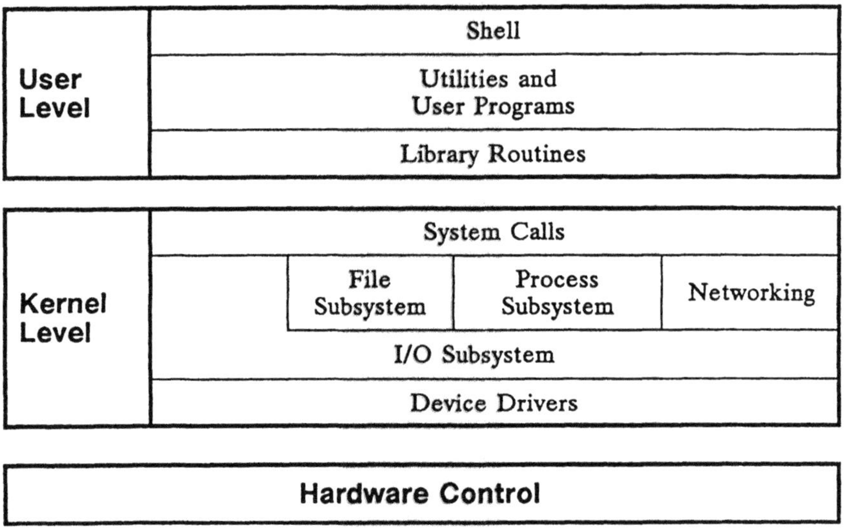

Figure 3.2 - Layered presentation of the UNIX operating system

In the user-level of the operating system, the user opens and closes files (which may be actual data files, or may be special files that correspond to system devices), reads and writes data, and so forth.

The *kernel level* of the operating system is accessed through system calls, which may be called directly by utility programs or user processes; or may be called through library routines. Kernel-level processes (or functions) handle the details of interacting with the internal structures of files, processes, and devices. The *hardware control level* of the system is accessed through kernel-level processes, usually drivers.

The discussions in this book will frequently refer to user-level activities versus kernel-level activities. One of the features which makes UNIX operating systems so popular is that most of the kernel is written in C language. Since C language is a high-level language it is also used for user-level programming. However, there are fundamental differences between user-level and kernel-level code:

- Each user-level program is coded separately, with its own **main** routine that controls the flow of execution. The entire kernel, however, has one

main routine, and all other kernel-level processes operate as functions of that routine.

- Each user-level process may be "paged out" of main memory, while a kernel-level process is never paged out.

- Each user-level process executes in a private area of user-address space and is generally unaffected by other user-level processes. All kernel-level processes, however, have full access to the address space of all other kernel-level processes.

System calls are the highest level of the kernel, and are the means by which a user-level process requests services from the kernel. System calls can be accessed directly from a C language or a Fortran program, or indirectly (by calling a C subroutine) from a program written in another language. To the programmer, system calls are indistinguishable from library routine calls.

All system calls take the form of functions, in that they can return a value. A return value of -1 usually indicates unsuccessful execution. When a call returns -1, an external variable called **errno** describes the nature of the problem.

Library routines are part of the user level. In most cases, library routines call system calls. For example, the **fopen** library routine calls the **open** system call; the **sleep** library routine calls the **alarm**, **pause**, and **signal** system calls. As a general rule, library routines execute a bit more slowly than the corresponding system calls, but also are safer for the novice programmer since they usually include some checks and clean up operations that the programmer would otherwise need to code.

The structure of the REAL/IX kernel, which except for the real-time features is identical to the UNIX kernel [Bach86], is presented in Figure 3.3. The block diagram shown in Figure 3.3, presents various REAL/IX modules, major real-time performance enhancements, and the relationship between the modules.

Three levels are shown in Figure 3.3: user, kernel, and hardware. The system call interface and libraries represent a connection between user programs and the kernel. System calls look like ordinary C function calls, and libraries map these function calls to the primitives needed to enter the operating system. Assembly language programs can invoke system calls directly without a system call library.

The system calls are partitioned into those that interact with the process control subsystem, the file subsystem, and the I/O subsystem.

The process control subsystem is responsible for interprocess communication, process scheduling and memory management. The process control subsystem and file subsystem interact when loading a file into memory for execution.

The file subsystem manages files, allocates file space, administers free space, and controls access to files.

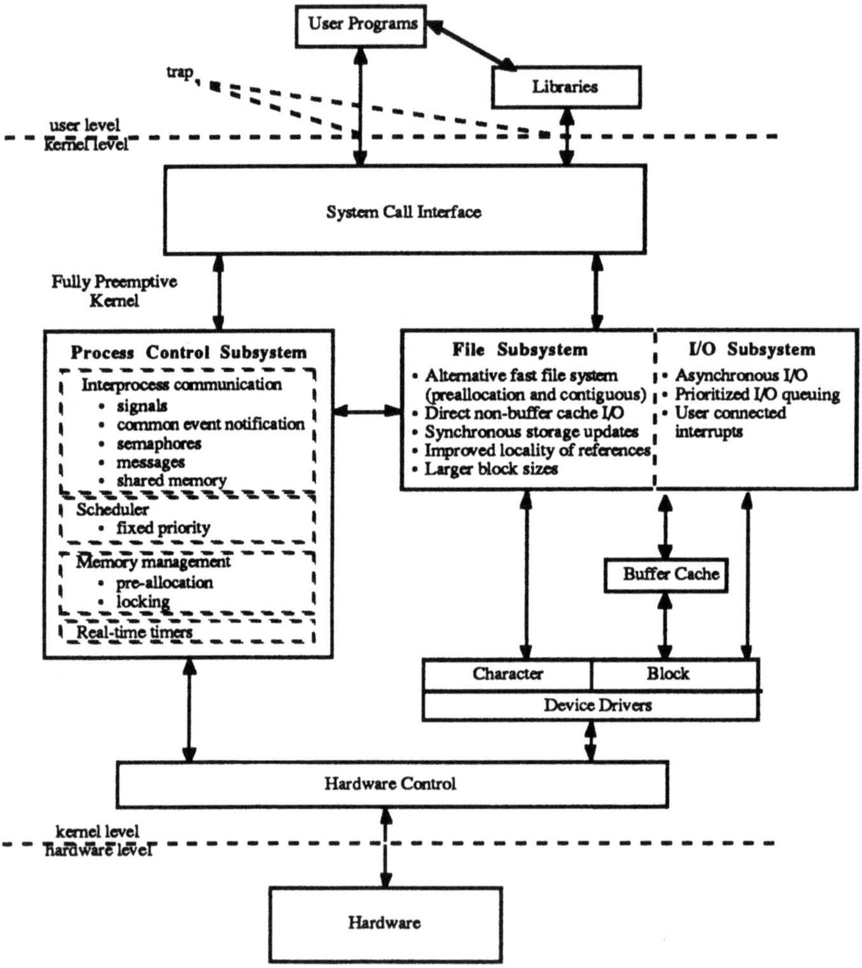

Figure 3.3 Block diagram of the REAL/IX kernel

Most user-level I/O is performed through the file subsystem. The I/O subsystem handles the actual interaction with the device. Each device on the system is represented by one or more special device files that can be addressed like any other files.

The REAL/IX operating system recognizes three basic privileges: regular, superuser, and real-time. Regular privileges are the standard privileges that allow the user to execute the commands and to only affect his or her own files and processes (or those whose owners have granted access). Superuser privileges are the traditional administrative privileges which allow access to all files and processes on the system. There are a number of administrative functions that can only be executed by the superuser. Real-time privileges can be assigned to a user or to a process and these privileges are required to use a number of the special features for real-time programming. Restricted assignment of these privileges ensures that a time-sharing program cannot inadvertently affect the real-time responsiveness of the system.

Real-time users and processes have more privileges than regular users, but fewer privileges than the superuser. A superuser can do anything that a real-time user can. Some examples of actions that are allowed for both real-time and superusers are: change the priority of an executing real-time process, initiate an asynchronous I/O operation, set the file descriptor of an opened file to bypass the buffer cache, and preallocate memory for the stack region of the program's data space.

Only superusers can do the following: access files owned by other users and groups; modify administrative files, including files for system initialization, message-of-the-day and accounting; run **sysgen** or modify any files involved in system configuration (this implies that drivers can only be installed by a superuser); shutdown the system; modify user logins and groups; and give real-time privileges to a user.

Real-time privileges are controlled by a system table that is loaded with the **setrtusers** command, usually during boot time. Processes executed by a user who is listed in this table are allowed to become real-time processes when the **setrt** system call is issued.

3.2 PROCESS SUBSYSTEM

The REAL/IX operating system supports all process subsystem facilities of UNIX System V, plus enhancements to provide an appropriate execution environment for real-time processes.

3.2.1 Process Concept

In UNIX terminology, a *program* is the set of instructions and data coded and compiled by the programmer, and a *process* is one execution of a program [Bach86]. Some other operating systems use the term *task* for what we call a process. In UNIX operating systems, many processes may concurrently execute the same program.

Processes execute at either user level or kernel level.

- Each user-level process runs in its own address space, separated from all other processes. Other processes may communicate with it through one of the facilities discussed in Section 3.5, and a process executing at a higher priority may prevent it from executing, but otherwise it is totally separated from other processes.

- All kernel-level processes execute as functions of the kernel **main** routine. While it is possible to synchronize kernel processes to prevent concurrent access of kernel resources, any kernel process can access the address space of any other executing process. For this reason, it is important that kernel-level processes (including user-installed system calls and drivers) use defined functions as much as possible, access kernel data structures appropriately, use kernel semaphores and spin locks as needed, and be tested thoroughly before being installed.

Each process is represented by two memory segments, called the *text* (or code) segment and the *data* segment, and a set of data structures that are referred to as the *process environment*. A text segment contains code and constant data and is shared by all processes running the same program.

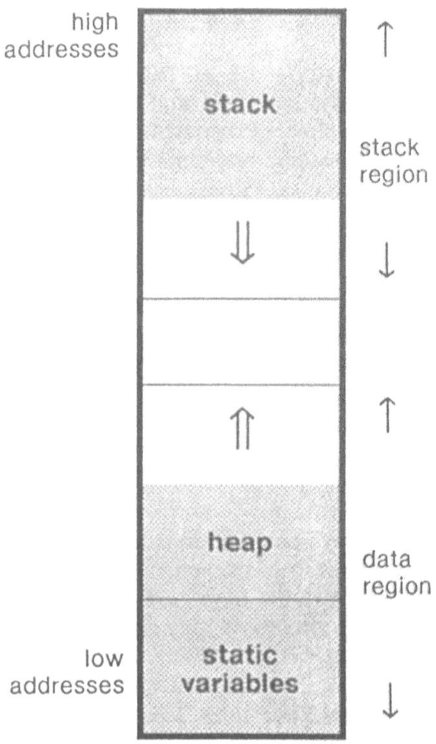

The data region begins at the low address of the space and grows upward; the stack region begins at the high address and goes down.

The actual stack and heap segments are always slightly smaller than the region that is allocated for them, as illustrated in the Figure.

Figure 3.4 - Data segment of executing process

The data segment of an executing process is composed of two regions: the stack region and the data region. The data region contains the process' static variables, and may also contain a dynamic data structure known as a *heap*. The data region begins at the low address of the space and grows upward; the stack region begins at the high address and grows downward. The actual stack and heap areas are always slightly smaller than the region that is allocated for them, as illustrated in Figure 3.4.

The process environment records the information the kernel needs to manage the process, such as register contents, priority, open files, and so forth. To maintain system integrity, a process cannot address its environment directly, but can use system calls to modify it.

3.2.2 Process Creation and Termination

One of the fundamental differences between the UNIX operating system and other operating systems is its reliance on processes that are spawned from other processes, called child processes. A number of standard system services exist as ordinary utility processes rather than being embedded in the operating system. When the operating system is first booted, it creates the **init** process, which is the parent process of all shell processes created when users log in. If a command is issued from the terminal (such as **cat**, to list the contents of a file), that process is a child process of the shell program. On UNIX operating systems, processes often use other processes rather than a subroutine. Of course, processes also create processes to run portions of algorithms in parallel, as they would on other operating systems, but the use of a process as something similar to a subroutine is characteristic of UNIX operating systems and their associated programming style.

3.2.3 Forking Child Processes

A new process is created with a **fork** system call. This call creates a child process, which is effectively a duplicate of the parent process that created it. This is implemented using a copy-on-write scheme, where data pages are copied only when a write operation is requested, thus avoiding unnecessary copying. The **fork** system call copies the parent's data and stack segments (or *regions*) plus its environment to the child process. The child shares its parent's text segment, which conserves memory space (all programs in the real-time UNIX system are reentrant). Child processes initialize more quickly than the original process, since they only have to modify parts of the inherited environment rather than recreate the entire environment.

The **fork** system call returns values to both the parent and child processes, but returns a different value to each. The parent receives the process id (PID) of the child, which can never be 0, and the child receives 0. The program uses these return values to determine which is the child process and which is the parent process (since they are both executing the same program) and takes different branches in the codc for each.

After checking the value returned by **fork**, the parent and child processes execute different branches of the same program in parallel. If the child process needs to execute a different program, it issues an **exec** call. The **exec** call replaces the text and data segments of its caller with those of a new program read from a file specified in the call. The **exec** call does not alter its caller's environment. A child process may be executing a different program, but it still has access to its parent's files, although they may have been modified by the child process between the **fork** and the **exec**.

A child issues an **exit** system call to terminate normally. This call takes a parameter whose value is returned to the child's parent. A child may also be terminated abnormally by a *signal* issued by the kernel, a user, or another process. When a child process terminates, either normally or abnormally, the operating system sends a SIGCLD signal to the parent process. Signals are discussed in more detail in Section 3.5.

3.2.4 Waiting for a Child Process to Terminate

Meanwhile, the parent process is free to continue execution in parallel with the child process. If the parent process needs to wait for the child process to terminate, it issues the **wait** system call. **wait** returns the process id of the terminated child process (which allows one parent process to spawn several children and specify the one for which it is waiting) and the status code passed by the child process when it exits.

Whether or not the parent waits for the child process to terminate, it receives a SIGCLD signal when the child process terminates. The parent process can catch this signal, then issue a **wait** to learn what happened to the child process.

3.2.5 Process States

In the REAL/IX operating system, there are eight process states and they can be viewed with the **ps -efl** command. These states, with the **ps** descriptor shown in parentheses, are:

1. The process is runnable when the kernel schedules it, although it is not currently running (R).

2. The *zombie* state, where the process has issued the **exit** system call and no longer exists, but it leaves a record containing an exit code and some timing statistics for its parent process to collect. The zombie state is the final state of a process.

3. The process has been stopped by a signal (T).

4. The process is newly created and is in a transitional state. The process exists, but is neither blocked nor runnable. This state is the start state for all processes except process 0 (I).

5. The process is blocked awaiting memory availability (X).

6. The process is executing in either kernel or user mode (O).

7. The process is blocked awaiting some event. It cannot be unblocked by a signal (D).

8. The process is blocked awaiting some event. It can be unblocked by a signal (S). This is usually the most common state.

The process state diagram is shown in Figure 3.5.

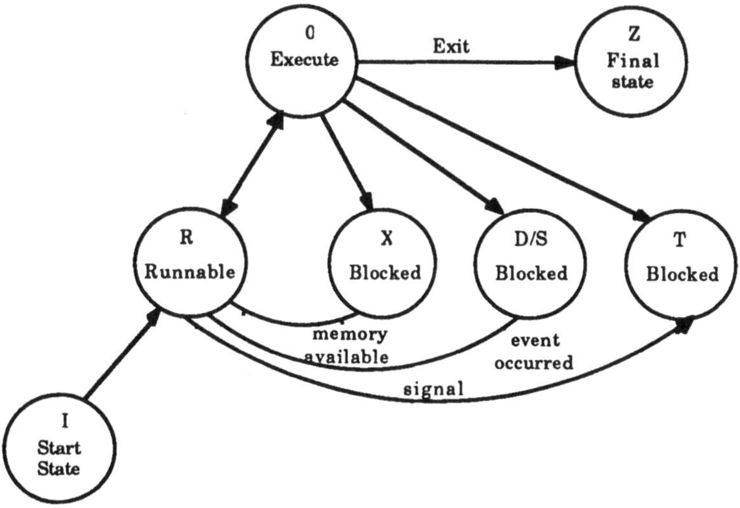

Figure 3.5 - Diagram of REAL/IX process states

3.3 MEMORY MANAGEMENT

The memory management subsystem allocates memory resources among all executing processes on the system.

3.3.1 Data Structures

Every executing process has three memory management data structures (*proc*, *user*, and *pregion*) associated with it:

- proc structure (defined in the *proc.h* header file).

  All proc structures are listed in the kernel's process table, whose size is determined at **sysgen** time. The kernel's process table is always in memory (never paged out). So the proc structures contain information the kernel may need while a process is paged out, such as its priority, its process group and parent process, address of the "u" page, and addresses used for sleep functionality.

- user block (or *u area*, defined in the *user.h* header file).

  The user block is never paged out on the REAL/IX operating system, but because some other varieties of the UNIX operating system do page them out, the convention is to include no information in user blocks that the kernel needs when the user block might be paged out. The user block for the currently executing process is always located at a specific location in virtual memory. When the kernel does a context switch, the *u area* for the currently running process is mapped out of the fixed address, and the *u area* for the process that is about to run is mapped into the fixed address. Each user block has a pointer to the corresponding proc structure.

- *process region* (or pregion) structure.

  The entries in the process' pregion table point to entries in the system's region table, each of which describes a logical segment of memory. Each pregion table has a fixed number of entries, usually three (for text, data, and stack) plus the number of shared memory segments for the process. All processes executing the same program have a pregion pointer to the same text segment in the system's region table. When sharing memory, the pregion structure for the process that initialized the shared memory segment points to the entry in the region table. The pregion structure for all other processes that access that shared memory segment point to the same region entry.

These structures are illustrated in Figure 3.6.

Note that for the two processes whose pregion tables are shown using the same shared memory segment, both point to the same *pregion* entry for the shared memory.

The **fork** and **exec** system calls are intimately associated with the memory management data structures. When a process **forks**, the kernel:

(1) makes a new entry in its process table for the child process, copying most of its contents from the parent's proc structure,

(2) copies the parent's pregion table to the pregion table it allocates for the child,

(3) allocates new pregion entries and page descriptors for the child's data and stack segments,

(4) allocates new pregion entries for the child's text and shared memory segments. (These regions share the parent's corresponding physical pages as long as both processes only read the pages.),

(5) if either the child process or the parent process writes to one of the pages for data or stack, the kernel makes a separate copy of that physical page for the child process.

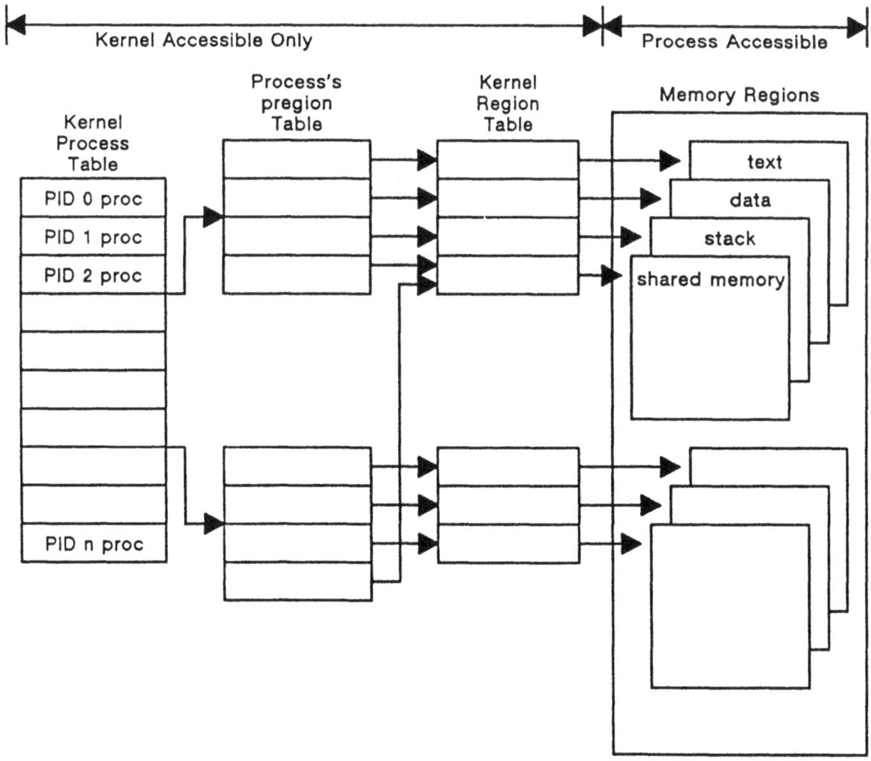

Figure 3.6 - Memory management data structures

A running process refers to memory with virtual addresses, which essentially consist of a virtual page number and a byte offset into the page. The hardware's memory management unit (MMU) translates the virtual page number into a physical page frame number, adds the offset, and sends the resulting physical address to memory.

The key to performing the virtual-to-physical address translation, or mapping, is the page map maintained in kernel memory and defined in *immu.h*. As discussed earlier, each process has its own page table, containing one entry for each of its pages. When the process is running, its page table is loaded into the page map.

3.3.2 Paging

When the number of processes exceeds the number that can be resident in memory, the kernel moves less-active pages (that are not locked in main memory) to disk memory from main memory. This maintains overall good system performance, although this procedure may slow the response of an individual process.

The **vhand** daemon is responsible for paging operations. When less than 10% of the available memory is free, **vhand** makes "aging passes". When less than 1% of the available memory is free, **vhand** pages out the least recently used pages on the system until 5% of memory is free.

The free list contains page frames that are eligible to be reused. Page frames are added to the head of the free list when they are no longer needed, and to the tail of the free list when they may be needed again. For example, when the last process executing a program terminates, the process' stack, data, user page, and page table frames can be of no use to another process, and so they are added to the head of the free list. The frames containing the code pages may be used if another process executes the program, so they are added to the tail of the free list. If another process executes the program while the code pages are on the free list, the kernel will reclaim them rather than bring them in from the object file or from the swap device. Page frames are allocated only from the head of the free list so that pages that may be needed again stay associated with page frames for as long as possible.

Note that frames containing kernel code and data are on neither the swap list nor the free list because no part of the kernel is ever paged out.

A page fault is an attempt to access a page that the pager has marked invalid, and invokes the kernel's page fault handler. The page fault handler takes different actions depending on where the invalid page is:

(a) If the page is on the free list, the page fault handler unlinks the associated page frame from the free list, marks it valid, and resumes the process. Reclaiming a page frame from the free list in this manner does not block the faulting process and is faster than a disk read, although the overhead incurred may still be unacceptable for critical real-time processes.

(b) If the page is paged out (in other words, the frame it formerly occupied has been allocated to another page), the page fault handler blocks the faulting process and schedules a disk read to retrieve the page from the swap device. Later, when the page has been read, the kernel allocates a frame from the head of the free list, updates the frame address in the process' page table, marks the page valid, and unblocks the process.

The combined actions of the pager and the page fault handler tend to keep frequently-accessed pages associated with page frames, while infrequently-used pages tend to migrate to the swap device. The pager moves page frames to the free list if they have not been accessed recently, so they can eventually be reallocated. Concurrently, page faults taken on these pages nullify the pager's efforts. If a page is accessed frequently, the pager will never see it marked as non-accessed and will never add it to the free list. If a page is accessed often, it may be added to the free list, but will be rapidly reclaimed by the page fault handler before it gets to the head of the list. Only the least-used pages get to the head of the free list and therefore have to be read from disk before they are used. The free list thus serves both as a source of available page frames and a cache of recently discarded pages that can be reclaimed quickly.

3.3.3 Allocating Memory

REAL/IX memory allocation is similar to that on the standard UNIX operating system, but includes extensions to provide explicit control over memory allocation in critical real-time application programs. These extensions provide the real-time programmer with complete control over the demand-paging subsystem. To guarantee response time, users are allowed to pre-page and lock all pages (instructions, data, shared memory, and stack) of a program into memory. At the programmer's option, the operating system will notify a real-time process of any attempts to grow the stack or data portions of the process' data segment.

The underlying philosophy of memory allocation is different for real-time than for time-sharing processes. The time-sharing philosophy is to avoid consuming any more memory than is absolutely necessary, so that all processes have equal access to memory resources. For critical real-time processes, the emphasis is on providing optimal performance for the program. Consequently, real-time programs typically preallocate a generous amount of memory and lock all resources they might need into memory.

The REAL/IX operating system uses demand paging, so the operating system does not allocate any memory for a process when it is initialized. Rather, the process is allowed to start executing at its entry point, which causes the process to page fault text and data pages as they are referenced. As the data segment (which is composed of the stack and data regions) outgrows the memory, the system allocates more physical pages. This scheme conserves memory and is appropriate for many applications, but the overhead incurred is unacceptable for critical real-time programs.

Most UNIX operating systems provide the **brk** and **sbrk** system calls to preallocate virtual space for the data region. The end of the data segment is called the *break*. **brk** and **sbrk** allow you to specify a new location for the break, with **brk** specifying an absolute address and **sbrk** specifying an address relative to the current break.

The REAL/IX operating system also provides the **stkexp** system call to preallocate virtual space for the stack. Users can specify either the absolute size of the stack or the increment by which the stack is to grow.

For programs that need memory allocated for data space, the **malloc** mechanisms are a simple, general-purpose memory allocation package. Real-time programs should call **malloc** only during the initialization part of the program, or use **brk** or **sbrk** to preallocate data space before calling **malloc**.

3.3.4 Locking Pages in Memory

Paging enables the operating system to provide good performance to a number of programs executing at the same time. However, the overhead associated with accessing processes or data that have been paged out is significantly more than the overhead involved in accessing processes or data that are resident in memory.

The **plock** system call allows users to lock text and data segments into memory. The **shmctl SHM_LOCK** system call allows the user to lock shared memory segments into memory. These calls lock segments into memory when they are first accessed. They can be used with the system calls that preallocate memory, or the user can allow the operating system to allocate memory as needed.

Critical real-time processes can lock segments into memory during process initialization with the **resident** system call, so that the first attempt to access a segment does not incur the overhead of loading it into memory. The **resident** call requires that memory be preallocated as discussed above. For critical real-time processes that preallocate memory, expanding memory beyond the preallocated limits is usually considered a fault, although the action taken for such a fault is at the discretion of the programmer. If desired, the **resident** call will post an event (as discussed in the following chapter) to the process if the memory allocated is inadequate for the stack or data region.

3.4 PROCESS SCHEDULING

Scheduling determines how the CPU is allocated to executing processes. Each executing process has a priority that determines its position on the run queue. In the REAL/IX operating system, the run queue consists of 256 process priority "slots", divided into two major parts as illustrated in Figure 3.7. Processes executing at priorities 128 through 255 (time-slice priorities) utilize a time-sharing scheduler implemented in the **onesec**[1] process. Processes executing at priorities 0 through 127 (real-time priorities) utilize a process priority scheduler implemented

---

1 The **onesec** process replaces the UNIX System V's **sched** process and is always Process 0. It runs roughly once a second and provides many housekeeping functions (including priority recomputation) that are traditionally performed by the clock interrupt handler. The priority of **onesec** is controlled by a tunable parameter.

internally. Each of these schedulers utilize different scheduling algorithms as discussed below.

Processes are scheduled according to the following rules:

- A process runs only when no other process at a higher priority is runnable.

- Once a process with a real-time priority (0 through 127) has control of a CPU, it retains possession of that CPU until it is preempted by a process running at a higher priority or relinquishes the CPU by making a call that causes a context switch, or blocks to await some event, such as I/O completion, or its time slice expires (by default, the time slice is 11 years, but this can be changed with the **setslice** system call).

- Because the operating system has a preemptive kernel, a running process can be preempted at any time if a process at a higher priority becomes runnable.

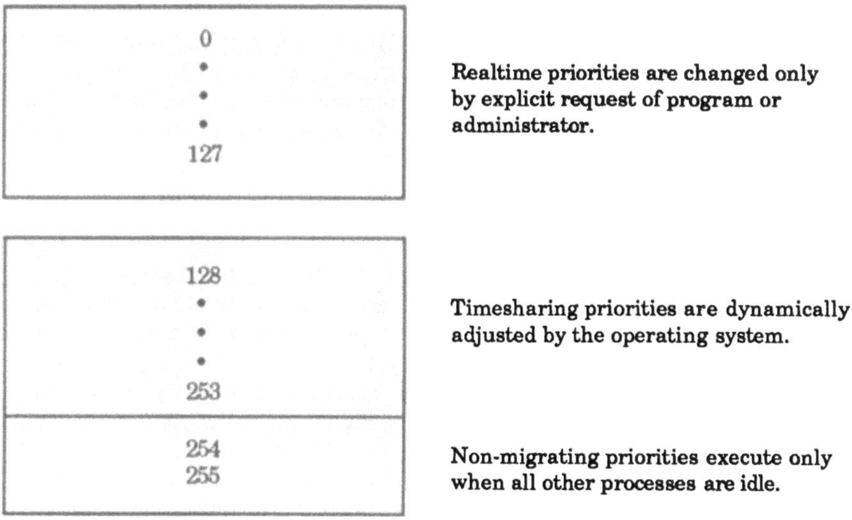

Figure 3.7 - REAL/IX process priorities

The process table for each executing process includes scheduling parameters used by the kernel to determine the order in which processes are executed. These parameters are determined differently for time-sharing and fixed-priority scheduled processes.

Time-Sharing Scheduling

Processes executing at priorities 128 through 255 utilize a time-sharing scheduler similar to that on other UNIX operating systems. The operating system varies the priorities of executing processes according to a specific algorithm. For instance, interactive processes gravitate towards higher priorities (since their actual run times are relatively small compared to their wait times), and processes that recently consumed a large amount of the CPU are relegated to lower priorities. The only control a process has over its priority is with the **nice** system call and **nice** command which lowers the relative priority of a process or, if issued by the superuser, can grant the process a more favorable priority.

The kernel allocates the CPU to a process for a time quantum, which is determined by the MAXSLICE tunable kernel parameter. If the process has not released the CPU at the end of that time quantum, it is preempted and fed back into the queue at the same priority. When the kernel again allocates the CPU to the process, the process resumes execution from the point where it was suspended. Once a second, those time-sharing processes that have consistently used their whole quantum are shuffled to lower priorities.

This time-slice scheduler has the advantage of equitably distributing the CPU among all executing processes. It is not adequate for critical real-time processes, which need to execute in a determinate (preferably fast) time frame. For this reason, the REAL/IX system supplements the traditional time-sharing scheduler with the fixed-priority scheduler.

Fixed-Priority Scheduling

Processes executing at priorities 0 through 127 utilize a fixed-priority scheduler. A process establishes its own priority with the **setpri** system call. The operating system will never automatically change the priority of a process executing at a real-time priority except during a boost operation. Only the process itself or a user with real-time or superuser privileges can change the priority. A process will execute only if there are no processes with higher priorities that are runnable at this time.

Runnable processes at the same priority are arranged in a circular, doubly-linked list. A round-robin scheduling scheme is used for processes at the same priority, with the ability for a process to relinquish its time slice to another process at the same priority. A process can also use the **setslice** system call to establish quantums; the default value is 11 years.

The fixed-priority scheduler allows a critical real-time process to "hog" the CPU as long as necessary to finish. If processes at high real-time priorities are using the CPU, low-priority real-time processes and time-share processes may never get to execute. Note that a process scheduled at priority 100 will run just as fast as a process scheduled at priority 1 if no processes are scheduled at a higher priority. Because a high-priority "runaway" process may never surrender the CPU, it is recommended that the console or a user terminal be set to run at priority 0 or 1 and no other processes (other than critical system processes) run at that priority, to ensure that the user can always regain control of the system.

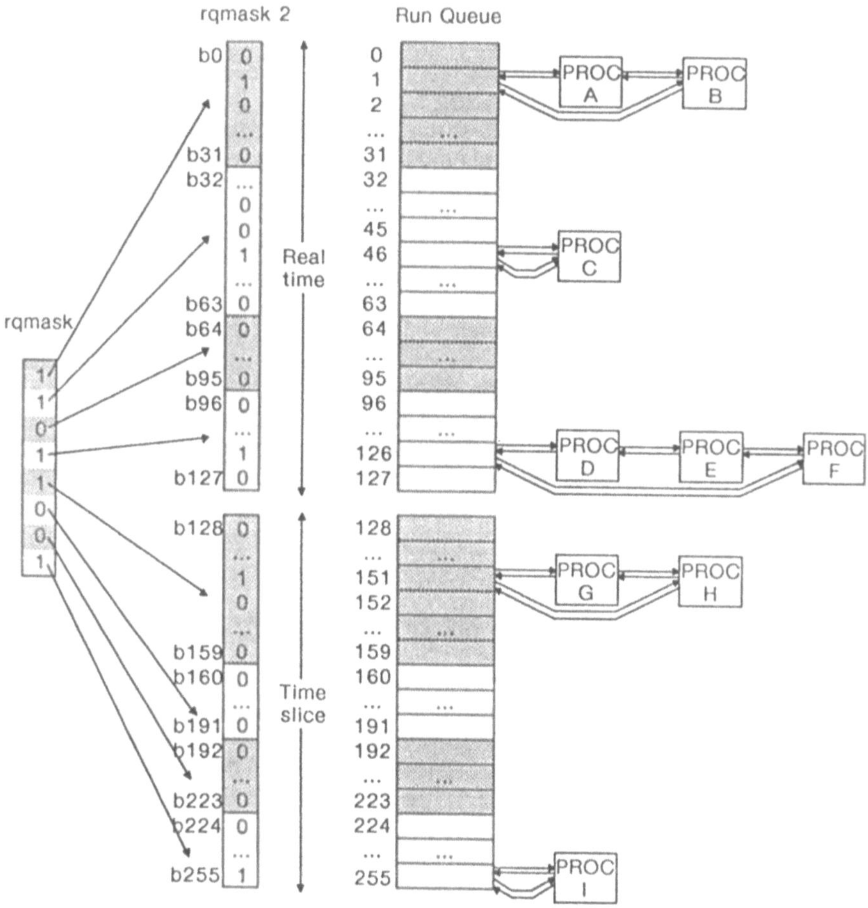

Figure 3.8 - REAL/IX run queue organization

To enable the operating system to search the queue efficiently, two bit mask schemes are implemented. The **rqmask2** scheme contains 8 bit masks, each of which is 32 bits long. Each bit corresponds to one slot in the queue; if a bit is set to 1, there are one or more runnable processes at that priority. The **rqmask** is an

8-bit mask, with one bit for each bit mask in **rqmask2**. If there are any runnable processes at priorities 0 through 31, the first bit is set. If there are any runnable processes at priorities 32 through 63, the second bit is set, and so forth. The run queue organization is illustrated in Figure 3.8.

3.4.1 Data Structure Integrity

The REAL/IX operating system uses spin locks and suspend locks (or kernel semaphores) to ensure data structure integrity in the preemptive kernel. If two processes access the same global data structure, it is important that the first process completes any update of that structure before the second process accesses it. In other UNIX kernels, this is handled by disabling interrupts to prevent an interrupt handler from accessing a data structure that was being manipulated by process-level kernel code. If the preemptive kernel were implemented without locks, a higher-priority process could cause a context switch from a lower-priority process even though it is in the process of updating a data structure, and thus corrupt the structure.

In a non-preemptive uniprocessor environment, data structure integrity can be preserved by manipulating processor execution levels to prevent interrupts when updating a structure, but this is inadequate for a multiprocessor configuration because the interrupt handler or another process may be executing on a different processor than the process-level routines. The locking mechanisms enable execution on a multiprocessor configuration, where all processors operate on a symmetrical, peer-to-peer basis and each processor can simultaneously execute user-level code, process-level kernel code, and interrupt-level kernel code.

Synchronization in Compatibility Mode

Other UNIX systems provide kernel-level synchronization with the **sleep/wakeup** functions to block and unblock a process, and the **spl** (set priority level) function to disable interrupts. The REAL/IX system provides three compatibility modes that allow drivers to be ported from UNIX System V without rewriting the synchronization facilities. The three modes are:

- Non-preemptible - kernel preemption is turned off when the process is running.
- Major-device semaphoring - one semaphore is set for the major device (that is, the driver itself). This is implemented in the switch table, so that only one instance of the driver entry point can execute at a time.
- Minor-device semaphoring - one semaphore is set for each minor device (that is, for each actual device controlled by the driver).

Drivers installed using these compatibility modes may not realize the full performance enhancements provided by rewriting the drivers to use kernel semaphores and spin locks, but should perform at a level similar to their performance level on UNIX System V.

Kernel Level Semaphores

Suspend locks, or kernel semaphores, are used when the lock time is relatively long (implemented by switching to another runnable process while the desired resource is busy). They can be used to limit the number of processes that access a kernel resource simultaneously or to block a process until a specified event occurs (in lieu of the **sleep/wakeup** functions of traditional UNIX operating systems).

The value of a semaphore is decremented with the **psema** or **cpsema** (conditional psema) functions. The difference between these two functions is that if the resource is not available, **psema** blocks and waits for the resource to become available, and **cpsema** returns without gaining access to the resource.

Value of Kernel (Suspend Lock) Semaphore		
<0	**0**	**>0**
One or more processes are blocked waiting access to this semaphore (and the resource it controls). The absolute value of the semaphore is the number of processes that are blocked.	The semaphore (and the resource it controls) may be in use, but no processes are blocked on it.	The resource controlled by the semaphore is available. The value of the semaphore indicates the number of resources available.
A process that issues a psema on the semaphore will block; a process that issues a cpsema on the process will return without accessing the resource.		The value of the semaphore indicates the number of processes that can access the resource without blocking.

Figure 3.9 - Values of kernel semaphores

The value of a semaphore is incremented with the **vsema** or **cvsema** (conditional vsema) functions. The difference between these two functions is that **vsema** increments the value of the semaphore unconditionally (thus unblocking a process that may be blocked waiting for it), whereas **cvsema** increments the value of the semaphore only if a process is blocked on that semaphore.

The value to which a specific semaphore is initialized determines its use. Semaphores used only to block processes, such as while waiting for an I/O operation to complete, are initialized to 0. In this case, the first process to issue a **psema** will block. Semaphores used to control access to a kernel resource are initialized to the number of resources available (for instance, the number of buffers in the pool), so that processes do not block unless the resource is exhausted.

Whatever the initial value of a semaphore, its effect is determined by its value at any given time. Figure 3.9 summarizes the meaning of kernel semaphore values.

Spin Locks

Spin locks are used when the lock time is very small (typically less than or equal to the time of two context switches). For uniprocessor configurations, spin locks are equivalent to disable/enable interrupt instructions, while in multiprocessor configurations they actually stall the CPU.

To understand spin locks better, consider the example illustrated in Figure 3.10. Processes MP1 and MP2 share a common interest in a piece of code and are executing on separate processors. MP1 enters the region and sets a spin lock with the **spsema** function. When MP2 attempts to enter the same region, it finds the lock set, and so loops on the lock instruction until MP1 releases the protected regions with the **svsema** function.

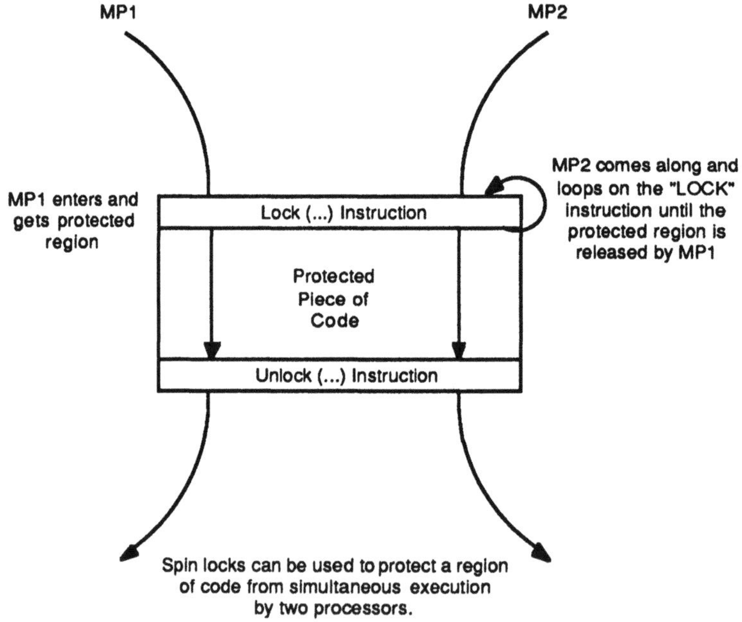

Figure 3.10 - REAL/IX spin locks

3.4.2 Timers

The operating system uses timers to schedule "housekeeping" operations that must be run periodically and to provide a mechanism through which real-time processes can schedule events.

System Clock

The system clock is the primary source for system synchronization. A clock interrupt is generated on every clock tick. The clock interrupt handler is activated by this interrupt, and maintains the user and system times and the current date. It also provides a triggering mechanism for process interval timers, profiling, and driver **timeout** functions.

The clock interrupt handler differs from that on most other UNIX operating systems in that the interrupt blocking time has been bounded to never block interrupts longer than 100 microseconds. To ensure this real-time constraint, some of the traditional interrupt handler functions have been moved to high-priority processes (daemons) that are triggered from the clock interrupt with a **vsema** or **cvsema** operation. These daemons include:

onesec	maintains free page counts, calculates new process priorities for time-slice processes, and unblocks other daemons.
vhand	processes paging operations
bdflush	flushes I/O buffers that have been around too long
timeproc	handles driver **timeout** functions
timedaemon	handles real-time timer expirations
ttydaemon	handles interrupts for the line discipline

Timing Functions

Typical UNIX timing functions supported by the real-time operating system are:

time	returns the value of time in seconds
gettimer	returns the value of time in seconds or nanoseconds
stime	sets the system time measured in seconds
alarm	sends SIGALRM to the calling process after a specified number of seconds have elapsed
pause	suspends a process until a signal is received
sleep	library routine that suspends execution of a process for a specified number of seconds or until a signal is received

Real-time Timers

Real-time processes need tight control over timing constraints in order to schedule specific events to occur in the system. These timers must be flexible, providing the real-time application with the ability to use either absolute or relative time. They must also provide the ability to schedule events in increments of seconds (like other UNIX timer functions) or microseconds for critical real-time applications.

The REAL/IX operating system provides a set of timers to support the requirements of real-time processes for scheduling events within the system. This timer implementation provides two types of timer mechanisms which real-time applications can access through system calls:

(1) **system-wide real-time timers** provide the application with the ability to read, write, and get the resolution of a system timer. This type of timer corresponds to the system time-of-day clock and represents the current time in seconds and nanoseconds since January 1, 1970. This timer is ascending in nature and is updated by the system at the frequency of the system clock. This system timer provides access to the system time in a unique format (seconds and nanoseconds), and is used to provide the process interval timers with a method of obtaining the current system time in readily usable format.

(2) **process interval timers** are designed to be used by one or more real-time processes to schedule system events within a very fine time scale, from a few seconds down to 1/256th of a second. The interval timers can be set by a real-time process to expire based on a time value that is relative to the current system time, or a time value that represents an absolute time in the future. These timers can be set to be "one-shot" or periodic.

A list of free process interval timers is defined at system generation (sysgen) time. The interval timers from this list can be allocated by real-time processes during process initialization or during normal execution. By using sysgen parameters, the timer mechanism can be customized for a particular application that requires varying amounts of timers to be available for process allocation.

To use a process interval timer, a real-time process does the following:

1. Issues a **gettimerid** system call to obtain access to a process interval timer. **gettimerid** gets a unique timer identifier from the free pool of process interval timers.

2. Sets a timer expiration value and activates the process interval timer.

Activating the timer actually means putting the timer for this process in an active timer queue of all process interval timers active on the system. The active timer queue is ordered so that the next entry to expire is positioned at the top of the queue.

The clock interrupt handler checks the first timer in the queue to determine if the specified expiration time is equal to the current system time. If so, a timer expiration has occurred and the **timedaemon** daemon is unblocked with a **vsema** operation. The **timedaemon** removes the expired timer from the active queue, reschedules the timer in the queue if it is a periodic timer, and posts an event to the appropriate process. The **timedaemon** then blocks (with a **psema** operation). The **timedaemon** only executes in response to a process timer expiration, so no additional overhead is incurred if no timers are being used.

The priority of the **timedaemon** is set by a tunable parameter, but should usually remain at a priority higher than the highest priority process that may request a time expiration. This ensures that timer expiration events are never delayed by another executing process on the system.

3.5 INTERPROCESS COMMUNICATION

The REAL/IX system supports a number of mechanisms that allow a user-level or kernel-level process to communicate with a user-level process. These include traditional system utilities and specific facilities to support the functionality required in real-time applications:

(1) signal mechanism
(2) common event notification that enhances the signaling facility
(3) shared memory, messages, and user-level semaphores
(4) binary semaphores, a very fast interprocess communication facility

In addition, the system supports pipes and named pipes. While these are useful for occasional transfers of small amounts of information between processes because they are so easy to code, they are generally too slow to be appropriate for real-time applications, and so are not discussed here.

3.5.1 Signal Mechanism

The signal mechanism is the traditional method of notifying a process that something has happened in one program that affects another program. Signals are part of the UNIX System V environment and they are always asynchronous (meaning that the receiving process never knows when it may receive a signal). The user-level program includes code to determine the action to take when a signal is received (terminate the process, ignore the signal, or catch the signal and execute a subroutine). The receiving process does not know which process sent the signal, and will react only to the first signal received. Subsequent signals are silently ignored.

The REAL/IX signal mechanism functions just like the traditional signal mechanism. While some internal modifications have been made to provide better performance in the real-time environment, signal-handling code from other UNIX systems will usually run without modification on the system.

Signals are sent and received as follows:

1. When the process is initialized, an array of signal-handling fields is set up in the *u area* associated with the process. Each field corresponds to a signal defined in the system, and contains the address of the user function that corresponds to the signal number (in other words, directions on the action to take when a signal of that type is received). The fields for any signals for which signal-handling functions are not provided are set to 0, causing the process to exit when that type of signal is received.

2. The receiving process uses the **sigset** system call to define the function to be executed when a signal of the specified type is received.

3. The sending process sends a signal to another process (or group of processes), identified by PID.

4. The appropriate signal-handling field in the *u area* of the receiving process is marked that a signal has been received. If the process is not currently executing a critical region of code, the designated action is taken immediately and the signal is cleared from the proc structure. If the process is executing a critical region of code, the signal is not handled and cleared until the process exits from the critical region.

5. As long as a process has an outstanding signal associated with it, subsequent signals of the same type sent to the process are silently discarded.

Signals can be sent in the following scenarios:

- sent by the kernel to a user-level process (for example, a segmentation-violation signal, which the kernel sends when a process attempts to access memory outside of its address space)

- sent by a user-level process to itself (for example, an alarm clock signal, where a user-level process sets the clock and when the alarm goes off, a signal is sent)

- sent by a user-level process to another user-level process (for example, a termination signal, when one of several related processes decides to terminate the whole family)

- sent by a driver to user-level programs on behalf of the user (for example, when the user presses the DEL or BREAK key to abnormally terminate processing)

A user-level program sends a signal to another user-level program or group of programs with the **kill** system call or the **kill** command.

Signals can arrive at any time during process execution. Signal-handling functionality is coded into the receiving process using

1. the **sigset** system call to define the action to take (ignore the signal, terminate the process, or execute a specified function that is defined in the program). If the receiving process does not include a signal-handling routine, the program will exit any time it receives a signal.

2. the **sighold** and **sigset** system calls to establish critical regions of code.

3.5.2 Common Event Notification

The REAL/IX kernel supplements the traditional signal mechanism with a high-performance event notification facility that provides several features not found in signals. It can handle notifications synchronously as well as asynchronously, and can queue multiple signals sent to one process. This feature is important for real-time applications, which typically need to respond to several events. It is a notification method for asynchronous I/O completions, connected interrupts, timer expirations, and resident memory violations, and can also be used for any application-specific needs.

Events are posted to a user-level process by itself or by another user-level process (using the **evpost** system call) or by the kernel. A 32-bit data item can be associated with each event posted. It is received along with the event identifier. Typically, the data item is a pointer to some common memory location. When an event is posted, it is queued onto a list of events associated with the receiving process. Each event queue is associated with a unique, per-process event identifier. Like signals, these event queues are private to the receiving process. Hence, an event posted to a queue can be delivered only to the process that created the queue. Because they are queued, events posted to the same event queue cannot be lost.

The receiving process determines whether the event is delivered synchronously or asynchronously when it creates the event identifier (*eid*). For synchronous delivery, the process uses the **evrcv** system call to receive the first posted event on a single event queue or the **evrcvl** system call to receive the first event in a specific list of event queues, as illustrated in Figure 3.11.

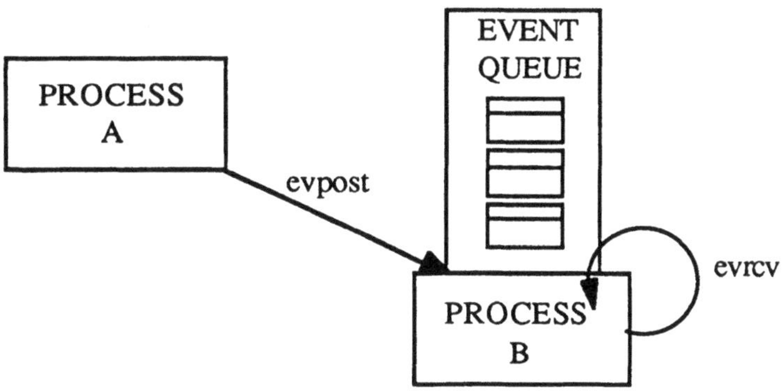

Figure 3.11 - Handling events synchronously

If no events are outstanding when the system call is made, the process can specify whether to wait until an event is posted or to return immediately with an indication that no event was available.

For asynchronous delivery, process notification is similar to the traditional signal mechanism, except that subsequent events will be delivered. When the receiving process creates the *eid* for the specific signal number (as defined on **sigset**), it specifies the function to be executed when that signal is received. Asynchronous delivery implies that the receiving process has no control over when the signal is received (except to block all signals). As soon as the signal (asynchronous event) is received, the receiving process will handle it, as illustrated in Figure 3.12.

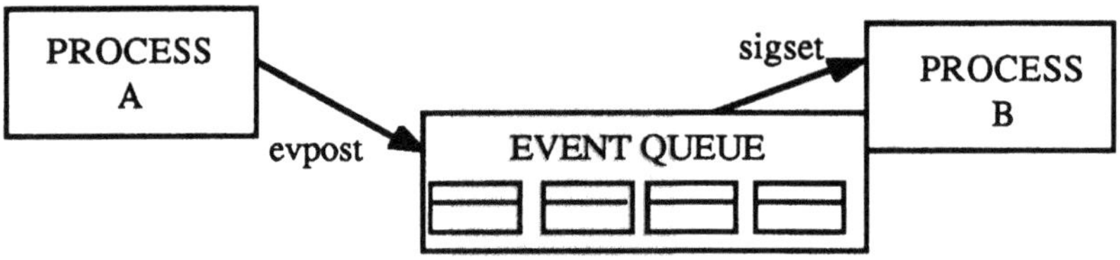

Figure 3.12 - Handling events asynchronously

The receiving process can create any number of separate event queues, each of which can have its own method of delivery and limit on the number of outstanding queued events.

One process can receive signals as well as synchronous and asynchronous events. In general, all programs should include signal-handling functionality, since the kernel or another user-level process may send it a signal. A limited number of processes (defined by the tunable parameter EVTMAXPRC) can receive and handle events. The event mechanism is used for critical real-time programs that require this functionality.

Any process executing on the system can post an event, as long as the process has the appropriate privileges:

a. executed by the superuser or a real-time user,

b. the real or effective UID of the sending process matches the real or effective UID of the receiving process.

3.5.3 Shared Memory

The fastest interprocess communication is through shared memory, where cooperating processes map the same area of memory into their address space. When one process writes to a location in the shared area, the data can be read immediately by any other process that has this location mapped in its address space. The time required to access this location is no more than a normal memory reference. All system overhead (other than address translation) associated with this type of message passing facility is eliminated.

The system calls for manipulating shared memory are **shmget**, **shmat**, **shmdt**, and **shmctl**.

The **shmget** call creates a new region of shared memory or returns an existing one; the **shmat** call logically attaches a region to the virtual address space of a process; the **shmdt** call detaches a region from the virtual address space of a process; and the **shmctl** call manipulates various parameters associated with the shared memory.

3.5.4 User-Level Semaphores

Semaphores, which can be implemented either at the kernel or user level, ensure data integrity between processes executing on separate processors, as described in Section 3.4.1.

For user-level semaphores, the REAL/IX system includes a binary semaphore mechanism which is faster than the traditional PC semaphore mechanism since it avoids unnecessary system call overhead. This fast binary semaphore facility provides the synchronization mechanism required to make shared memory a viable, fast interprocess communication facility.

3.6 FILE SUBSYSTEM

The file subsystem controls access to data files as well as devices. It provides a hierarchical organization for files and directories, buffering of data (and the ability to bypass buffering for critical real-time I/O operations), and control of file access.

3.6.1 File Types

A file is the basic unit of the file subsystem. Files can represent character or binary information, but all files are stored identically as a sequence of bytes. There are four basic file types.

Regular	one dimensional array of bytes used to store data, text, or programs.
Pipe	similar to *regular* files in how they represent unformatted information, and unique in that reads from them are destructive. This file is used to communicate between processes.
Special	used to interface between the process and device. These files reside in the */dev* directory.
Directory	used to organize regular, pipe, special, and other directory files. They hold file names and references to information about the files. Only the operating system can write to them. Users can modify directories by making a request to the operating system.

The REAL/IX file subsystem uses three entities to maintain user and system files and directories. These are:

1. **Directory Tree:** all accessible directories and file systems, used when giving path names.

2. **File Systems:** independent collections of files and directories, each of which is located on the same partition (or contiguous partitions) of a disk device.

3. **Directories**: reside within a file system and are used to further organize user and system files. They contain the names of the files and references to the remainder of the information about this file. This reference is called the **inumber** and is used to locate the **inode** for the file being accessed.

3.6.2 File Listings

The **ls** command is used to list files in a directory. A number of options are available to provide additional information and specify the format of the output.

This listing provides the following information:

mode	the first character identifies the type of file. **-** is a regular file; **d** is a directory; **e** is an extent-based file. Special device files use **c** for a character-access file and **b** for a block-access file. Special device files are discussed more in Section 3.7 on the I/O subsystem. The remaining nine characters define the file access permissions as discussed in the next section.
links	the number of names linked to this file.
owner and group	identifies who can access the file as owner and who can access the file as group. Use the **chgrp** command to change the group, and the **chown** command to change the owner of a file.
size	logical size of the file in bytes. For special device files, this field contains the major and minor device numbers.
date and time	date and time of last file modification.
file name	the common name used to access this file.

3.6.3 File Permissions

File permissions determine who may read, write, and execute a file. Each file has an owner (changed with the **chown** command) and a group (changed with the **chgrp** command). The *mode* of a file is an octal mask that determines the access privileges for the owner (**u**), group (g), and world or other (**o**). It is displayed in the last nine characters of the leftmost column of the output from the **ls -l** command. The format of the output is three sets of three characters each, defining read, write, and execute permissions for the owner, group, and "other", as illustrated below:

rwx	rwx	rwx
owner	*group*	*other*

For permissions that are not granted to that class of user, a dash (-) replaces the letter. For instance, **r--** permissions indicate read privileges but no write or execute permissions. Initial file permissions are determined by the **umask** value set in the */etc/profile* or *$HOME/.profile* file. They can be changed with the **chmod** command. **chmod** can use either the single letter representation or a three digit number, where each digit corresponds to the owner, group, and other, respectively. The value of each digit is determined by summing the number corresponding to the permissions:

4 read permissions (r)
2 write permissions (w)
1 execute permissions (x)

So, for example, **777** represents the permissions shown above (read, write, and execute permissions for the owner, group, and world). **640** gives the owner read and write permissions, the group read permissions, and no access permissions to other users. **chmod** can assign permissions in a format such as **chmod g+rw** (which adds read and write permissions for the group) or **chmod o-w** (which removes write permissions for other). Note that any executable file must have execute permissions and directories must have execute permissions to be used in a path name.

The user name shown in the **ls** output corresponds to a user ID assigned in the */etc/passwd* file. The group name corresponds to a group ID assigned in the */etc/passwd* file and populated in the */etc/group* file. The user and group shown in the **ls** output correspond to the "real" UID and GID.

Normally, a process runs with the permissions of the user who executes it. A program can use the **setuid** and **setgid** system calls to set the "effective" UID and GID. When the **setuid** bit is on, the process runs with the permissions of the real owner, and when the **setgid** bit is on, the process runs with the permissions of the real group. This is used, for instance, to have a file that can be updated by a number of users, but only through a specific command (not through an editor or other utility). The program can give execute permissions to anyone, then internally reset the effective UID or GID so it can access a file that has restricted permissions.

3.6.4 User View of a File System

A file system is a combination of directories and files descending from a common directory. The combination of directories and files makes up a file system. Figure 3.13 shows the relationship between directories and files in a REAL/IX file system. The directories are represented by circles and files are represented with lines beneath the directories.

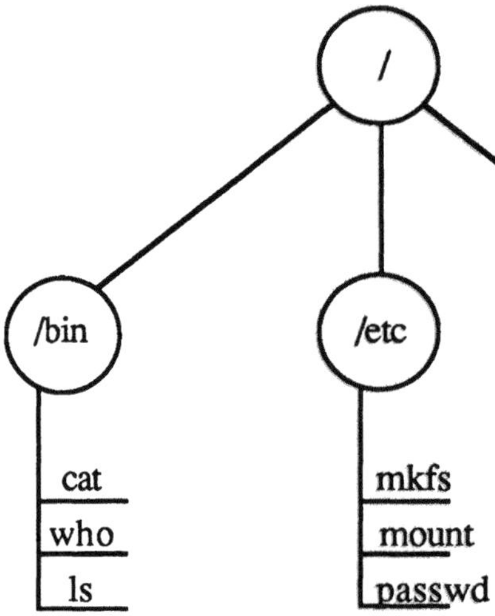

Figure 3.13 - A REAL/IX file system

The starting point of any UNIX file is a directory that serves as its root. One file system is itself referred to by that name, *root*_ and is the topmost directory on the system. The *root* directory of the *root* file system is represented by a single slash (/). The file system diagrammed in Figure 3.13 is a *root* file system, with subdirectories */bin, /etc*, and */usr*.

A *full path name* for a file gives the location of a file in relationship to *root*, for instance, */bin/cat*. A *relative path name* for a file gives the location of that file in relationship to the user's present working directory. Therefore, if the user's present working directory is *root*, he could refer to *bin/cat*.

Relative path names use . (dot) to refer to the present working directory and .. (dot dot) to refer to the directory above the present working directory. Therefore, if the user's present working directory is */etc*, he could use the relative path name *../bin/cat* to refer to this file.

Another file system can be mounted under the *root* file system. Figure 3.14 shows such a file system.

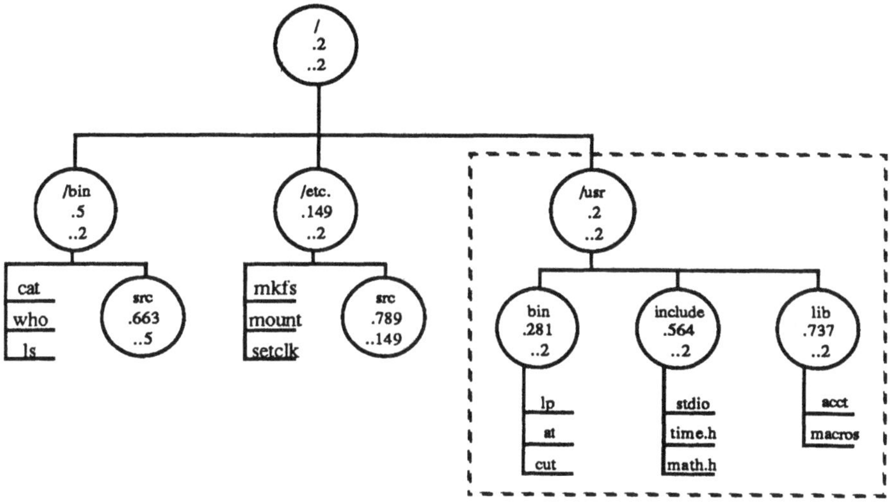

Figure 3.14 - Adding another file system to root

A directory such as */usr* can be referred to as a "leaf" or "mount point", since it forms the connection between the *root* file system and another mountable file system. It can also be referred to as a "child" of /, or the parent of the */usr* file system. For a complete list of all file systems mounted on your machine, use the **/etc/mount** command.

Every file in a file system has a unique number, called the *inumber*, associated with it. An inumber is used as an index into the *ilist*, which is a collection of information nodes (*inodes*) for that file system. This is described more fully later in this chapter. Here we are concerned with the inumbers of two file names that exist in every directory and hold the file system together: . for the directory itself and .. , which points to the parent directory. The directory entry for . contains the inumber of the directory itself, and the entry for .. contains the inumber of the parent directory, which is the same number as that given to the . file in the parent directory. This interrelationship between the . and .. files gives the file system structure its cohesion.

The file system structure illustrated in Figure 3.14 shows the inumbers of . and .. for the various directories. The inumber of both the . file and the .. file in all mount-point directories is 2. Notice that the .. inumber of all files descending directly from *root (/)* or */usr* is 2. Generally, the inumber of the .. file in */etc/src* is the same as the inumber for the . file in */etc*. The only time this is not true is when a directory is the mount point of a file system, in which case the inumbers of both . and .. are 2.

3.6.5 Accessing Files in Programs

User-level programs access files through system calls (which may be accessed through library routines). These calls go through the file system and (if so programmed) the system buffer cache. Below the buffer cache, the I/O subsystem (described in Section 3.7) handles the interaction with the disk device where the file data is stored. The REAL/IX operating system supports two file system architectures which are accessed through the file system switch. These two architectures are discussed later in this section. Figure 3.15 illustrates the flow of data and the flow of control for file access.

The REAL/IX operating system supports two file system architectures, called S5 and F5. The S5 architecture is the same as that in UNIX System V. The F5 architecture provides faster file access for real-time and time-share processes. The file system architectures are discussed in more detail later in this section.

File Descriptors. When a file is first accessed with the **open** or **creat** system call, it is assigned a file descriptor. All subsequent file I/O uses this descriptor, which serves as a sort of handle on the file for the process. Each executing process has a *descriptor table* that contains an entry for each open file descriptor. Entries in the descriptor table are indexed from 0 to (n-1), where n is the value of the NOFILES tunable parameter that defines the maximum number of file descriptors an executing process can have at one time. The default value is 80.

I/O system calls other than **open** and **creat** use this index value to specify the target descriptor. Because the descriptor table is part of a process' environment, a child process inherits access to all of its parent's descriptors. However, because the child's environment is a copy of the parent's, the child process can alter its description table without affecting that of its parent.

New descriptors are assigned sequentially as is appropriate for the type of file. For regular files, each **open/create** operation creates one new file descriptor, but the **pipe** system call that creates a pipe creates two descriptors (one for the read end and one for the write end of the pipe). In all cases, the system call used returns the index value(s) of the newly created descriptor, which is used in subsequent I/O calls.

The **close** system call notifies the system that no more I/O will be done on this file descriptor and frees its slot in the descriptor table for reuse. A process can also manipulate table entries with the **dup** system call, which makes a duplicate of a descriptor in the first available slot. The original descriptor can then be closed and a new descriptor created in the original position. To restore the initial descriptor, it can be **duped** from its saved location, after closing the new descriptor.

Standard I/O and Redirection. Standard I/O defines file descriptors 0, 1, and 2 as referring to standard input (**stdin**), standard output (**stdout**), and standard error (**stderr**), respectively. Typically, programs read their input from the standard input, write their output to the standard output, and write diagnostic information to standard error. A process inherits descriptors from its parent, so the standard I/O files are already set up, and the new process merely needs to establish descriptors for the auxiliary files and devices it needs. Using the standard I/O descriptors automatically gives a program a large measure of universality. Since files, devices, and pipes all work essentially the same, a program will work with the standard I/O descriptors hooked up to any of them. As an example, a program that counts words in a text stream and writes the total to the standard output works equally well whether the input is taken from a terminal, from a file, or from another process. Likewise, the output can be written to a terminal, file, or another process.

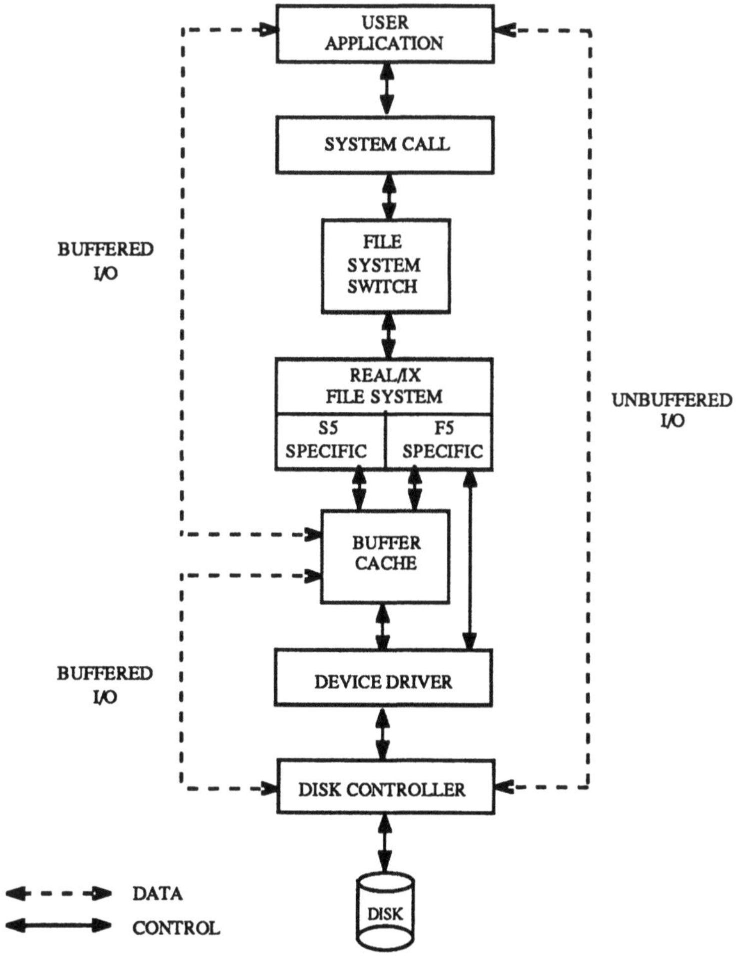

Figure 3.15 - REAL/IX file subsystem

Unless otherwise defined, the standard input is associated with the keyboard of the user who invokes the process. The standard output and standard error are associated with the user's display. Usually the standard error retains its association with the display, but often a new child process redirects its standard input and/or output before **exec**ing a program. This way, the **exec**ed program does not need to be concerned with the source of its input or the destination of its output. The most common example of this is the shell, which provides users with a very convenient notation for asking that the standard input, output, and error of a program be redirected before it is executed.

Asynchronous File I/O. Most UNIX kernels support only synchronous I/O operations, meaning that any I/O operation issued by a process causes that process to block until the I/O operation is complete. A real-time application needs the capability of overlapping I/O operations with process execution. The REAL/IX operating system supports asynchronous I/O operations for files and devices, enabling the process that initiated the I/O operation to continue the process execution stream once the I/O operation is queued to the device. When the I/O operation completes (either successfully or unsuccessfully), the initiating process is notified with either the common event notification mechanism or by polling a control block. The polling option saves the overhead of a system call.

The ability to overlap application processing and I/O operations initiated by the application program and to allow one process to simultaneously perform several separate I/O operations is required by a number of real-time applications. For instance, journalizing functions must be able to queue logging records for output without blocking the initiating process. Data acquisition processes may have two or more channels delivering intermittent data that must be read within a certain time. The process issues one asynchronous read on each channel. When one of the channels needs data collection, the process reads the data and posts it to secondary memory with an asynchronous write. The process is then free to carry out additional processing.

The REAL/IX system provides facilities for asynchronous read and write operations, and the ability to cancel an asynchronous I/O request. There are also optional initialization services that speed I/O throughput by preallocating and initializing various data structures.

The REAL/IX implementation of asynchronous I/O provides the following capabilities:

- Asynchronous I/O requests can be issued for both regular files and I/O devices.
- Multiple asynchronous read and write operations can be simultaneously queued to one file descriptor.
- One process can queue asynchronous read and write operations to several open file descriptors.
- To further improve I/O throughput, asynchronous I/O operations to the extended portion of extent-based files can bypass the buffer cache.

Unbuffered I/O functionality is implemented in the inode associated with a file descriptor, using **fcntl** requests. Unbuffered I/O can be emulated when required.

- Pending asynchronous I/O requests can be cancelled.
- Notification of asynchronous I/O completion is optional. If used, notification can be obtained through either polling or the common event notification method.
- Asynchronous I/O operations can be used with both sequential and random access devices.
- One driver and its associated devices can support both synchronous and asynchronous read and write operations.

Each asynchronous I/O operation establishes an asynchronous I/O control block (aiocb) structure, which contains information to control the I/O operations, such as the number of bytes to transfer and whether to post an event to the sending process when the I/O operation completes. When the I/O operation completes, the aiocb structure is updated, indicating either that the operation was successful or containing the error code of any error that may have occurred.

Asynchronous I/O operations to character devices are implemented using the **aio** entry point to **cdevsw**. The operating system sets up an **areq** kernel data structure, populated with appropriate information from aiocb, and the requesting process. This structure controls the data transfer, and is updated when the I/O transfer is completed. Neither the user-level process nor the driver blocks at any time; and since each I/O request generates a separate aiocb-areq pair of structures, additional asynchronous I/O requests can be initiated before the previous operation has completed.

Buffer Cache. Normally, file I/O operations use the system buffer cache as an intermediate storage area between user address space and the device itself. For instance, when writing a file, the data is actually written to the buffer cache. The operating system periodically flushes the contents of the buffer cache to the disk. Each buffer has a buffer header associated with it that holds the control information about the buffer such as the block and file system or origin for the data. This buffering scheme is defined in the *buf.h* header file. The number and size of buffers and the number of buffer headers and hash slots for the buffer cache are controlled by a series of tunable kernel parameters.

From the view of the driver that transfers data between the system buffer cache and the device, I/O operations that use the buffer cache are called *block I/O*, since data is transferred one block at a time. A block can range from 512 bytes to 131072 bytes, depending on the logical block size of the file system. The system buffering scheme allows drivers to transfer linked lists of data, although actual physical I/O is done one block at a time. Without this facility, an I/O operation would have to return after each buffer was transferred. For instance, when writing a six block file, the system would write one block, return, write one more block, return, and so forth. By using a linked list, the system looks for the next buffer when it finishes transferring the first block of data, and only returns when the entire six blocks are transferred. The system still performs six distinct operations, but it avoids the overhead of returning after each operation.

There are several advantages to the use of buffer cache:

(1) **Data caching** - The data remains in main memory as long as possible. This allows a user process to access the same data several times without performing physical I/O for each request. The user process is blocked for a very short time while waiting for the I/O, since it does not have to wait for the physical I/O operation.

(2) **Paging enabled** - If no buffering of data was done, a user process undergoing I/O would have to be locked in main memory until the device transferred data into or out of the user data space. Since there is a system buffer between the user data space and the device, the process can be paged out until the transfer between the device and the buffer is completed, then paged back in to transfer data between the buffer and user data space.

(3) **Consistency** - The operating system uses the same buffer cache as user processes when doing I/O with a file system, so there is only one view of what a file contains. This allows any process to access a file without worrying about timing. The buffer algorithms also help insure file system integrity, because they maintain a common, single image of disk blocks contained in the cache. If two processes simultaneously attempt to manipulate one disk block, the buffer algorithms serialize their access, preventing data corruption.

(4) **Portability** - Since I/O operations are done through the buffer cache, user-level programs do not have to worry about data alignment restrictions the hardware may impose. The kernel aligns data internally, so programs can be ported to new kernels without being rewritten to conform to new data alignment properties.

(5) **System Performance** - Use of the buffer cache can reduce the amount of disk traffic, thus increasing overall system throughput and decreasing average response time. Especially when transmitting small amounts of data, having the kernel buffer the data until it is economical to transmit it to or from the disk improves general system performance.

<u>Bypassing the Buffer Cache.</u> Use of the buffer cache has significant advantages for general applications, but it also has disadvantages for some real-time applications. Consequently, the REAL/IX operating system provides the capability of bypassing the buffer cache by setting a file control (**fcntl**) command on the file descriptor. I/O operations that bypass the buffer cache transfer information directly between user address space and the device.

The use of the buffer cache improves general system performance. Bypassing the buffer cache, on the other hand, may speed the time of individual I/O operations but will slow other I/O operations on the system.

Sharing Files. Two or more processes may share the same open file in one of the following ways:

- A child process inherits its parent's open files. The child and parent processes also share I/O pointers, so a **read** by one process changes the position in the file for both processes. Normally the child process takes over the files while it runs, and the parent process does nothing with the files until after the child process terminates.

- Two or more unrelated processes may open the same file at the same time, as long as they all have adequate permissions. In this case, each process has a separate I/O pointer, but a change to the contents of the file is seen by all processes that have the file open.

- Two or more file names can be linked to the same file, as long as both file names are in the same file system. The two linked files have the same inode, so any updates made to one file affect the contents seen by the other file.

If two or more processes update the same file at the same time, data may be lost or corrupted. For this reason, the system allows you to set read and write locks on a file or record with **fcntl** commands. A read lock prevents any process from write locking the protected area. A write lock prevents any process from read or write locking the protected area. These locks can be implemented so the process either fails when it attempts to set a lock against an already-locked area, or blocks until the existing lock is released.

3.6.6 File System Structure

The REAL/IX operating system supports two file system architectures, referred to as S5 and F5. The S5 architecture is the same as the file system structure in UNIX System V. The F5 file system architecture provides faster file access for both real-time and time-sharing applications. Both file system architectures are accessed through the same system calls and support the full range of logical block sizes.

The structure of the two file systems is similar, as illustrated in Figure 3.16.

The major sections, shown in Figure 3.16, are:

Superblock	Contains global information about the file system, such as the file system architecture being used, the size of the ilist, how many inodes are being used, the logical block size,

the total number of blocks in the file system, and the number of blocks being used. It also contains some status information about the file system, as explained below.

Ilist — A numbered collection of inodes for all files in the file system. An inode holding control and status information is associated with each file in the file system.

Bitmap (F5 only) — A map of all data storage blocks allocated to the file system. The operating system can scan this table to determine which blocks are free and which are not.

Data Storage Blocks — Storage for the data in the files and directories. These are referenced by number and maintained through the inodes of the files that use them.

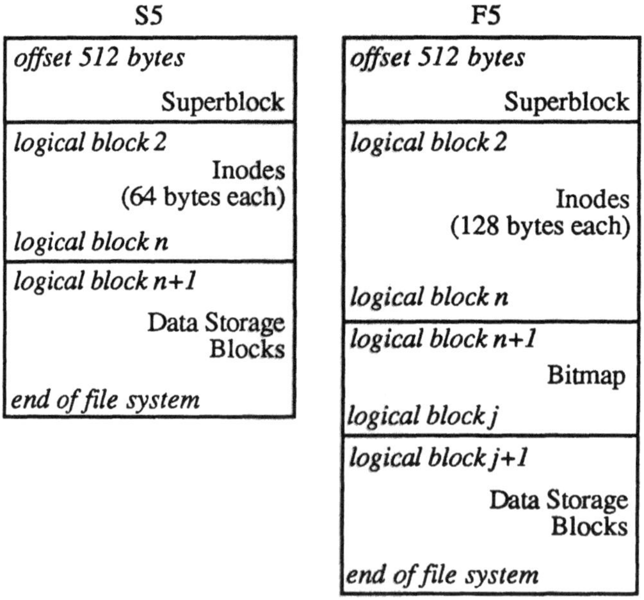

Figure 3.16 - Internal structure of a file system

To the operating system, a file system is an arrangement of logical blocks of disk space. The size of a logical block is determined for each file system at the time it is created, and can range from 512 to 131,072 bytes. It is held together by a system of inodes. Each regular file, pipe, special file, and directory has an inode associated with it. The inode contains all of the information about the file except its name (which is kept in a directory) and its contents (which are kept in the data storage blocks for the file system). Note that the inodes for special files do not point to data storage blocks, but rather store the major and minor number of the device.

All the inodes for a file system are stored contiguously starting at logical block number 2 of the file system, in a list called the *ilist*. The number of inodes each block in the *ilist* can hold is determined by the file system architecture being used (S5 inodes are 64 bytes each and F5 inodes are 128 bytes each) and the logical block size of the file system. For instance, each block in an S5 file system that uses 512-byte, logical blocks can hold 8 inodes (which are 64 bytes each), and each block in an F5 file system that uses 4096-byte logical blocks can hold 32 inodes (which are 128 bytes each). The number of inodes specified at the time the file system is created determines the number of blocks dedicated to the inode list.

The *inumber* gives the starting point for the inode as an offset into the list. It is not kept as part of the inode for a file, but is calculated when the inode is to be accessed. To access the inumber, use the **stat** or **estat** system call or the **ls -i** command.

An inode for a file contains:

Mode	the file type (regular, directory, special, or pipe), the execution bits (sticky bit, set user and group IDs), and access permissions for the owner, group, and others. If this field is null, the inode is not in use.
Number of Links	number of times this file is referenced in a directory, or the number of links to the file. Unnamed pipes have a zero value in this field.
Owner and Group IDs	indicate the owner and group identification for the file and are used when checking access permissions for the file. Both of these are numeric values. The translation to character strings can be found in the */etc/passwd* and */etc/group* files.
Size	the number of bytes in the file. If the current offset in the file is the same as the size of the file, the user is at the end of the file. For a pipe file, this field shows the number of bytes written but not yet read. For a special device file, this field shows the major and minor numbers of the device.
Access Times	three times are kept: the last time the file was modified, the last time the file was read, and the last time the inode was altered. A simple

	read of a file does not affect the modification time but does affect the access time.
Data Block Addresses	an array of 13 data block numbers used to access the (non-contiguous) data blocks for the file.
Extent List (F5)	a list of up to 4 extents of contiguous data blocks allocated for the file.
Last Written (F5)	the last block written to the file.
Flags (F5)	determine how space will be automatically allocated for writes beyond the extent-based portion of the file and whether space should shrink on **creat/trunc** operations.

The first 512-bytes of the file system (the first physical block) is never used in REAL/IX file systems. This is a vestige from older file system architectures that needed this area for bootstrap information.

The superblock occupies the second physical block of the file system. Note that, for file systems that use logical blocks larger than the 512-bytes physical block, this leaves the rest of the first logical block unused before the ilist begins at logical block 2. The superblock is read into memory when the file system is mounted, and is updated on the disk periodically by the **bdflush** daemon. For synchronous file systems, the super block is updated every time a write operation is initiated.

The super block contains the following status information.

Sizes

- *size of the inode list:* the total number of inodes available in the file system. This number must be less than 65,500.
- *size of the file system:* the total number of logical blocks in the file system, including the super block, inode list, and data blocks. The size of the data bock collection can be derived from this number.

Counts of Available File System Space

- *free inodes:* the total number of inodes available for allocation
- *free blocks:* the total number of storage blocks available for allocation

Memory-Resident Flags

- *modification ("dirty") flag:* This flag is set when the super block in main memory is modified. When **sync** runs, it checks for this flag and, if set, updates the super block on disk and clears the flag. If this flag is not set, **sync** does not update the file system or the super block.

- *read-only flag:* This flag is set when the file system is mounted as a read-only file system. If it is set, any attempt to write to a file in this file system will fail. This flag is frequently set on file systems that contain only source code, or when debugging device drivers to ensure that no writes are accidently done to files in the file system. This flag can also be set when backing up a file system while the system is in the multi-user state.

File System Description Information

- *magic number:* indicates the file system architecture being used. This is S5FsMAGIC for S5 file systems and F5FsMAGIC for F5 file systems.

- *logical block size (type):* indicates the logical block size of the file system. 1 indicates a 512-byte logical file, 2 indicates a 1024-byte logical file, and so forth up to 9, which indicates a 131,072-byte (128K) logical file size.

The super block also contains two array fields used for allocating inodes and storage blocks, each of which has a corresponding lock field used to lock the arrays when they are being manipulated.

3.6.7 Accessing Data Storage Blocks

UNIX operating systems do not require that files be created with an initial allocation. In fact, on most UNIX systems, this is not possible. Rather, a file is created when opened for writing for the first time, and space for the data is allocated as writes are done to the file, one block at a time. As a file expands, free blocks are allocated for the file and associated with the file's inode, and as the file shrinks, data blocks that are no longer needed are deallocated from the file and made available to other files in the file system. This conserves space in the file system, since the maximum waste for each file is less than the size of one logical block.

The drawback of the standard scheme is that executing processes must absorb the overhead of allocating and deallocating data storage blocks for their files. In addition, the blocks associated with a file may be scattered around the disk, which increases file access time. This overhead is not excessive for most standard applications, but may be unacceptable for critical real-time processes. For this reason, the F5 file system architecture allows up to four *extents* to be allocated for each file. An extent is a chunk of contiguous data blocks that are preallocated when the file is created.

The inode of each file has pointers to the data storage blocks associated with that file. Inodes in both the S5 and F5 file system architectures include 13 disk block addresses that point to the non-contiguous data blocks allocated for that file. In addition, the F5 file system has four extent addresses that point to the extents allocated to the file. A file in an F5 file system can use only the data block addresses, only the extents, or a combination of the two to access data block addresses. The data stored in a storage block that is part of an extent is referred to as the *extent-based part of the file.* Certain operations are supported only on extent-based parts of files.

Data Block Address Array. The inode's data block address array points to the data storage blocks associated with all S5 files and the non-extent based files in F5 file systems. It contains 13 blocks:

blocks 0-9	point to the first 10 data storage blocks associated with the file.
block 10	for files that are larger than 10 blocks, points to an indirect block, which in turn points to the block addresses of another set of data blocks associated with the file.
block 11	for files that contain more blocks than can be accessed through the single indirection of block 10, points to a double indirect block that contains the addresses of a set of indirect blocks, each of which contains the addresses of another set of data blocks.
block 12	for even larger files, points to a triple indirect block that contains the addresses of a set of double indirect blocks that point to sets of indirect blocks that point to the data blocks.

This scheme is illustrate in Figure 3.17. Data storage blocks are shaded, and indirect blocks are shown unshaded.

The number of data blocks accessed by each indirect block varies depending on the logical block size of the file system. The number can be calculated by dividing the logical block size by four, which is the size of one pointer. Given that the number of bytes of data that can be stored in each data block also increases for the larger logical block sizes, you can see that double and triple indirection is seldom needed but, if it is used, one can incur a noticeable amount of excess overhead in file access.

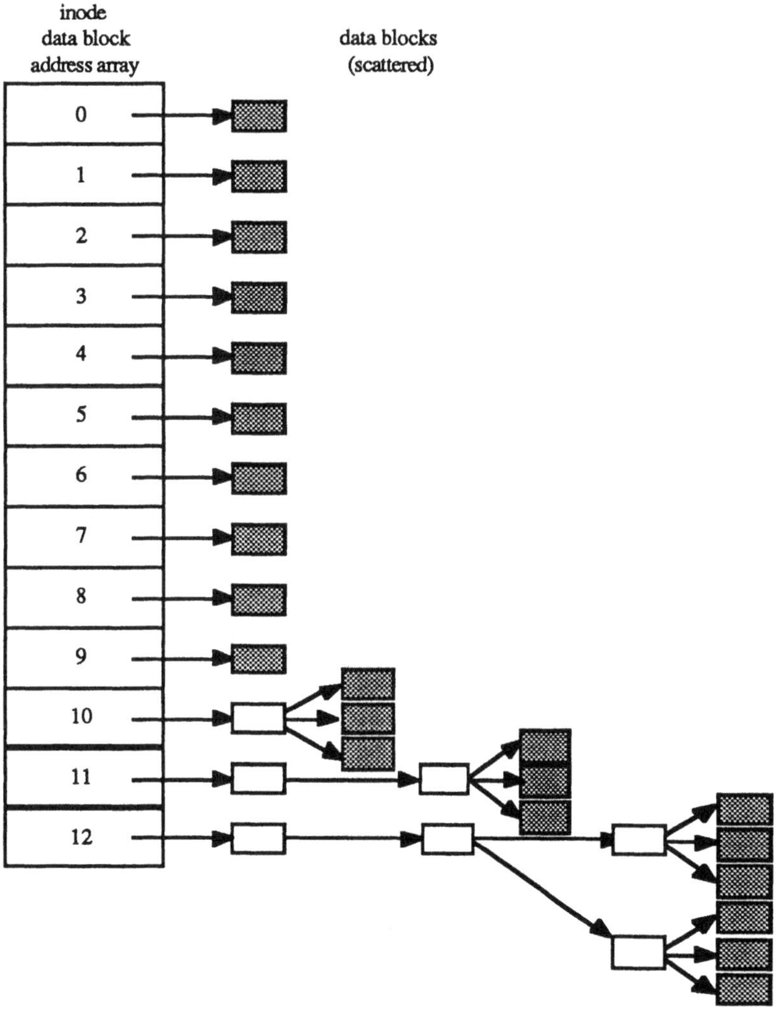

Figure 3.17 - Accessing non-contiguous data blocks

Inodes for files in F5 file systems have an extent list in addition to the data block address array discussed above. An extent is a set of preallocated, contiguous data blocks. The operating system does not impose a limit on the number of data blocks that can be allocated to one extent beyond the limit of the size of the file system. In fact, the operating system will allow you to create a file system that contains one file with one extent that contains all the data storage blocks allocated for the file system.

Each extent is identified by the physical offset into the file system of the first block and a running sum of the number of data blocks allocated to all extents for the file, as illustrated in Figure 3.18.

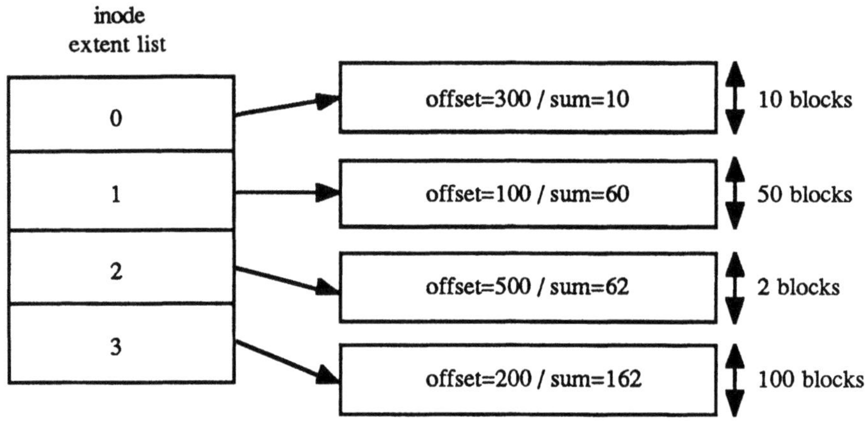

Figure 3.18 - Accessing extents (contiguous data blocks)

In this figure, the first extent begins at block 300 and contains 10 data storage blocks, so the sum is 10. The second extent begins at block 100, and contains 50 data storage blocks, so the running sum is 60, which is the number of data blocks allocated to the first and second extents. The sum for the fourth extent represents the total number of data storage blocks allocated to all extents for the file (162 in this example). Summing the extents make loops self-terminating, and thus more efficient. If no extents are used, the offset and sum for all extents are 0. The offset and sum for the extents can be viewed using the **ls -E** command.

Inodes in files in F5 file systems also contain additional flags that describe the allocation mechanism. These can be viewed with either the **ls -e** or **ls -E** command:

- c — file has contiguous extents.
- s — physical space will shrink (in non-contiguous fashion) on truncates and creates. The default is to not shrink.
- g — grow file for writes beyond the end of physical space. If not set, writes beyond the last active extent will fail.

The **prealloc** command or system call can be used to allocate contiguous file space to a file, specify where the extent should be physically located on the disk, and set the flags that control allocation. The **trunc** system call truncates a file to a specified size. The **estat** and **efstat** system calls provide statistical information (such as file size and number of links) for files in F5 file systems similar to that returned by the **stat** and **fstat** system calls for S5 file systems, as well as information on the extents.

3.6.8 Accessing Free Inodes and Data Blocks

Each time a file is created, the operating system must allocate an inode and an appropriate number of data blocks to the file. Inodes are allocated in the same way for both file system architectures, using an array of free inodes stored in the super block. Data blocks are identified and allocated using different schemes for each architecture, with S5 file systems using a linked list with a cache kept in the super block and F5 file systems using a bitmap of free blocks stored outside the superblock.

Allocating and Deallocating Inodes. The super block's free inode array contains the inumbers of 100 free inodes, although many more may be available on the file system. An index points to the next available slot in the array. When a file is created, an inode must be allocated. If no inodes are available for allocation, the **open** or **creat** system call will fail.

The operating system takes the following steps to allocate an inode:

1. Lock the free inode array.
2. Decrement the index into the free inode array and use it to find the inumber of the next available inode. Free inodes are identified by a zero value for the **mode** field.
3. If the free inode array empties, go to the ilist on disk and look for free inodes. As they are found, put their numbers in the array of free inumbers until the array is filled (100 inumbers) or, if the file system has less than 100 available inodes, until all available inodes are listed in the free inode array.
4. Read the inode into main memory.
5. Assign appropriate header information to the inode.
6. Unlock the free inumber array and unblock any processes that were blocked while waiting for the array.

When an **unlink** system call removes the last link to a file, the inode for that file is removed and its inumber is added back to the free inode array.

If the array is already full (has 100 inumbers in it), the operating system compares the number of the newly deallocated inode against the number in the first slot of the free inumber array. The lower of the two numbers is put (remains) in the first slot. The higher of the two numbers is added to the ilist on disk. By ensuring in this way that the lowest numbered inode available is in the first slot of the free inumber array, unnecessary searches are eliminated.

Allocating and Deallocating Free Blocks. Free blocks are data storage blocks that do not currently contain inodes, indirect address blocks, file extents, or data and are not part of the directory tree structure. Free blocks are each one logical block long. For S5 file systems, the super block's free block array contains the data block numbers of 50 free data blocks, forming the beginning of a free list of data block numbers. This array is used as a stack whenever the file system needs to allocate another data block. To repopulate the free block array, the operating system uses address zero as a pointer to a free block that contains an additional 50 addresses. This algorithm is extremely fast but tends to scatter data over time.

For F5 file systems, a bitmap of all free data blocks in the file system is stored outside the super block. To allocate data blocks for a file, the operating system can quickly search this bitmap to identify free data blocks. This is slower, but tends to localize disk accesses to a particular file, and also enables the operating system to quickly identify contiguous blocks available to be allocated for extents.

3.6.9 File System Access Tables

When a file system is identified to the operating system with a **mount** command, the operating system makes an entry in the mount table and reads the super block into an internal buffer maintained by the kernel. Parts of the super block that are needed in memory are the lists of free inodes and storage blocks and the flags and time fields that are constantly being modified.

Three system tables maintain information about all files that are opened or referenced. These are:

1. **System Inode Table**: contains information from the inodes for each open or referenced file. The operating system maintains one system inode table for all processes. It is part of the operating system's address space.

2. **System File Table**: contains information about opens of files. Each time a file is opened, an entry is allocated in this table that identifies the way the file was opened and the user's current offset in the file. Like the system inode table, this table is part of the operating system's address space.

3. **User Area File Descriptor Table**: A table of pointers to entries in the system file table. One of these tables for each process resides in the user's user area.

Figure 3.19 shows how these tables string together. The following sections describe these tables in more detail.

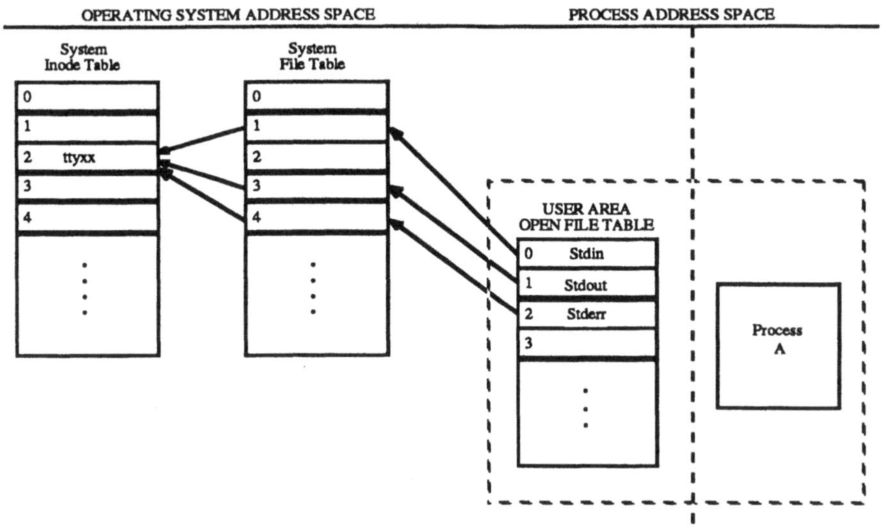

Figure 3.19 - File system tables and their pointers

The System Inode Table. The system inode table holds most information from the disk version of the inode, as well as the following:

1. **device**: identifies the device on which the file system resides. This indicates the file system of which the file is a part.

2. **inumber**: along with **device**, locates the file in the current file hierarchy. The location of the inode is calculated each time the file is referenced using the inumber as an offset, and is not stored in the disk version of the inode.

3. **reference count**: number of times the file was opened or referenced. In other words, how many pointers from the system file table point at this entry. When a table entry is shared, the reference count shows how many processes are sharing the entry. When this number drops to zero, the file is no longer being referenced and the entry can be deallocated.

4. **last logical block read**: used by the system to determine if the file is being read sequentially. If it is, the operating system invokes the read-ahead feature each time a read is done. This causes the block n+1 to be queued for reading when the block n is read.

5. **hash list pointers**: used for locating used inode table entries and maintaining a free list of inode table entries.

6. **flags**: indicate whether the file represents a shared-text *a.out* file, a locked inode, a modified file, or a mount-point directory. Other flags

specify if synchronous writes are to be done to this file and if someone is waiting for this inode to be unlocked.

Notice that the system inode table does not contain any time stamps, which are part of the disk version of the inode.

Several linked lists are used to provide easy access to system inode table entries currently in use and to keep a list of free inode table entries for use when allocating entries while opening and referencing files. These lists are present in all systems based on UNIX System V to decrease the time required to manipulate new files:

- **System Inode Table Free List**: starts at an operating system variable, which points to an unused system inode table entry, which points to another, and so on until all free table entries are on the free list. The link pointer of the last entry has a null pointer as its value.

- **System Inode Table Hash Lists**: consist of pointers to inode table entries, each of which starts a hash list of inode table entries. This reduces the average number of entries inspected when looking for a file in the table by breaking the total number of used entries into a series of lists specified by the NINODE kernel parameter. These lists are maintained through an inode hash table.

  The inumber and device are hashed to find an entry in the hash table. This entry points to an entry in the system inode table which is the head of the hash list. If the file is represented by an entry in the inode table, it will be on this hash list.

The System File Table. The system file table contains information about the opening of files on the system. Each time a file is opened, an entry is allocated and populated in the system file table. A system file table entry contains the following information:

a) **reference count**: indication of how many file descriptors are pointing to this entry. These may be from one or more processes. If two processes are pointing to the same system file table entry, they must be related through a **fork** and the file must have been opened before the **fork**.

b) **current offset**: indication, in bytes, of the user's position within the file.

c) **flags**: used to record how the file was opened. They include the following values:

   - read: the file can be accessed for reading

   - write: the file is available for writing

- append: before each write to the file, the current offset will be set equal to the size of the file. Therefore, if two or more users are appending to the same file, they will always append to the end of the file, not just starting at the end.

- no delay: if the file being opened is a named pipe, reads to an empty pipe will not cause the process to be put to sleep, nor will writes to a full pipe. Instead, an error will be returned.

d) **pointer to system inode table entry**: link to the remainder of the information about the file; an access pathway to the data blocks for the file.

The user area File Descriptor Table. The user area file descriptor table is part of the user area and contains pointers to entries in the system file table, which in turn points to entries in the system inode table. Each entry is referenced by a file descriptor (described above) and corresponds to an open file. The size of this table is determined by the kernel parameter NOFILES. The default value of NOFILES is 80, which allows each process to have up to 80 files open concurrently, including **stdin**, **stdout**, and **stderr**. The **dup** system call copies one entry in the file descriptor table to another.

3.6.10 Using the File Access Tables

To illustrate how the file access tables work, the following sections describe the internal system activities related to the **open**, **creat**, **read**, and **write** system calls.

open

The **open** system call opens an existing file and returns a file descriptor. As a simple example of the **open** system call, assume that the argument to **open** is the path */a/b*.

1. The operating system sees that the path name starts with a slash, so in the user area there is a pointer to the inode table entry for the *root* directory's inode.

2. Using the *root* inode, the system does a linear scan of the *root* directory file looking for an entry "a". When "a" is found, the operating system picks up the inumber associated with "a".

3. The inumber gives the offset into the ilist in which the inode for "a" is stored. At that location, the system determines that "a" is a directory by looking at the file type.

4. That directory is searched linearly until an entry "b" is found.

5. The "b" is found, its inumber is picked up and used as an index into the ilist to find the inode for "b".

6. The inode for "b" is copied to the system inode table, and the reference count is incremented.

7. The system file table entry is allocated, the pointer to the system inode table is set, the offset for the I/O pointer is set to zero to indicate the beginning of the file, and the reference count is initialized.

8. The user area file descriptor table entry is allocated with a pointer set to the entry in the system file table.

The algorithm for locating the inode of a file illustrates why it is advisable to keep directories small. Search time is also speeded up by keeping subdirectory names near the beginning of a directory file, which the **dcopy** command does.

creat

The **creat** system call creates a new file and returns a file descriptor. It functions like the **open** system call, with three additional steps at the beginning:

1. The super block is referenced for a free inode.

2. The mode of the file is established (by combining the system defaults with the complement of a **umask** entry) and entered in the inode.

3. Using the inumber, the system goes through a directory search similar to that used in the **open** system call, except that here the last portion of the path name is written by the system into the directory that is the next to last portion of the path name, and the inumber of the newly-created file is stored with it.

read and write

The **read, write, aread** and **awrite** system calls take a file descriptor as an argument, and follow these steps:

1. Using the file descriptor as an index, the file descriptor table is read to get a pointer to the system file table.

2. The user buffer address and number of bytes to read/write are supplied as arguments to the call. The correct offset into the buffer is read from the system file table entry. For the **aread** and **awrite** system calls, the offset can be modified by settings within the aiocb control block.

3. For read operations, the inode is found by following the pointer from the system file table entry to the system inode table. The operating system copies the data from storage to the user's buffer.

4. For write operations, the same pointer chain is followed, but the system writes into the data blocks. If new blocks are needed, they are obtained by the system from the file system's list of free blocks.

5. The read or write operation will take place, provided the file is not locked by another process.

6. Before the system call returns to the user, the number of bytes read or written is added to the offset in the system file table.

Files Shared by Related Processes. If related processes are sharing an open file (as is the case after a **fork**), they also share the same file descriptor and entry in the system file table.

Unrelated processes that access the same file have separate file descriptors and separate entries in the system file table. Because they executed separate **open** calls, they may be reading from or writing to different places in the file.

In both cases, the entry in the inode table is shared. The correct offset at which the read or write operations should take place is tracked by the offset entry in the system file table.

Path Name Conversion. The directory search and path name conversion take place only when the file is opened. For subsequent access of the file, the system supplies a file descriptor which is an index into the file descriptor table in the user's process area. The file descriptor table points to the system file table entry where the pointer to the system inode table is picked up. Given the inode, the system can find the data blocks that make up the file.

3.7 I/O SUBSYSTEM

Most user-level I/O is done through the file subsystem. The I/O subsystem handles actual interaction with the device.

3.7.1 Device I/O

One of the virtues of UNIX operating systems is that I/O requests to devices look very much like I/O requests to regular files. Each device on the system is represented by one or more *special device files* that can be addressed like any other file. The operating system uses the information in the special device file to locate the appropriate *device driver*, which is coded to handle the device-specific requests.

All device I/O is directed to a special device file in the */dev* directory. Special device files are created by the superuser with the **mknod** command. Each special device file is either "block" type or "character" type, identified by a "b" or a "c" in the first field of the permissions field.

Block drivers, which transfer data between user address space and the device through the system buffer cache, are normally written for disk drives and other mass storage devices capable of handling data in blocks.

Character drivers, the typical choice for interactive terminals and process control devices, are normally written for devices that send and receive information one character at a time.

One device often has more than one special device file associated with it. For example, a disk device has a block special device file that is used for normal user I/O operations, as well as a character special device file that is used for administrative operations such as backups, file system checking and repair, and disk formatting. As another example, one device may have more than one name by which it is accessed, such as the *console*, which is also accessed as *contty* and *systty*. In this case, the three names are represented by three special device files that are linked together.

Special device files store the major and minor device number in the inode field that holds file size information for regular files. The major device number is an index used by the operating system to identify the driver that controls this device; the minor number is used by the driver to identify which particular device or subdevice controlled by the driver is being accessed.

Device drivers are kernel-level processes that isolate low-level, device-specific details from system calls. Because there are so many details for each device, it is impractical to design the kernel to handle all possible devices. Instead, a device driver is included for each configured device.

The main outline of any driver is a set of *entry-point routines* that are named in a specific way (Figure 3.20). Each driver is assigned a two- to four-character prefix, which is combined with prescribed suffixes (such as **open, close, read, write,** and so forth) to form the names of the driver entry point routines. So, if the driver's prefix is **xxxx**, the driver might have entry-point routines named **xxxxopen, xxxxclose, xxxxread, xxxxwrite**, and so forth. These routines may call subordinate routines, for which the naming conventions are less strict.

The driver routines are accessed through two *device switch tables*: **cdevsw** for character special device files, and **bdevsw** for block special device files. These tables are built by sysgen, and are basically matrices with a row for each driver and a column for each type of entry point routine. The tables are indexed by the major device number. So, if the user-level program issues a **read** system call against a character device with major number 53, the operating system looks in the **cdevsw** table for major number 53, and finds that the appropriate routine is **xxxxread**.

The switch tables are used to access the driver's *base-level* routines, which execute synchronously in response to user-level program requests. Most hardware device drivers also have an *interrupt level*, which executes in response to interrupts generated by the hardware device itself. Interrupts are the primary mechanism through which devices communicate with the operating system. They may signal that some abnormal condition (such as a device out of calibration or temperature out of range) has occurred.

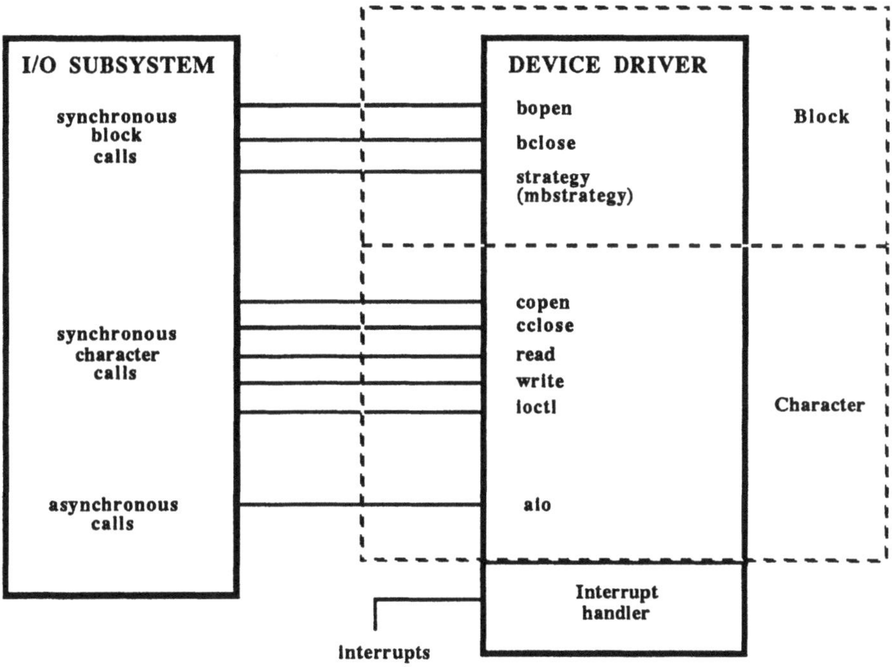

Figure 3.20 - Driver entry points

Interrupt routines are accessed through an interrupt vector file, *m68kvec.s*. **sysgen** builds this file, which associates the interrupt received with the appropriate interrupt handling routine using the driver prefix and a specific name for the interrupt handling routine much as the switch tables described above do.

Direct I/O allows a user program to control devices directly, thus saving the system overhead associated with other I/O (whether synchronous or asynchronous) such as system call entry and exit. The user process maps the device registers into its address space with the **shmget** and **shmat** system calls. Once mapped in, the process can read and write these registers like any other variable, thus gaining complete control over the device operations.

Configuring a device into the operating system is the process of providing information about a driver and any associated devices and tunable parameters to the system. In the REAL/IX operating system, this is done using the administrative **sysgen** command, which is an interactive menu-driven program that automatically updates the appropriate system files.

The REAL/IX system supports priority queuing of disk I/O associated with real-time processes. This means that:

- For processes running at real-time priorities, disk I/O associated with higher-priority processes executes before disk I/O associated with lower-priority processes, regardless of the order in which the I/O requests were queued. Disk I/O associated with processes executing at the same priority is executed according to a FIFO algorithm.

- For processes running at time-sharing priorities, disk I/O operations execute only when there are no competing requests from processes executing at real-time priorities, and are scheduled according to a FIFO algorithm as in the traditional kernel. In the system, the first queued are the first to run.

The traditional scheme for scheduling disk I/O provides fair-share accesses to all processes, but can result in disk "bottlenecks" that would subvert the benefits of the real-time scheduler. Ensuring high disk I/O throughput for high-priority processes is essential for providing deterministic response times for critical real-time programs.

No system calls are associated with this feature. Real-time processes that want to change the priority of their disk I/O operations should change the priority of the process before initiating the I/O operation.

3.7.2 I/O Transfer Methods

All user I/O is done against data in buffers in user address space. This information is moved to the device itself using one of three schemes:

1. lock the data in user space and transfer directly to the device.

2. do an intermediate transfer to local driver data space in the kernel.

3. do an intermediate transfer using a kernel buffering scheme, either the system buffer cache or a private buffering scheme defined just for the application.

Figure 3.21 illustrates these three schemes.

Method #1 is the fastest data transfer method, but should only be used with devices that have adequate data storage on the controller and allow a restart after an error (such as network, printer, and some robotics devices). The data must always be locked in user address space before beginning the I/O transfer to ensure that it is not paged out. Method #2 is useful for occasional transfers of small amounts of data.

Most I/O operations for data files use Method #3 with the system buffer cache. Each buffer consists of two distinct parts: the buffer itself, which is a region of kernel memory allocated for data storage, and the buffer header that provides control information for the operations. This control information includes the number of characters to transfer, whether this is a read or write operation, and status information. By default, each buffer holds 1024 bytes of information. Tunable parameters allow you to reconfigure the number of buffers and to specify storage sizes ranging from 1K to 128K bytes.

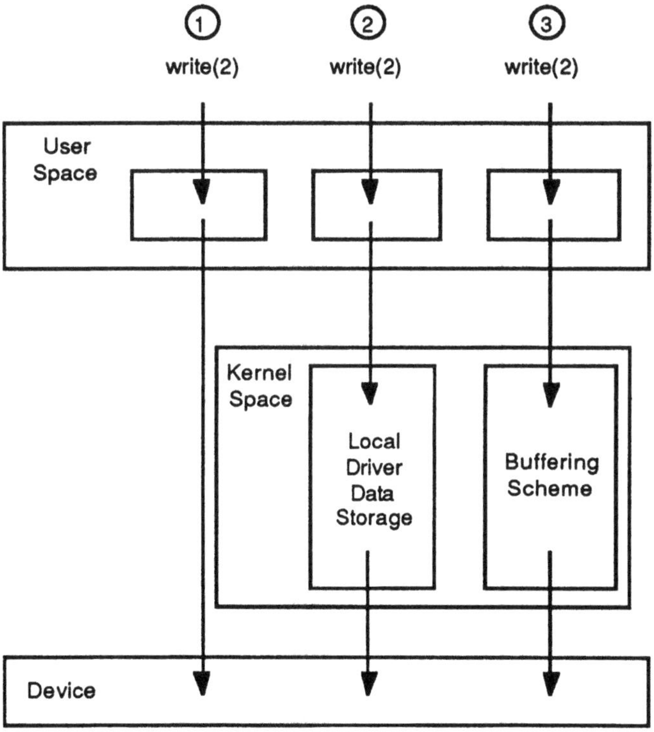

Figure 3.21 - Three methods of I/O transfer

3.7.3 Initiating I/O Operations

Most I/O operations are controlled by two or more paired structures, one of which is a user-level control block, the other of which is a kernel-level control block. The user-level process populates the user-level control block, and the operating system transfers the appropriate information to the parallel kernel-level structure, then later transfers new information from the kernel-level structure back to the user-level structure. The reason for these paired control blocks is that the interrupt level of the kernel, which must update the control structure when the I/O transfer is complete (or if it fails because of a device error), can never access a data structure that is also accessed by user-level processes.

There are two types of I/O operations in the REAL/IX operating system: synchronous (or blocking) and asynchronous (or non-blocking). Synchronous I/O operations are all that is supported on many UNIX operating systems. After the process issues the synchronous I/O request, it blocks and does nothing more until the I/O operation completes. The asynchronous I/O interface is provided to support real-time applications (such as a journalizing program) that can (and should) continue execution while waiting for the previous I/O request to complete.

Section 3.6 discusses how I/O requests interact with a file descriptor at the user level. The following sections describe how the I/O transfers to the device itself are performed.

<u>Synchronous (Blocking) I/O Operations</u>. Synchronous I/O transfers are requested with the **read** and **write** system calls. These in turn activate the appropriate driver entry point routines: **read** and **write** for character devices, **strategy** for block devices.

For I/O operations that use the system buffer cache, the information in the user-level buffer is transferred to a parallel buffer in the kernel-level buffer cache. For other operations, the information may be transferred into some area of kernel memory, or the user-level address space that contains the data may be locked. Regardless of whether the data itself is copied into kernel address space, the control block information is usually transferred into a kernel structure.

The driver routine then validates the request and handles the device-specific details required to transfer the data. After initiating the I/O transfer, the process blocks to await completion of the transfer. The device will signal that the I/O operation has completed, and the driver's interrupt handler will catch this signal and unblock the driver routine that initiated the I/O request. The driver routine in turn unblocks the associated user-level process as described below.

For data transfers that use the system buffer cache, used buffers are returned to the system's list of free buffers after the I/O transfer is completed. These buffers will be reused according to a least-recently-used algorithm.

<u>Asynchronous (Non-Blocking) I/O Operations</u>. Asynchronous I/O operations are initiated with the **aread** and **awrite** system calls, which in turn call the **aio** driver entry point routine. Asynchronous I/O operations may or may not use the buffer header associated with the system buffer cache, but they always use a pair of control block structures. aiocb is the user-level control block and areq is the kernel-level control block.

When these structures have been validated and populated with information on the data to be transferred, the operating system begins the I/O transfer. The process does not block, and may indeed initiate other asynchronous I/O operations before the first one completes.

When the I/O transfer completes, the driver's interrupt handler catches the device's completion interrupt and issues a function call that updates the kernel-level control structure. The operating system then transfers this completion information to the user-level structure, which effectively notifies the associated user-level process.

Each active asynchronous I/O transfer has its own pair of control blocks, but many pairs may be associated with one process. In general, the interface is optimized for applications where a process repeatedly does similar transfers and can reuse control structures. Once used, the control block structures are returned to the process' pool of available structures, but they are never returned to the system-wide pool of control structures until the process exits or explicitly frees them.

3.7.4 Device Interrupts

An interrupt is any service request that causes the CPU to stop its current execution stream and to execute an instruction stream that services the interrupt. When the CPU finishes servicing the interrupt, it returns to the original stream and resumes execution at the point it left off.

Hardware devices use interrupt requests to signal a range of conditions. For traditional computer peripherals, interrupts signal successful device connections, write acknowledgements, data availability, and read/write completion. For other devices such as process control devices, interrupts tell the CPU that something has happened on the device. Driver interrupt routines are responsible for determining the cause of the hardware interrupt and executing the instructions to handle the interrupt appropriately. The ability to handle such interrupts in a predictable time frame is a key element of a real-time operating system environment.

In addition to hardware interrupts, the operating system handles two other types of interrupts:

1. Exceptions, which are conditions that interrupt the current processing of the CPU and require special fault handler processing for recovery. Examples of exceptions include floating point divide-by-zero operations, bus errors, and illegal instructions. Fault handlers are responsible for executing instructions to handle the specific fault, and for restarting the interrupted instruction sequence once the fault is handled.

2. Software interrupts (Programmed Interrupt Requests or PIRs), which are generated by writing an integer into a logical register address assigned to the interrupt vector table. These are used by the operating system but are not available for general use.

The REAL/IX system uses Motorola's MC68030 microprocessor, which accepts eight levels of interrupts. The level indicates the degree of priority given the interrupt by the CPU. The higher the priority, the quicker the system will service the interrupt when multiple interrupts are pending. Level 7 is the highest priority, level 1 is the lowest priority. Level 0 indicates that no interrupts are pending.

The Interrupt Priority Level (IPL) for the requesting device is determined by the device itself and is identified to the operating system in **sysgen**.

An interrupt vector is an entry to the interrupt vector table that is assigned to an interrupt by the **sysgen** process. The interrupt vector table resides in kernel space in main memory and associates interrupts with their appropriate interrupt routines. Every hardware device has at least one interrupt vector table entry. Each entry is assigned an *interrupt vector number* that associates the interrupt with the text address identifying the starting address of the interrupt handler for that interrupt. When an interrupt occurs, the CPU associates the interrupt with its interrupt vector number, fetches the starting address of the interrupt handler, and executes the address to service the interrupt.

Each device has at least one interrupt vector assigned to it. **sysgen** creates an internal interrupt vector table and stores it in the *m68kvec.s* file, which the system uses to identify which interrupt vector is associated with which device. There are 256 interrupt vector table entries, of which 192 are available for user devices.

3.7.4.1 Interrupt Handling

Interrupts are always asynchronous events; in other words, they can arrive in the driver at any time. If an interrupt occurs that is at a higher priority than whatever is executing at the time, control switches to the interrupt handler to service the interrupt, then returns to whatever was executing before. However, user-level programs are usually notified of the results of the interrupt synchronously, through return codes that the driver writes to the user structure.

When a driver's interrupt routine receives an interrupt, it determines what type of interrupt it is and then handles it. Interrupt handling typically involves one or more of the following:

1. issuing a function call (**vsema** or **wakeup**) to unblock the appropriate base-level routine of the driver, which in turn resumes execution. The base-level routine will eventually issue a return code that notifies the user-level process that the I/O is complete.

2. sending a signal or posting an event to the appropriate user process(es) associated with this device.

3. updating the **u_error** member of the user structure to notify the user-level process that an error occurred.

These conventions for handling interrupts are used for most traditional computer peripherals, where most interrupts indicate that some hardware action requested by the base level of the driver has completed. Many devices associated with real-time applications require that the operating system handle other types of interrupts.

3.7.4.2 Connected Interrupts

Connected interrupts provide a consistent interrupt notification interface for hardware interrupts. Real-time applications that benefit from connected interrupts are characterized by having devices that generate interrupts that are not directly associated with an I/O operation and must be serviced rapidly, even if some other processes are delayed. When the interrupt handling routine receives an interrupt, it updates data structures. The user-level process is notified of the interrupt either through the common event notification facility or by polling a process memory location. This provides the deterministic interrupt notification required by real-time applications.

Although most control of the connected interrupt mechanism is in the user-level program, using the facility requires special coding in both the device driver and the associated user-level program. The following scenario summarizes how the mechanism works:

1. The user-level program populates a **cintrio** structure, which specifies whether notification will be by polling, through the common event notification mechanism, or through **cisema**; whether notification is to occur for every interrupt or whether each interrupt must be acknowledged before the user-level program is notified of subsequent interrupts from that device is specified. If the notification method is polling, the memory location to be polled is also specified. The **cintrio** structure also includes one member whose use can be tailored to the specific needs of the driver and application.

2. When the user-level program issues the CI_CONNECT **ioctl** command, the operating system creates a cintr data structure in the kernel where it can be accessed by the connected interrupt interface functions.

3. When the driver's interrupt routine receives an interrupt, it uses the **cintrnotify** kernel function to notify the associated user-level process.

4. The operating system updates the **cintrio** structure appropriately. This effectively notifies the associated user-level process of the interrupt, as illustrated in Figure 3.22.

User-level programs use a set of IOCTL commands (documented on the **cintrio** manual page) to control connected interrupts. Drivers implement the connected interrupt mechanism with the **cintrget**, **cintrnotify**, **cintrctl**, and **cintrelse** kernel functions.

Using direct I/O with the connected interrupt mechanism makes it possible to implement a device driver as a user-level process. This is useful for applications where tight control over the device is required.

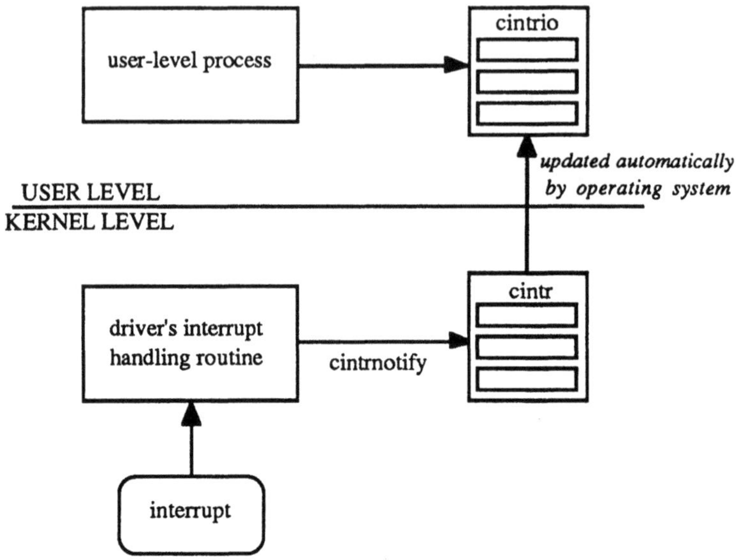

Figure 3.22 - Connected interrupt notification

3.7.4.3 Handling Interrupts for Asynchronous I/O Operations

Job completion interrupts for asynchronous I/O operations are handled differently than those for synchronous I/O operations, where a process is blocked awaiting the completion of the operation. When the interrupt routine receives the interrupt and determines that it is associated with an asynchronous I/O operation, it updates appropriate members of the areq structure. The operating system then updates the corresponding aiocb structure, thus notifying the associated user-level process.

3.7.5 Drivers for Real-Time Applications

Technically speaking, there is no such thing as a "real-time driver". There are, however, drivers that support the performance requirements of real-time applications, and drivers for devices that are associated with real-time applications. These real-time drivers should meet the following criteria:

- allow for preemption
- have low interrupt latencies
- be written to minimize contention for resources, which may cause processes to block for longer periods of time
- support real-time features as appropriate

In addition, a number of internal enhancements should be made to the UNIX System V kernel to improve driver performance. For example, on UNIX System V, error messages written to the console by drivers may degrade performance by increasing interrupt latencies. The REAL/IX system includes a daemon that writes the error messages to the console and to an internal kernel structure. Consequently, these error messages have virtually no effect on system latencies.

Drivers written for devices that are used specifically for real-time applications (such as an analog or digital process control board) can meet more stringent performance requirements by never blocking and by using specific real-time features such as connected interrupts. In many cases, the best approach is to use direct I/O control of the board, and have a kernel-level driver that is written mainly to support interrupts generated by the board.

Summary

This chapter has presented an overview of the basic concepts and capabilities of a real-time UNIX operating system. These attributes were premised on providing real-time capabilities while maintaining the standard UNIX system functions and environment. In the next chapter, the detailed features and use of an operating system based upon the concepts outlined in this chapter, are presented.

CHAPTER 4

Designing Real-Time Applications

In Chapter 3, the concept of the REAL/IX operating system, a fully preemptive real-time UNIX operating system, is described. In this chapter, the guidelines for designing real-time applications using the REAL/IX environment are given. The chapter begins with general programming guidelines, scheduling processes, and real-time memory allocation. Special emphasis is given to interprocess communication mechanisms, file systems, and device interfaces. This chapter includes a number of example programs.

4.1 PROGRAMMING GUIDELINES

Developing real-time applications requires careful thought at all stages. In the design phase, it is important to identify the following:

(a) Performance requirements against which the completed application can be tested.

(b) The precise functionality required, and which functionality can be isolated into separate programs. Only the most critical functionality should be coded for processes that will execute at high, fixed priorities and be locked in memory.

(c) The interprocess communications that are required.

- Shared memory provides the fastest interprocess communication, but also consumes system memory. When using shared memory, one must choose which process will own the shared memory segment, which processes can have read/write access to the shared memory, and whether to use semaphores, binary semaphores, or messages to coordinate access to the shared memory segment.

- Only two signals can be defined specifically for an application.

(d) What are the file access requirements for the application? If file-access is a critical part of the application, consider using the F5 file system for the application files. Isolating the data files in a private application file system enables you to optimize the file system logical block size for the application and, mounting the file system synchronously reduces contention for the file system.

(e) If the real-time application uses an application-specific device (such as a process control board), design the board interface, noting that:

- Direct I/O, with the kernel driver dedicated only to handling interrupts, is often the most efficient method to access the board. Controlling the device completely with a kernel driver may provide greater flexibility in controlling complex devices.

- Using connected interrupts is usually the preferred method for handling interrupts from application-specific devices. Determine the number of connected interrupt structures that are required (usually one for each type of interrupt the board issues) and whether the user level process should be notified with the common event mechanism or through polling. Events are more appropriate if the board needs to queue multiple interrupts, pass data from the board, and can afford a context switch to other executing processes. Polling is usually a little faster, and is the preferred method if the board does not need to queue multiple interrupts, does not need to pass data (or can afford some loss of data when passing information), or this is the only application executing on the system.

4.1.1 Real-Time Program Structure

Real-time programs typically have three distinct sections: one that initializes and preallocates resources required by the process, one that prepares the process for real-time execution by locking resources in memory and setting the process' priority, and one that contains the bulk of the functionality of the program. Although not all features are used in all applications, the pseudo-code, in Figure 4.1, illustrates a typical program structure.

Before executing the process, preallocate file space that is required for the application, and be sure the UID has real-time privileges or is a superuser. If appropriate, create a script in the */etc/rc2.d* directory to begin execution of the process when the system is booted. Application scripts should execute after all system scripts in *rc2.d*.

```
Global definitions and declarations
        #include lines
        Code to detach IPC structures gracefullyon exit

main {
        Initialization code
                definition of signal-handling functions
                create shared memory segments
                create semaphores, binary semaphores, or messages
                        to control access to shared memory
                initialize event structures (evget)
                initialize connected interrupt structures
                open files and devices required
                initialize asynchronous I/O structures (arinit,
                        awinit)
                initialize process interval timers (gettimerid)
                generate child processes (exec and fork)

        Preparation for real-time execution
                set process interval timers (absinterval or
                        incinterval)
                lock process in memory (plock and resident )
                lock shared memory segments in memory (shmctl)
                set execute priority for a fixed priority

        Process functionality
                This is application-dependent and is usually a loop or
                series of loops that:
                        read and write to files (synchronously or
                            asynchronously), using the buffer cache
                            or bypassing it, and so forth),
                        manipulate device registers or communicate
                            to the device with an ioctl call,
                        react to interrupts that happen on the device
                        communicate with other processes
                        subroutines that execute at a precise time
}
```

Figure 4.1 - The structure of a real-time program

4.1.2 Development Procedure

Some general guidelines for the development phase are:

(1) During development, compile your program with the **-g** option. This causes the compiler to generate the information required by the symbolic debugger, **sdb**. The **-g** option should not be used to compile the program for performance testing and production.

(2) If your application uses application-specific system calls and kernel-level drivers, it is advantageous to use the DEBUG kernel for the initial testing phase.

In most cases, it is recommended that real-time applications be developed using the following steps. These rules are not hard and fast, and may not work for all applications, but are a good starting point.

1. Develop the file interfaces.

2. If the application interfaces an application-specific board, develop that interface next.

   - Develop and test the base-level of the driver or the user-level process that communicates to the device.

   - Develop the interrupt-handling code. This always requires a kernel-level driver, and usually also requires setting up the user-level process to handle connected interrupts.

3. Thoroughly test the functionality of the application before incorporating the features that are critical for achieving full real-time performance. This is important since the features listed below can cause serious problems if they are used with code that has bugs.

   - Running the process at a high, fixed priority, especially priorities higher than the **prfdaemon, bdflush,** and **ttydaemon.**

     It is recommended that users always have a shell executing at a higher priority than any application process, and this shell should be run on a terminal on an **m332xt??** port rather than the console or one of the **scc?** ports that are controlled by the **ttydaemon**; this is especially critical when testing the application, to ensure that you can regain control of the system under any conditions.

     It is important to understand that the operating system does not force a process running at a high, fixed priority to give up the CPU (unless a higher-priority process needs to run). If a high-priority process goes into a loop, the only way to recover the system is to reboot it, unless you have a shell at a higher priority. If the process is executed by a script in the *rc2.d* directory, even rebooting may not be enough to regain the system.

   - Preallocating file space that does not grow or shrink.

Table 4.1
Real-Time Tasks, System Calls and Commands

Real-Time Programming Task	System Call, Command, or Data Structure	Section Where Applied
Assign real-time privileges to a user	setrtusers setrtusers	Scheduling Processes
Set and remove real-time privileges for a process	setrt clrrt	
Set and check the priority of a process	getpri setpri	
Voluntarily give up CPU	relinquish	
Set the CPU time slice size	setslice	
Suspend or resume a real-time process	suspend resume resume swtch	
Schedule processes to run at a precise time and/or at precise intervals	absinterval incinterval getinterval gettimer gettimerid reltimerid resabs resinc restimer settimer itimerstruc timestruc	Scheduling Processes
Using common event notification mechanism	evctl evget evpost evrcv evrcvl evrel	Interprocess Communications
Using binary semaphores	bsget bsfree bslk bslkc bsunlk	
Prellocate and lock memory	resident stkexp	Real-Time Memory Allocation

Table 4.1 cont'd

Real-Time Programming Task	System Call, Command, or Data Structure	Section Where Applied
Preallocate and truncate contiguous file space	prealloc prealloc trunc	Using Files
Check file status	estat efstat	
Initiate asynchronous I/O operations Use connected interrupts	arinit awinit aread awrite acancel arwfree aio comp_aio comp_cancel_aio aiocb areq	Interfacing Devices
Use connected interrupts	cintrio cintrctl cintrget cintrnotify cintrelse	Interfacing Devices
Add system calls to the kernel	sysent	Writing System Calls

Allowing the system to modify the file size is usually the easiest way to determine the amount of file space that is required; you can then preallocate an appropriate amount of space.

- Locking the process and shared memory segments in memory, allocating physical shared memory segments, or specifying the virtual address at which a process attaches the shared memory segment.

4.1.3 Using System Calls

Table 4.1 presents a task-oriented overview of the real-time tasks, system calls, and commands available for developing applications in the REAL/IX environment.

A number of the system calls supported on the REAL/IX operating system should not be used in real-time applications except during initialization. These system calls may block or have some other function that could degrade the determinism of the real-time response.

The system calls presented in Table 4.2 are not recommended for real-time applications that have stringent performance requirements except during process initialization:

Table 4.2
System Calls Not Recommended for Real-Time Applications

access	getuid	shmat
acct	link	shmdt
brk, sbrk	mkdir	signal
chdir	mknod	sigset
chmod	mount	stat,fstat
chown	msgctl	statfs, fstatfs
chroot	msgget	sync
close	open	sysfs
creat	pipe	times
dup	plock	uadmin
exit	profil	ulimit
fcntl	ptrace	umask
fork	read	umountuname
getdents	rmdir	unlink
getpgrp	semget	ustat
getpid	setpgrp	utime
getppid	setgid	wait
geteuid	setuid	write
getgid	shmctl	
getegid	shmget	

4.1.4 Performance Hints

The **gprof** or **prof** commands can be used to analyze the efficiency and performance of the user's application. They are used to check to see where the application is spending significant amounts of time and whether additional tuning is necessary. In addition to using the special practices for real-time performance, it is important to remember the standard performance pitfalls that are also relevant to non-real-time programming:

- CPU loops waiting on a condition.

- Using too many system calls to transfer information. For instance, 1 read of 2048 characters is more efficient than 2048 reads of 1 character each.

- Poor locality of reference (such as an excessive number of **goto** statements).

- Excessive use of shell programming.

In addition, the following is suggested:

- Create application-specific system calls for applications rather than using archived library routines.

- Use the REAL/IX library software. For example, use **perror**(3C) for reporting system call errors, **getopt**(3C) for parsing command-line options, and **malloc**(3C) and (3X) for allocating memory dynamically.

- Allocate all resources and do **exec**, **fork**, and **open** calls during the initialization stage of the program.

- When calling **read** or **write**, make the request size the same as the file system logical block size. Use **estat** or **efstat** to get the block size on F5 file systems; use **stat** and **fstat** to get the block size on S5 file systems.

4.2 SCHEDULING PROCESSES

As described in Section 3.4, scheduling determines how the CPU is allocated to executing processes. REAL/IX implements both time-sharing and fixed-priority scheduling. Two main points which summarize how processes are scheduled under REAL/IX are:

1. A process runs only when no other process at a higher priority is runnable, and

2. Once a process with a real-time priority (0 through 127) has control of a CPU, it will retain possession of the CPU until it is preempted by a process running at a higher priority, or it relinquishes the CPU by making a call that causes a context switch.

A running process can be preempted at any time if a process at a higher priority becomes runnable. A single example given below illustrates kernel preemption and scheduling. In this example, process A is running at priority 16, while process B at priority 30. The following are critical time intervals, as shown in Figure 4.2:

1. Process A executes first, since it is running at a higher priority. It will hold onto the CPU until it relinquishes it (or is preempted by a process at a higher priority).

2. Process A initiates a blocking I/O operation.

3. The corresponding driver routine is called to initiate the data transfer. While waiting for the device, the driver issues a **psema**(D3X) kernel function call, which relinquishes the CPU.

4. Since Process A has relinquished the CPU, Process B can now execute. Process B issues a system call which causes the corresponding kernel service code to execute.

5. While Process B's kernel code is executing, the I/O completion interrupt is received by the interrupt handler associated with Process A. The interrupt handler issues a **vsema**(D3X) kernel function call, which makes Process A runnable.

6. At the end of the interrupt, Process A preempts Process B, even though Process B has not relinquished the CPU. Process B remains in the kernel and is runnable, but will not resume execution until there is no runnable program at a higher priority.

7. The base level of the driver associated with Process A returns to the user-level Process A, which continues its execution after the I/O function completes.

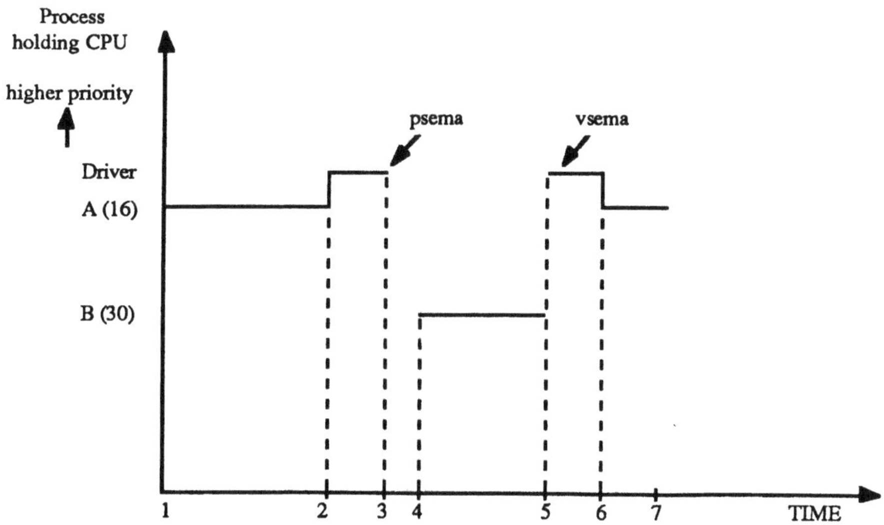

Figure 4.2 - Example of kernel preemption and scheduling

4.2.1 Selecting Process Priorities

Process priorities must be selected very carefully to ensure that a less-critical process never prevents a more-critical process from running and that all executing processes receive adequate run time for their needs. Time-sharing systems usually ensure that all processes eventually get some run time, but a real-time operating system does not offer such protections.

Table 4.3 shows how the 256 priority levels are distributed and lists some of the standard system daemons and processes with their default priorities.

Table 4.3 - Default Priorities of System Processes

Priority	Process	Function
0	**timeproc** (PRITIMEPRC)	executes timeout functions.
	ttydaemon (PRITTYDAEMON)	manages line discipline interrupts for console and serial port drivers on the CPU.
	timedaemon (PRITIMEDAEMON)	manages realtime interval timer expirations.
1–94	-----	non-migrating realtime priorities available for general use.
95	**bdflush** (PRIBDFLUSH)	flushes dirty buffers.
	onesec (PRIONSEC)	controls time-sharing processes (priorities 128–255).
	prfdaemon (PRIPRFDAEMON)	writes error messages from the kernel to the console.
	vhand (PRIVHAND)	pages out pages of memory.
96–127	-----	non-migrating realtime priorities available for general use.
128–253	-----	time-sharing priorities available for general use.
254	-----	non-migrating priority available for general use.
255	idle	used by idle task in system.

The following guidelines should be followed when setting and changing process priorities:

1. By default, the **timeproc** process that handles timeout requests runs at priority 0. Exercise extreme caution when changing this priority. If another process runs at a higher priority and dominates the CPU, signals from terminals may not work and timeout processing may be delayed. This can cause serious problems if, for instance, a device decides to reset

itself as a result of not receiving a response from the host in the expected amount of time.

2. The **timedaemon** must run at a priority greater than or equal to the priority of the highest priority real-time process that uses real-time interval timers. In general, this priority should not be changed.

3. The **ttydaemon** must run at a higher priority than any process that accesses a driver using the line discipline. The priority of this daemon is seldom changed, but can be moved to a lower priority as long as its priority is greater than or equal to that of the highest-priority process that accesses the console or any other device that uses the line discipline. Note that there are some possible hardware ramifications if the value of this daemon is changed.

4. In the REAL/IX operating system, process 0 is the **onesec** process, which replaces UNIX System V's **sched** scheduling program. It runs roughly once a second, and provides many housekeeping functions (including priority recomputation) that are traditionally performed by the clock interrupt handler. By default, **onesec** runs at priority 95; its priority can be changed if necessary, but his should be done very carefully.

5. Avoid using priorities 0 through 15 for application programs. This will provide greater flexibility for future configurations, without degrading performance (a process runs as fast at priority 20 as at priority 1 if there are no processes with priorities 1 through 19).

6. In general, the console (for one user terminal) should always run at a higher priority than any other user process and no other processes should run at that priority. This is especially important when testing and debugging code, but always a good idea, since it ensures that the user always has a way to regain control of the system. It is emphasized that this shell should be for emergency use only.

7. Balance the priorities of all processes executing the system. Under a real-time scheduler, it is quite possible for a real-time process to completely dominate the CPU and cause a low-priority job to be completely locked out of the CPU. When needed, the **setpri** command can be used to change priorities "on the fly".

4.2.2 Setting Real-Time Privileges

Before programs are executed at a real-time priority level, the user should first obtain privileges. This is done with either the **setrtusers** command or the **setrtusers** system call, both of which must be issued by a user (or process) with superuser privileges. **setrtusers** loads the system real-time privilege table with the list of user ID's that are allowed real-time privileges.

Real-time privileges must also be given to processes in order to perform such real-time operations as resuming a process or changing the priority of a process. There are three ways in which a process may effectively gain real-time privileges.

1. Any process with superuser privileges can execute at a real-time priority since superuser privileges automatically override any restrictions. In this case, a system check of the real-time privileged users table is bypassed.

2. Real-time privileges are inherited by a child process if the parent process has real-time privileges.

3. The **setrt** system call can be used to give the calling process the necessary real-time privileges. When **setrt** is used, the system checks to see if the user's ID appears in the kernel's real-time privileged users table (previously set with **setrtusers**). In contrast, the system call **clrrt** is used to remove real-time privileges from a calling process. Since system services check for real-time privileges before they check superuser privileges, they will execute faster. **setrt** is the preferred method of assigning real-time privileges to a process.

4.2.3 Changing Process Priority

Table 4.4 shows the system calls that can be used to change or affect the priority of a process.

Table 4.4
System Calls to Change or Affect Process Priority

System Call	Function
setpri(pid, pri)	set scheduling priority
getpri(pid)	get scheduling priority of the specified process
suspend	suspend the calling process
resume(pid)	resume a suspended process
swtch(pid)	equivalent of **resume/suspend**
setslice(pid, slice)	set CPU time slice size
relinquish	relinquish time slice to another process at the same priority

The **setpri** system call sets the scheduling priority of a process. The first argument, *pid*, is the process ID of the target process (the process to be changed) and the second argument *pri* is the new scheduling priority to be assigned to the target process. The range of valid process priorities that can be assigned is 0-255 (0-127 for real-time processes, 128-255 for time-sharing processes). Lower numbers indicate higher priorities. The priority of a real-time process is fixed unless explicitly changed with the **setpri** call. Processes that are set within the time slice range will have their priorities automatically adjusted by the system. The current priority of any process can be retrieved with the **getpri** system call. For both **setpri** and **getpri**, if the target process is the process initiating the call (calling process), then *pid* is zero.

The following are characteristics of the **setpri** system call:

- If *pid* is non-zero, the requesting process must have real-time privileges (granted by the **setrt** system call).
- If *pid* is zero, the calling process must have real-time privileges to make its own priority more favorable.
- In all cases, permission checks are bypassed if the effective user ID of the requesting process is superuser.

Processes can be suspended or resumed with the user of the **suspend**, **resume**, and **swtch** system calls. **suspend** causes the calling process to be suspended; it will remain suspended until a **resume** or **swtch** system call is performed by another process. The **resume** system call will resume a previously suspended process (indicated by the argument *pid*). If the target process was suspended with a **suspend** or **swtch** system call, it will resume normal execution once **resume** has completed and it becomes the highest runnable process in the system.

The **swtch** call is the equivalent of executing **resume** and **suspend** system calls respectively as in:

> **resume**(*pid*);
> **suspend**

swtch saves the overhead of one system call by resuming the target process and immediately suspending the calling process. The target process will resume execution when it becomes the highest priority process in the system.

The **setslice** call sets the CPU time slice size of the process indicated by *pid*. The argument *slice* is the new CPU time slice, specified in ticks, to be assigned to the target process. The range of valid slice sizes is 1 to 2^{31}-1 (a little over a year with a 60 Hz system clock). A process will not share the CPU with another process of the same priority until the time slice of the first process expires, or when some other event in the system causes the CPU to be rescheduled (such as an I/O completion of a higher priority process).

The **relinquish** call instructs the calling process to relinquish the CPU to another process at the same priority. When executed, **relinquish** causes a context switch to occur from the calling process to the next process that is runnable at the same priority. If no other processes are runnable at that priority, the calling process will immediately switch back to itself. Since processes are scheduled in a round-robin fashion within a priority level, the calling process will not run again until all other runnable processes at that level have run.

```
/* measure the cost of a context switch */

#include <stdio.h>
#include <sys/types.h>

main()
{
        register i;
        register time_t t;
        register time_t overhead;

        if (setrt() < 0) { /* acquire realtime privileges */
                perror("setrt");
                exit(1);
        }
        if (setslice(0, 0x7FFFFFFF) < 0) { /* no time slice expirations */
                perror("setslice");
                exit(1);
        }
        if (setpri(0, 1) < 0) { /* get a good priority */
                perror("setpri");
                exit(1);
        }
        i = 1000000; /* a million times so result is in microseconds */
        t = time(0);
        while (--i)
                getpid();
        overhead = time(0) - t; /* calculate loop syscall overhead */
        i = 500000; /* each process will do 1/2 */
        /*
         * Pass CPU back and forth
         * between parent and child.
         */
        if (fork() == 00) {
                while (--i)
                        relinquish();
        } else {
                t = time(0);
                while (--i)
                        relinquish();
                wait(0);
                printf("context switch = %d microseconds\n",
                        (time(0) - t ) - overhead);
        }
        exit(0);
}
```

Figure 4.3 - The example program illustrates the use of the **relinquish** system call

The example program in Figure 4.3 illustrates the use of the **relinquish** system call by creating two processes and measuring the cost of the context switch as the CPU is relinquished. The example also uses several other system calls previously discussed including **setrt**, **setslice**, and **setpr**.

The priority of a running process can be changed with the shell command **setpri**, executable only by a real-time user or a superuser. **setpri** *pid pri*, sets the scheduling priority of the target process (similar to **setpri**). Arguments *pid* and *pri* are the process ID and priority level of the target process, respectively.

A suspended process can be resumed from the shell with the **resume** command. This command also works like its system call counterpart, **resume**, and resumes the process indicated by the argument *pid*.

4.2.4 Monitoring the Run Queue

Standard UNIX System tools can be used to monitor the real-time priority run queue. The primary tool is the **ps** command. As an example, consider the following section of **ps** output:

```
$ps  -el

  F S   UID    PID  PPID C    PRI   NI  ADDR    SZ  WCHAN  TTY       TIME COMMAND

 11 D     0      0    0 0     95   20  c460c    1  12462c  ?         0:00onesec
 10 S     0      1    0 0    188   20  c470a   10       0  ?         4:05init
 11 D     0      2    0 0     95   20  c4808    0  1248f4  ?         0:05vhand
 11 D     0      3    0 0     95   20  c4906    0  124588  ?         0:40bdflush
 11 D     0      4    0 0      0   20  c4a04    0  12463c  ?         0:00timeproy
 10 S     0   1290    1 0    156   20  c4ff8    8   de796  m332x11   0:00getty
 10 S     0  14347    1 0    156   20  c50f6    8   dec96  m332x20   0:00getty
 10 S     0  13464    1 0     15   20  c5ddc   18  122588  console   0:01ksh
 10 S   305   4891    1 0    188   20  c60d6   19   c6156  m332x23   0:05ksh
 10 S   309     27    0 0     19    0  e4274   48   dedd6  m332x21   0:15robot1
```

Note the following points:

- Processes with priorities in the range 128-253 are scheduled just as they would be under time-sharing UNIX, only the priority is +128. For instance, **init** sleeps at priority 60 under time-sharing UNIX, but at priority 188 on REAL/IX. The operating system automatically shifts the priority of these processes.
- The **onesec** process is PID 0; on UNIX System V, the scheduler would be PID 0. **onesec** runs at priority 95.
- **robot1** (PID 27) is a real-time process running at priority 19. It is currently sleeping, which allows processes at less favorable priorities to run. However, should it become runnable, the only process in the listing that could preempt it is the **ksh** at the console (running at priority 15).

4.2.5 Real-Time Timers

As presented in Section 3.4.2, real-time timers provide the real-time application with the abilities: (a) to use either absolute or relative time, and (b) to schedule events in increments of seconds or microseconds. The REAL/IX timer concept provides two types of timer mechanisms: (a) system-wide real-time timers, and (b) process interval timers, described in 3.4.2.

Tables 4.5 and 4.6 summarize the system calls used for system-wide real-time timers and process interval timers, respectively.

A list of free process interval timers is defined at system generation (**sysgen**) time. The interval timers from this list can be allocated by real-time processes during process initialization or during normal execution. By using **sysgen** parameters, the timer mechanism can be customized for a particular application that requires varying amounts of timers to be available for process allocation.

Table 4.5
System Calls and Structures for System-Wide Timers

System Call or Structure	Description
settimer (*timer_type*, *tp*)	Sets the value of the system-wide real-time timer, specified by *timer_type*, to the value pointed to by *tp*. The argument *tp* is a pointer to a timerstruc structure (**timestruc**) where the timer value is taken from.
gettimer (*timer_type*, *tp*)	Returns the current value of the system-wide real-time timer specified by *timer_type*. The argument ***tp*** is a pointer to a timer structure (**timestruc**) where the timer value is to be placed.
restimer (timer_type, res, maxval)	Returns the resolution (***res***) and maximum value (*maxval*) of the system-wide real-time timer specified by *timer_type*. *res* and *maxval* are pointers to **timestruc**, where the resolution and maximum time value are placed.
timestruc	Format of time (in seconds and nanoseconds) for system-wide real-time timers.

Table 4.6
System Calls and Structures for Process Interval Timers

System Call or Structure	Description
gettimerid *(timer_type, event_type, eid)*	Allocates a process interval timer to the calling real-time process and assigns a unique identifier to the timer. *timer_type* identifies the system-wide real-time timer associated with this identifier. *event_type* is the type of event mechanism used to deliver an event when an expiration occurs. The timer expiration event is sent to the process via the *eid* value.
absinterval (*timerid,value, ovalue*) **incinterval** (*timerid,value, ovalue*)	Sets the expiration time of the process interval timer, *timerid* to an absolute time value (**absinterval**) or to a time value relative to the current time (**incinterval**). *value* is the time value to be set; *ovalue* is set to the time value being used on timer expiration reloads.
getinterval (*timerid, value*)	Gets a time value for the process interval timer described by *timerid* and returned by **gettimerid**. *value* is a pointer to an itimerstruc where the amount of time remaining before expiration and the current interval value (if one exists) are stored.
reltimerid (*timerid*)	Deactivates and releases the process interval timer *timerid* previously allocated to the process via a **gettimerid** system call. Any outstanding events associated with *timerid* are cancelled and the timer is freed.
resabs(*timerid,res, max*) **resinc** (*timerid, res, max*)	Returns the resolution and maximum absolute (**resabs**) or increment (**resinc**) time value for the process interval timer *timerid*. These values are used by **absinterval** and **incinterval**. *res* and *max* are pointers to a timestruc structure where the resolution and maximum time value are placed.
itimerstruc	Format of time value (in seconds and nanoseconds) for process interval timers.

To use a process interval timer, a real-time process does the following:

1. Obtain an event identifier from the **evget** system call.

2. Issue a **gettimerid** system call to obtain access to a process interval timer. **gettimerid** gets a unique timer identifier from the free pool of process interval timers.

3. Set a timer expiration value and activate the process interval timer.

   - To set the value to an absolute time, use the **absinterval** system call.

   - To set the value to a time relative to the current system time, use the **incinterval** system call. The **gettimer** system call returns the current system time; the return value can be used with **incinterval**, or **incinterval** can set the value relative to "now".

4. Use the **evrcv** system call to receive the timer expiration event.

Activating the timer actually means putting the timer for this process in an active timer queue of all process interval timers active on the system. The active timer queue is ordered so that the next entry to expire is positioned at the top of the queue.

The clock interrupt handler checks the first timer in the queue to determine if the specified expiration time is equal to the current system time. If so, a timer expiration has occurred and the **timedaemon** daemon is unblocked with a **vsema** operation. The **timedaemon** removes the expired timer from the active queue, reschedules the timer in the queue if it is a periodic timer, and posts a timer expiration event to the appropriate process. The **timedaemon** then blocks (with a **psema** operation). The **timedaemon** only executes in response to a process timer expiration, so no additional overhead is incurred if no timers are being used.

The priority of the **timedaemon** is set by a tunable parameter, but should usually remain at a priority higher than the highest priority process that may request a time expiration. This ensures that timer expiration events are never delayed by another executing process on the system.

4.2.5.1 Example program: Using the **incinterval** system call

The following example program, shown in Figure 4.4, demonstrates how to set up a one-shot process interval timer using the **incinterval** system call. The expiration time is 1/2 second, set relative to the current time.

The FORTRAN example, in Figure 4.5, is similar to the C example just described. It is presented only to show how one might accomplish this task in the FORTRAN language using system calls and C library routines.

```
/*
 * Timer test for process interval timers:  "timer_test".
 */
#include <stdio.h>
#include "sys/time.h"
#include "sys/lock.h"
#include "sys/evt.h"

extern int errno;

int sec = 0;          /* wakeup time */
int nsec = 500000000; /* set expiration time to 1/2 second */

int isec = 0;  /* interval wakeup time */
int insec = 0;



main()
{
      int eid, tid;
      struct event event;               /* define a local event structure */
      struct itimerstruc timval;        /* define local timer structs */
      struct itimerstruc oimval;
      struct itimerstruc *tval, *oval; /* setup pointer to timer structs */


      if (setrt() == -1) {
            fprintf(stderr, "timer_test: failed setrt\n");
            exit(1);
            }
      if (setpri(0,10) == -1) {
            fprintf(stderr, "timer_test: failed setpri\n");
            exit(1);
            }
      if (plock(PROCLOCK) == -1) {
            fprintf(stderr, "timer_test: failed plock\n");
            exit(1);
            }
      if (resident(0,0) == -1) {
            fprintf(stderr, "timer_test: failed resident\n");
            exit(1);
            }


      /* get a unique event id for this process */

      if ((eid = evget(EVT_QUEUE, 1, 0, 0)) == -1) {
            printf("Error on evget: %d\n", errno);
            exit(1);
      }
```

Figure 4.4 - The example C program which illustrates how to set up a one-shot interval timer using the **incinterval** system call

```
    /* get a unique timer id for this process */

    if ((tid = gettimerid(TIMEOFDAY, MODCOMP_EVENTS, eid)) == -1) {
          printf("Error from gettimerid test: %d\n", errno);
          exit(1);
    }

    tval = &timval;   /* initialize pointers to timer structures */
    oval = &oimval;

    tval->it_value.tv_sec = sec;        /* move desired future expiration */
                                        /* time into structure */
    tval->it_value.tv_nsec = nsec;
    tval->it_interval.tv_sec = isec;
    tval->it_interval.tv_nsec = insec;

    /* call the incinterval syscall to put the timer on the
     * active timer queue.
     */

    if (incinterval(tid, tval, oval) == -1) {
          printf("Error from incinterval test: %d\n", errno);
          exit(1);
    }

    /* wait here for the timer to expire, when it does the event
     * will be sent here.
     */

    evrcv(1, &event);
    printf("\n ** timer_test one-shot expired **\n");

    /* now return the timer to the free pool of timers */

    if (reltimerid(tid)) {
          printf("Error from reltimerid test: %d\n", errno);
          exit(1);
    }
    printf("\n\t timer_test test complete !!!\n");
    exit(0);

}
```

Figure 4.4 - cont'd

```
C
C  Fortran program that uses the realtime extensions
C
      PROGRAM TESTRT
C
C  Declare all interface functions
C
      INTEGER*4 SETRT, SETPRI, PLOCK, RESIDENT, EVGET, GETTIMERID
      INTEGER*4 RELTIMERID
C
C  Declare parameter variables so that this reads somewhat like
C  the C equivalent.  These variables take the place of the variables
C  from the C #include files.
C
      INTEGER*4 EVT_QUEUE, EVT_SIGNAL
      INTEGER*4 TIMEOFDAY, MODCOMP_EVENTS
      INTEGER*4 PROCLOCK
C
C  Declare general use variables
C
      INTEGER*4 ISETRT, ISETPRI, IPLOCK, IRESID, IRELTMR
C
C  Define common blocks
C
      INTEGER*4 EID, TID
      COMMON /EVENTID/EID, TID
C
C
C  Initialize constants for calling realtime extensions
C
      DATA EVT_SIGNAL/1/, EVT_QUEUE/2/
      DATA TIMEOFDAY/1/, MODCOMP_EVENTS/1/
      DATA PROCLOCK/1/
C
C  Initialize realtime extensions
C
C  Set process for realtime privileges
C
      ISETRT = SETRT()
      IF (ISETRT.LT.0) THEN
     WRITE(6,*)'Failed to set process to real time.
     WRITE(6,*)'ISETRT =  ,ISETRT
     STOP
   ENDIF
```

Figure 4.5 - The FORTRAN example program to set up a one-shot interval timer

```
C
C  Set priority to a realtime priority of 20
C
      ISETPRI = SETPRI(0,20)
      IF (ISETPRI.LT.0) THEN
         WRITE(6,*)'Failed to set priority.
         WRITE(6,*)'ISETPRI = ',ISETPRI
         STOP
      ENDIF
C
C  Lock text and data segments into memory
C
      IPLOCK = PLOCK(PROCLOCK)
      IF (IPLOCK.LT.0) THEN
         WRITE(6,*)'Failed to lock text and data segments into memory.
         WRITE(6,*)'IPLOCK = ',IPLOCK
         STOP
      ENDIF
C
C  Make all locked segments resident in memory
C
      IRESID = RESIDENT(0,0)
      IF (IRESID.LT.0) THEN
         WRITE(6,*)'Failed to make locked segments resident in memory.
         WRITE(6,*)'IRESID = ',IRESID
         STOP
      ENDIF
C
C  Get an event identifier
C
      EID = EVGET(EVT_QUEUE,10,0,0)
      IF (EID.LT.0) THEN
         WRITE(6,*)'Failed to get an event identifier.
         WRITE(6,*)'EID = ',EID
         STOP
      ENDIF
C
C  Get an identifier for the process interval timer
C
      TID = GETTIMERID(TIMEOFDAY,MODCOMP_EVENTS,EID)
      IF (TID.LT.0) THEN
         WRITE(6,*)'Failed to get process interval timer id.
         WRITE(6,*)'TID = ',TID
         STOP
      ENDIF
```

Figure 4.5 - cont'd

```
C
C  Call subroutine to set and wait for event timer
C
      WRITE(6,*)'Set and wait for event timer.
      CALL WAIT(500000000)
C
C  Release timer
C
      IRELTIMER = RELTIMERID(TID)
      IF (IRELTIMER.LT.0) THEN
         WRITE(6,*)'Failed to successfully release timer.
         WRITE(6,*)'IRELTIMER = ',IRELTIMER
         STOP
      ENDIF
C
      WRITE(6,*)'Successfully set and waited for timer!'
      END
C
C
C -------------------------------------------------------------------
C  Subroutine to set and then wait for the event timer
C
      SUBROUTINE WAIT(WAITVAL)
C
C  Declare all interface functions
C
      INTEGER*4 INCINTERVAL, EVRCV, SIGNAL, ALARM, PAUSE
      INTEGER*4 WAITVAL
C
C  Declare variables for interfacing to system routines
C
C       TVAL1(1) = timer interval in seconds
C            (2) = timer interval in nanoseconds
C            (3) = current value in seconds
C            (4) = current value in nanoseconds
C
C       TVAL2(1) = timer interval in seconds
C            (2) = timer interval in nanoseconds
C            (3) = current value in seconds
C            (4) = current value in nanoseconds
C
C       EVID(1) = event identifier = EV_EID
C       EVID(2) = event poster identification = EV_TYPE
C       DATAITEM = posted data item
C       WAITVAL = duration of wait time in nanoseconds
```

Figure 4.5 - cont'd

```
C
      INTEGER*4 TVAL1(4), TVAL2(4)
      INTEGER*4 EVRCV_RTN(2), DATAITEM
      INTEGER*2 EVID(2), EV_EID, EV_TYPE
      EQUIVALENCE (EVRCV_RTN(1),EVID(1))
      EQUIVALENCE (EVID(1),EV_EID)
      EQUIVALENCE (EVID(2),EV_TYPE)
      EQUIVALENCE (EVRCV_RTN(2),DATAITEM)
C
C  Declare general variables
C
      INTEGER*4 INTERVAL, IEVRCV
C
C  Define common blocks
C
      INTEGER*4 EID, TID
C
      COMMON /EVENTID/EID, TID
C
C  Set the expiration time for the process interval timer - tid
C
      TVAL1(4) = WAITVAL
      INTERVAL = INCINTERVAL(TID,TVAL1,TVAL2)
      IF (INTERVAL.LT.0) THEN
         WRITE(6,*)'Failed to set interval time.
         WRITE(6,*)'INTERVAL =   ,INTERVAL
         STOP
      ENDIF
C
C  Wait for the timer to expire and receive the event
C
      IEVRCV = EVRCV(1,EVRCV_RTN)
      IF (IEVRCV.LT.0) THEN
         WRITE(6,*)'Failed to successfully receive the event.'
         WRITE(6,*)'IEVRCV = ',IEVRCV
         STOP
      ENDIF
      RETURN
      END
```

Figure 4.5 - cont'd

4.3 REAL-TIME MEMORY ALLOCATION

The underlying philosophy of memory management is different for real-time and time-sharing programs. The time-sharing philosophy is to avoid consuming any more memory than is absolutely necessary so that all processes have equal access to memory resources. For critical real-time programs, the emphasis is on providing optimal performance for the program. Consequently, real-time programs typically preallocate a generous amount of memory and lock all resources they might need into memory.

REAL/IX memory allocation is similar to that of UNIX System V, with extensions to provide explicit control over memory allocation in critical real-time applications. This section discusses how memory is allocated for REAL/IX user-level processes, how to determine the memory needs of a program, and how the REAL/IX resident program support facilities provide the special controls over memory allocation required in many real-time applications.

As described in Section 3.2, the data segment of an executing process is composed of two regions, the stack region and the data region (see Figure 3.3). The data region contains the process' static variables, and may also contain a dynamic data structure known as a heap. The traditional UNIX system supports dynamic data allocation with the **brk** and **sbrk** system calls that expand or contract the data region. These can be called explicitly, but are more often accessed by a library heap package, such as **malloc**.

When the process is initialized, the operating system allocates memory for the stack and data regions. As the stack or data segment outgrows that memory, the system allocates more physical pages. This scheme conserves memory and is appropriate for many applications, but the overhead incurred is unacceptable for critical real-time programs. For this reason, the REAL/IX system supplements the **brk/sbrk** system calls that allocate memory for the data region with the **stkexp** system call that allocates memory for the stack region.

The REAL/IX operating system, like UNIX System V, is a virtual operating system, meaning that pages of memory not currently being accessed may be paged out of memory to a swap area on the disk if another process needs more memory. While the virtual memory concept makes more efficient use of memory, real-time performance is adversely affected when a program must wait for data to be swapped back into memory. The traditional UNIX system call, **plock**, locks data into memory. The **shmctl** system call used with the SHM_LOCK command locks shared memory segments into memory. While **plock** and **shmctl** will lock resources into memory, they do not force pages to be loaded into memory in the first place. To accomplish this, they are supplemented with the REAL/IX **resident** call, so that the program is guaranteed to be available the first time it is accessed as well as later.

4.3.1 Controlling Memory Allocation

The resident program support facilities provide the control over memory allocation for critical real-time programs. This function can be summarized as follows:

1. preallocate memory for the stack and data regions or the program's data space,

2. load and lock text, data, and shared memory segments into memory,

3. post an event to the process if the stack or data segment expands beyond the preallocated region.

The resident program support facilities are used together to provide real-time memory management for critical real-time programs. Other programs execute using traditional UNIX system memory management techniques.

Memory is preallocated by user applications with the system calls listed in Table 4.7.

Table 4.7
System Calls for Allocating Memory

System Call	Function
int brk (*endds*)	expand heap region so that *endds* is the first address beyond the heap region (absolute)
char sbrk(*incr*)	expand data region by *incr* bytes (relative)
int stkexp (*incr, flags*)	expand stack region If *flags* is STKSZ: expand to *incr* bytes (absolute) with no *flags* argument, expand by *incr* bytes (relative)

These calls should be used in critical real-time programs to avoid the overhead of natural stack growth and its accompanying performance degradation.

The size of the data and stack regions can be specified in absolute or relative terms. **brk** specifies the absolute size of the data regions, and **stkexp** with the STKSZ flag specifies the absolute size of the stack region. **sbrk** and **stkexp** specify the expansion as *incr* bytes (rounded to the next highest page boundary) beyond the current region.

Memory for the stack and data region is always allocated in pages. The NBPC parameter (defined in <sys/param.h>) is the number of bytes per page. For **sbrk** and **stkexp**, *incr* is rounded up to the nearest page boundary.

The **sbrk** and **stkexp** calls return the old size of the data and stack region, respectively. Using 0 as the *incr*, these calls return the current size, as shown below:

```
datasz=(sbrk(0));         /* return current size of data region */
stksz=(stkexp(0,0));      /* return current size of stack region */
```

Application programs are often written using the library call **malloc** to allocate dynamic data storage space in the data segment instead of using **brk**. In this case, **brk** or **sbrk** should NOT be used to preallocate memory. Instead, all data structures should be preallocated using **malloc**.

The amount of memory that can be preallocated using these calls is limited by the sysgen tunable parameter MAXUMEM, which specifies the maximum virtual memory that can be allocated to any process.

4.3.2 Locking Pages into Memory

Pages are locked into memory with the system calls listed in Table 4.8

The **plock** and **shmctl** calls lock the segments into memory. These calls are used just as in UNIX System V, so the segments will be loaded into memory only when they are first accessed. If followed by the **resident** call, all text, data, and shared memory segments that are locked by **plock** and **shmctl** are loaded into memory during process initialization rather than the first time they are accessed.

The **resident** call takes a *flags* argument and, if *flags* == EVT_POST, an event identifier *eid* (that must be initialized before calling **resident**). This is used to notify the process of real-time memory violations, as discussed below.

Table 4.8
System Calls for Locking Pages into Memory

System Call	Function
plock(PROCLOCK)	lock text and data segments into memory
shmctl (*shmid*,*SHM_LOCK*,*buf*)	lock shared memory segment into memory
resident(*flags*, *eid*)	load text, data, and shared memory segments into memory.

The amount of memory that can be locked by any process is limited to the total size of available physical memory (displayed during the initial bootstrap of the operating system) minus the number of pages specified by the MINPAGMEM sysgen tunable parameter. MINPAGMEM pages are reserved for use by the paged virtual memory mechanism, to ensure that any non-resident processes on the system can continue to execute without excessive paging. MINPAGMEM should be set to twice the maximum number of non-resident processes required for a particular installation. This will allow more resident memory on systems that do not require many non-resident processes. However, MINPAGMEM should always be greater than the MINAVAILRMEM sysgen tunable parameter.

For real-time processes that are critical enough to warrant preallocating memory in this fashion, dynamically expanding memory beyond these limits is usually considered a fault. The action taken for such a fault is at the discretion of the programmer. Programs that use the resident program support facilities may use the common event notification mechanism discussed in Section 4.4 to handle real-time memory violations.

4.3.3 Example Program: Preallocating Memory for a Process

This example, consisting of nine steps, makes a real-time process permanently resident in physical memory.

1. Include any files that you will need and declare global variables and functions.

```
#include <stdio.h>
#include <signal.h>
#include <sys/types.h>
#include <sys/ipc.h>
#include <sys/shm.h>
#include <sys/evt.h>
#include <sys/lock.h>

void rtviolate();
void sighand();

int shmid;

void
err_exit(s)
char *s;
{
/* detach shared memory segments gracefully*/
        perror(s);
        if (shmctl(shmid, IPC_RMID, (struct shmid_ds *)0) == -1)
                perror("shmctl(IPC_RMID)");
        exit(1);
}
```

```
int
main()
{
        int eid;
        char *shmptr;
        int maxstacksize = 0x10000;

        sigset(SIGHUP, sighand);
        sigset(SIGINT, sighand);
        sigset(SIGQUIT, sighand);
        sigset(SIGTERM, sighand);
        sigset(SIGSEGV, sighand);
```

2. Use **setrt** to set real-time privileges

```
if (setrt()) {
        perror("setrt");
        exit(1);
}

if ((shmid = shmget(IPC_PRIVATE, 0x10000, IPC_CREAT|0600)) ==  -1)
{
        perror("shmget");
        exit(1);
}
```

3. Attach any shared memory segments.

```
if (shmptr=(shmat(schmid, 0  0)) == -1)
        err_exit("shmat");
```

4. Use **brk** or **sbrk** to preallocate sufficient space for the data region. If you prefer to use **malloc**, then preallocate your data structures now using **malloc**. DO NOT use **brk** or **sbrk** if you intend to use **malloc**.

5. Use **stkexp** to preallocate sufficient space for the maximum size of the stack.

```
if (maxstacksize > stkexp(0, 0)) {
        if (stkexp(maxstacksize, STKSZ) == -1)
                err_exit("stkexp");
}
```

6. Use **plock** to lock the text, data, and stack segments.

```
if (plock(PROCLOCK))
    err_exit("plock");
```

7. Use **shmctl** with SHM_LOCK to lock any shared memory segments

```
if (shmctl(shmid, SHM_LOCK, (struct shmid_ds *)0) == -1)
    err_exit("shmctl(SHM_LOCK)");
```

8. Set the signal handler to be used for real-time violations. Use **evget** to initialize the event identifier that will notify the process of real-time violations if the stack or data region space is expanded beyond the preallocated sizes. The standard signal values (defined on the **sigset** man page) are not appropriate for this event, so use the user-defined signal SIGUSR1 with the fault-handling function.

```
if ((int)sigset(SIGUSR1, rtviolate) == -1)
    err_exit("sigset");

if ((eid = evget(EVT_SIGNAL, 0, SIGUSR1, rtviolate)) == -1)
    err_exit(evget");
```

9. Call **resident** to ensure all locked segments are physically resident in memory. Pass the event identifier as a parameter so that real-time violations will be delivered.

```
        if (resident(EVT_POST, eid))
                err_exit("resident");

        /*
         *          The main part of your program
         *          goes here.
         *
         */

        /* all segments are unlocked automatically on exit */
        if (shmctl(shmid, IPC_RMID, (struct shmid_ds *)0) == -1) {
                perror("shmctl(IPC_RMID)");
                exit(1);

        }
        return (0);
}
```

4.3.4 Example Program: Handling Real-Time Memory Violations

A real-time memory violation exists when a process requires more memory than has been preallocated for it. This is not, technically, an error condition, since the operating system is capable of allocating additional memory for the process. The example program, in Figure 4.6, illustrates one way of handling real-time memory violations.

```
void sighand(signum)
int signum;
{
        fprintf(stderr,"sighand>signal number %d caught\n", signum);
        if (shmctl(shmid, IPC_RMID, (struct shmid_ds *)0) == -1) {
                perror("shmctl(IPC_RMID)");
                exit(1);
        }
        exit(1);
}

void
rtviolate(signum, sigparm, e)
int signum;
int sigparm;
event_t e;
{
        if (signum != SIGUSR1) {
                fprintf(stderr,"rtviolate>unexpected signal number %d caught\n",
                signum);
                return;
        }

        if (e.ev_type != EVT_TYPE_RES) {
                fprintf(stderr,"rtviolate>unexpected ev_type %d received\n",
                e.ev_type);
                return;
        }
        if (e.ev_dataitem & STKGROW) {
                fprintf(stderr,"rtviolate>The stack has grown into a new
                page,\n");
                fprintf(stderr,"rtviolate>through natural stack growth.\n");
        }
        if (e.ev_dataitem & STKEXP) {
                fprintf(stderr,"rtviolate>The stack has grown into a new
                page,\n");
                fprintf(stderr,"rtviolate>through a call to stkexp(2).\n");
        }
        if (e.ev_dataitem & BRK) {
                fprintf(stderr,"rtviolate>The data region has grown into a new
                page,\n");
                fprintf(stderr,"rtviolate>through a call to brk(2).\n");
        }
        if (e.ev_dataitem & DATUNLOCK) {
                fprintf(stderr,"rtviolate>No more resident memory!  The data
                segment has been unlocked,\n");

                fprintf(stderr,"rtviolate>and is now subject to paging.\n");
        }
}
```

Figure 4.6 - Example: handling real-time memory violations

4.4 INTERPROCESS COMMUNICATIONS: PIPES, SIGNALS, AND EVENTS

As described in Section 3.5, the REAL/IX operating system provides several ways for processes to communicate with each other. These are:

1. pipes and named pipes,
2. signals,
3. event mechanism (a superset of signals),
4. semaphores,
5. messages, and
6. shared memory.

Shared file pointers and process tracing can also be used for interprocess communication. These methods are seldom appropriate for general use and so are not discussed here.

This section describes the first three mechanisms, while Section 4.5 discusses the IPC mechanisms for interprocess communications. The IPC mechanisms include semaphores, messages, and shared memory.

4.4.1 Pipes and Named Pipes

A pipe is a file-like structure that is used for one synchronized read/write operation. The **pipe** system call creates a pipe and returns two file descriptors: **fides**, which is opened for reading, and **fides** which is opened for writing. Reading and writing a pipe is similar to reading and writing a file, but with some significant differences:

- If the reader gets ahead of the writer, the reader just waits for more data.

- If the writer gets too far ahead of the reader, it sleeps until the reader has a chance to catch up. This helps to ensure that the kernel does not have too much data queued.

- Once a byte is read, it is discarded, so long-running processes connected with pipes do not fill up the file system.

Besides being slow, pipes have two major disadvantages: the processes communicating over a pipe must be related (typically, parent and child or two siblings); and they are not reliable when there are multiple readers or writers, since reads and writes are not guaranteed to be atomic.

FIFOs, or named pipes, were introduced in UNIX System III to solve these problems with pipes. FIFOs are special device files, created with the **mknod** system call. Although FIFOs are not faster than pipes, they can be accessed by any process that has appropriate permissions. This is possible since the bytes written or read by one system call are always contiguous.

Because FIFOs are as easy to program, they are useful for occasional transfers of small amounts of information between processes. However, they do not provide the performance typically required by real-time applications, and should be used sparingly in programs that require real-time performance.

4.4.2 Signals

As described in 3.5, signals are part of the traditional UNIX system environment and are always asynchronous (meaning that the receiving process never knows when it may receive a signal). The user-level program includes code to determine the action to take when a signal is received (terminate the process, ignore the signal, or catch the signal and execute a subroutine). The receiving process does not know which process sent the signal, and will react only to the first signal received; subsequent signals are silently ignored.

The procedures of sending and handling signals are described in 3.5.

A user-level program sends a signal to another user-level program with the **kill** system call. The synopsis is:

```
int kill(pid,signo)     /* send signal */
int pid;                /* process-ID of receiving process */
int signo;              /* signal number to send */
/* returns 0 if successful; returns -1 if an error occurs */
```

The *pid* can be either the actual process ID for the process to which the signal is sent or a value that has special meaning. Table 4.9 describes the valid values for *pid*.

The **kill** system call is usually issued using the **kill** command. Its main use as a system call *per se* is with **SIGTERM, SIGQUIT, SIGIOT** to cause a core dump for a certain error condition. It can also be used when testing the error-handling code of a program by simulating signals such as **SIGFPE** (floating-point exception).

User-defined signals are similar to other signals with the exception that they are never sent to a user by the operating system. These types of signals are used for developing portable programs. The signals defined for both **signal** and **sigset** include two user-defined signals, **SIGUSR1** and **SIGUSR2**.

Table 4.9
Valid Values for pid with kill

pid value	Meaning
actual PID	send signal to the process identified by *pid*.
0	send signal to all processes in the same process group as the sender. This is used with the **kill** command to kill all background processes. Processes in other process groups will not receive the signal.
-1	send signal to all processes whose real UID is equal to the effective UID of the sender. This can be used to kill all processes owned by the sender, regardless of process group. Note that, if superuser sends a **kill -1**, all processes except for the swapper (process 0) and **init** (process 1) are killed.
negative other than -1	send signal to all processes whose process group ID is equal to the absolute value of *pid*. This allows the sending process to terminate a subsystem such as a DBMS, a communication handler, or a print spooler, each of which may have a different process group.

4.4.3 Common Event Notification Mechanism

The concept of common event notification is described in 3.5. The REAL/IX common event notification mechanism is a superset of the traditional UNIX System V signal mechanism. Common events have multiple notification methods, can handle notifications synchronously as well as asynchronously, and can queue multiple signals sent to one process. Character drivers that use connected interrupts use the event mechanism to notify a user process of device interrupts.

One process can receive signals as well as synchronous and asynchronous events. In general, all programs should include signal-handling functionality, since the kernel or another user-level process may send it a signal. Only a limited number of processes on the system can use the common event notification mechanism. (The actual number is set by the tunable parameter EVTMAXPRC). It should be used in critical programs that need to handle synchronous or asynchronous events or need some other feature that the event mechanism supplies beyond that of

sigset or **msgrev**. Any process executing on the system can post an event, as long as that process has proper permissions.

4.4.3.1 Using Event Mechanism

This section discusses how to code user-level programs that use the event mechanism. Events can also be posted from kernel-level processes such as drivers, although only user-level processes can receive events.

To code a program to receive events:

1. Include the **evget** system call in the initialization routine to initialize the tables required. Use one **evget** call for each type of event that the program can receive.

2. If the process will handle events asynchronously, use the **evget** or **sigset** system call to specify how to handle them.

3. If the process will handle events synchronously, (polled or blocking), use the **evrcv** or **evrcvl** system call to receive and handle them.

4. Use the **evrel** system call to release the tables when they are no longer needed. The event tables are automatically released when the process terminates either normally or abnormally. Event tables are not inherited from a **fork** system call.

To code a program to send event notifications, use the **evpost** system call. **evpost** can be added to any process on the system that has appropriate permissions, not just those that are coded to receive events.

4.4.3.2 Posting an Event

The sending process posts an event to the process (identified by PID) with the **evpost** system call. This creates an event structure that identifies the *eid*, the type of posting (such as user-posted event, asynchronous I/O completion event, or timer expiration event) and a *dataitem*. *dataitem* can contain an index into a table containing more information, an offset or pointer into a shared memory block, a signal number, a file descriptor, or some other relevant information.

The event structure is a 64-bit block that can be queued to the process. Table 4.10 shows the members of this structure.

Table 4.10
Event Structure

Structure Member	Valid Values	Meaning
ev_eid (16 bits)	*any non-negative integer*	event identifier
ev_type (16 bits)	EVT_TYPE_USER	user-posted event
	EVT_TYPE_ASNCIO	asynchronous I/O completion event
	EVT_TYPE_TIMER	timer expiration event
	EVT_TYPE_INTR	connected interrupt occurred
	EVT_TYPE_RES	resident process violation
ev_dataitem (32 bits)	*any reasonable item*	posted dataitem

The **evpost** system call takes three arguments, as shown in the following synopsis:

```
int evpost (pid,eid,dataitem)
int pid;                /* process-ID of receiving process */
int eid;                /* eid to be posted */
long dataitem           /* data item to be posted with this event */
```

The meanings of these arguments are:

- *pid* is the process id of the process to which the event will be posted.
- *eid* is the event id of the event to be posted. This determines whether this event should be handled synchronously or asynchronously and, for events that are to be handled asynchronously, the action to be taken.
- *dataitem* is a piece of data to be associated with this event. For example, an index into a table that contains more information, another PID, a signal number, a file descriptor, an offset into a shared memory block, or a hardware address of a board generating an external event.

The PID used for posting an event must be the actual PID of the process. A *0* or negative value has no meaning to **evpost** and will result in an error.

The posting process must have super-user or real-time permissions (or **kill** privileges) to post to processes other than itself.

4.4.4.3 Handling Events Asynchronously

One process may handle some events synchronously and other events asynchronously. A separate **evget** system call must be issued for each *method* (synchronous or asynchronous).

Each event that is handled asynchronously is processed as follows:

1. The **proc** table for the specified PID associates the event with the appropriate process in much the same way a signal is associated with a process. If an event is posted to a process that does not exist or cannot receive events, the posting process receives an error message. Otherwise, the *eid* (event identifier) specified by the poster is queued onto the `sigp` list.

2. If the receiving process is not currently executing a critical region of code, the event is handled as prescribed by the fourth argument to the **evget** system call. If the process is executing a critical region of code, the event stays on the `sigp` queue until the process exits from the critical region, then handles the event.

3. As long as the event queue is not filled, subsequent events posted to the process will be added to the queue and handled in order.

The third and fourth arguments to **evget** (*signo* and *func*) determine how asynchronous events are handled. They are used only when the value of *method* is **EVT_SIGNAL**.

- *signo* is the signal that specifies the signal to be delivered to the event structure (for example, **SIGHUP**).

- *func* is the name of the signal-catching function, just as for **sigset**. It can have one of the following values:

0	The function to be invoked is the one specified by sigset.
pointer to a function	This arranges to catch the signal every signal but `SIGKILL` can be caught. The function is coded in the signal-catching program and called when the signal arrives.

Critical regions of code are regions that should not be interrupted before completion. The **sighold** and **sigrelse** calls can be used to protect critical regions of code from asynchronous events as well as signals.

If the same *signo* is used by both the traditional UNIX system signal mechanism and the event mechanism, the UNIX signal sending mechanism may not deliver sent signals. For this reason, the user may want to restrict use of the event mechanism to the use of the two user-defined signals **SIGUSR1** and **SIGUSR2**.

4.4.4.4 Handling Events Synchronously

Each event that is handled asynchronously is processed as follows:

1. The `proc` table for the specified PID associates the event with the appropriate process in much the same way a signal is associated with a process. If an event is posted to a process that does not exist or cannot receive events, the posting process receives an error message. Otherwise, the *eid* (event identifier) is queued onto the `sigp` list.

2. The receiving process issues the **evrcv** system call to receive the first event posted to the event. Alternately, it can use the **evrcvl** to receive the first event posted that matches a list specified in the program.

3. As long as the event queue is not filled, subsequent events posted to the process will be added to the queue and handled in order.

The REAL/IX system includes two routines for receiving and handling events synchronously:

- **evrcv** receives the first queued event posted to the process.

- **evrcvl** receives the first queued event posted to the process from a specified list.

The synopses of these two system calls are:

```
#include <sys/evt.h>

int evrcv (waitflg,event)
int waitflg;
event_t *event;
```

```
#include <sys/evt.h>

int evrcvl (evl,evcnt,waitflg,event)
int *evl;
int evcnt;
int waitflg;
event_t *event;
```

4.4.4.5 Receiving Events from a List

The **evrcvl** system call lets you receive only events whose identifiers are on a list. The first argument to **evrcvl** (*evl*) points to the list of up to 64 event identifiers; the second argument (*evcnt*) gives the number of event identifiers on this list. It must be at least 1 and no greater than 64.

A receiving process can define any number of lists. Such a list can be populated statically, for example:

int list[3]={1,2,3}

It is usually more useful to populate it after the **evget** call, or at some later time when the user knows exactly what he wants.

4.5 INTERPROCESS COMMUNICATIONS USING SHARED MEMORY

Section 4.4 discussed how processes communicate through pipes, signals, and the common event mechanism. Sections 4.5, 4.6, and 4.7 discuss the IPC mechanisms for interprocess communications. Shared memory, semaphores, and messages are called the IPC mechanisms because, in older releases of UNIX System V, they were sold as an add-on driver package. These drivers are included in the REAL/IX operating system, like the release of UNIX System V on which it is based. The IPC mechanisms include:

(1) shared memory	the fastest method of interprocess communication, where a region of memory is mapped into the address space of two or more processes. Each process accesses this memory region as local.
(2) semaphores	used to coordinate access to shared memory regions and data buses.
(3) binary semaphores	an alternate semaphore mechanism, which is faster than traditional semaphores, although in some cases it does not provide the full functionality that may be required.
(4) messages	processes communicate by exchanging data stored in buffers.

The shared memory mechanism is described in Section 4.5, while semaphores and messages are described in Sections 4.6 and 4.7, respectively.

The general approach to using IPC mechanisms is as follows:

1. One process (called the "owner" of the entity) issues the ***get** call to allocate the IPC entity or entities and associated data structures. This **get** call also determines access permissions for the IPC entity, these permissions access as much as file access permissions control access to files.

2. All other processes access the IPC entity by its ID, so the user must issue a ***get** call that does not initialize any structures to get the ID of the IPC entity.

3. Processes then use the IPC facility through the operations described on the ***op** page.

   - For shared memory, the operations allow the process to attach the shared memory region to their process so it can be read and/or written, and to detach the shared memory region from their process if it is no longer needed.

   - For messages, the operations allow the process to send and/or receive messages from the queue.

   - For semaphores and binary semaphores, the operations allow the process to decrement and increment the semaphore, thus preventing another process from accessing the resource while it is being updated.

4. If necessary, the **msgctl, semctl,** and **shmctl** calls allow any process with appropriate permissions to check and change the values of the controlling data structures. The ***ctl** command should always be used with the IPC_RMID command in the process that creates the IPC entity, to ensure that the memory associated with that entity is freed if the process exits.

5. The **ipcs** command can be used to get the status of any IPC entity. It uses the *key* from the ***get** call to identify the IPC entity being queried.

6. The **ipcrm** command can be used to remove a message queue, semaphore set, or shared memory ID from the system. This command should not be necessary if the IPC_RMID control command was issued, but does allow the administrator to recover the memory if the code omits the IPC_RMID call.

All IPC facilities require that processes supply a *key* in order to get the appropriate ID for the specific entity being accessed. This key can be anything that all processes agree on. If some control is not used, unrelated processes may unintentionally access each other's IPC entities.

The recommended approach is to use the **ftok**(3C) routine to form a unique key from a file name and an ID that uniquely identifies a project (if the project has a defined group in the */etc/group* file, the GID for that group is a good value for the ID). The file used as the first argument must correspond to an existing file on the system, such as the name of the executable file for the process that creates the IPC entity.

Each IPC has a system call used to allocate the structure (**shmget** for shared memory; **semget** for semaphores; **bsget** for binary semaphores; and **msgget** for messages). Each of these calls and the **msgsnd** call used to send a message takes a *flg* argument that determines the access permissions and operation mode for the IPC. A set of predefined constants for the operation modes are OR'd to the octal value of the permissions desired. Each predefined constant implies an octal value and the combined octal value determines the permissions and operation. These are summarized in Table 4.11.

Table 4.11 - IPC Flags

	Meaning	Predefined Constant	Octal Value
Access Permissions	read by owner	SHM_R MSG_R SEM_R	0 0 0 0 **4** 0 0
	write by owner	SHM_W MSG_W SEM_W BS_R	0 0 0 0 **2** 0 0
	read by group	*None*	0 0 0 0 0 **4** 0
	write by group		0 0 0 0 0 **2** 0
	read by other		0 0 0 0 0 0 **4**
	write by other		0 0 0 0 0 0 **2**
Operation (general)	entry currently allocated	IPC_ALLOC	0 **1** 0 0 0 0 0
	create entry	IPC_CREAT	0 0 0 **1** 0 0 0
	exclusive access (fail if key exists)	IPC_EXCL	0 0 0 **2** 0 0 0
	do not block to wait for a resource (fail if facility cannot be allocated without blocking)	IPC_NOWAIT	0 0 0 **4** 0 0 0
Operation (shared memory)	cache inhibit	IPC_CI	0 0 **1** 0 0 0 0
	do not clear segment when attached	IPC_NOCLEAR	0 0 **2** 0 0 0 0
	shared segment is physical	IPC_PHYS	0 0 **4** 0 0 0 0
	grow segment on next attach	SHM_INIT	0 0 0 **1** 0 0 0
	remove segment when no processes are attached	SHM_DEST	0 0 0 **2** 0 0 0
	attach with read-only permissions	SHM_RDONLY	0 0 **1** 0 0 0 0
	round attach address to SHMLBA	SHM_RND	0 0 **2** 0 0 0 0
Operation (messages)	preallocate space for messages	IPC_PREALC	0 0 **2** 0 0 0 0
	do not generate error if message is larger than MSGMAX	MSG_NOERROR	0 0 **1** 0 0 0 0

Note that each IPC data structure has access permissions that are similar to those used on files. Read and/or write permissions are allocated to the owner, group and/or other users. When the structure is created, its owner is the effective UID of the creating process and its group is the effective GID of the creating process. The UID and GID of the structure can be changed after it is created using the **shmctl**, **semctl**, or **msgctl** calls. If you do not define access permissions, only the superuser (who bypasses all permission controls) will be able to access the structure.

The typical usage is to use numbers to represent the permissions and the predefined constants to define operations. For example, the third argument to **shmget** is *shmflg*. To create a shared memory segment that has read and write permissions for the owner and group, the command is:

> **shmget**(*key*, *size*, 0660 | IPC_CREAT)

4.5.1 Using Shared Memory

The fastest method of interprocess communication is shared memory, where cooperating processes map the same area of virtual memory into their address space. When one process writes to a location in the shared area, the data is immediately available to any other process that has this location mapped in its address space. The time required to access this location is no more than that required for a normal memory reference.

Figure 3.5 in Section 3.3 illustrates how processes access shared memory regions. One process (the "owner" of the shared memory region) creates the shared memory region with the **shmget** system call. That process' region table points to this shared memory segment, just as it points to its text, data, and stack segments. A second process (the "attacher") then issues the **shmat** system call to attach to this segment. The pregion entry for the attacher process points to the owner's region table entry for the shared memory segment. Any number of processes can attach to this shared memory segment. When a process exits, or if it no longer needs access to the shared memory region, it can issue the **shmdt** system call to detach from that region.

When processes share memory, they must use semaphores, binary semaphores, or messages to coordinate access to the shared memory segment. These mechanisms are discussed later in this chapter.

The REAL/IX operating system supports the UNIX System V system calls for working with shared memory. Table 4.12 lists these system calls.

A process initially creates a shared memory segment facility using the **shmget** system call. On creation, this process sets the overall operation permissions for the shared memory segment facility, sets its size in bytes, and can specify that the shared memory segment is for reference only (read-only) on attachment. If the memory segment is not specified to be for reference only, all other processes with appropriate operation permissions can read from or write to the memory segment.

Table 4.12
Shared Memory System Calls

System Call	Description
shmid = **shmget**(*key, size, shmflg [physaddr]*)	Create shared memory region, identified by **shmid**, which is associated with *key*. The *size* is specified in bytes. *shmflg* controls permissions.
shmat(*shmid, shmaddr, shmflg*)	Attach a shared memory segment to the calling process. *shmaddr* determines the address at which the segment is attached; *shmflg* can be used to attach the segment for read-only access.
shmdt(*shmaddr*)	Detach the shared memory segment located at *shmaddr*.
shmctl(*shmid, cmd, buf*)	Perform various control operations, as specified by *cmd*, such as set access permissions for the shared memory region, lock/unlock the segment in memory, and remove the shared memory region from the system.

The **shmat** call (shared memory attach) allows processes to associate themselves with the shared memory segment if they have permission. They can then read or write as allowed. All processes that will access the shared memory segment, including the process that owns it, must attach it to their memory space.

The **shmdt** call (shared memory detach) allows processes to disassociate themselves from a shared memory segment. Therefore, they lose the ability to read from or write to the shared memory segment.

The original owner/creator of a shared memory segment can relinquish ownership to another process using the **shmctl** system call. However, the creating process remains the creator until the facility is removed or the system is reinitialized. Other processes with permission can perform other functions on the shared memory segment using the **shmctl** system call.

4.5.2 Creating a Shared Memory Segment

When designing an application, determine which process will be the owner of the shared memory segment. The code for that program should do the following, usually as part of its initialization:

1. Begin execution of the code at a non-real-time priority. In other words, do not issue a **setpri** call until after the shared memory segment has been allocated with **shmget**.

2. Set up code to explicitly free the shared memory segment if the process is aborted. Otherwise, the shared memory region is not freed and the memory remains allocated. If the process is rerun (especially if the process aborts and is restarted several times), the system may run out of memory because of the allocated shared memory segments left around. An example of code that frees the shared memory segment is:

```
perror(s);
if (shmctl(shmid, IPC_RMID, (struct shmid_ds *)0) == -1
    perror("schmctl(IPC_RMID)");
exit(1);
```

   This code is typically located with other global function definitions, immediately after global variable declarations, and before the **main** routine.

3. Create the shared memory segment, specifying the access permissions and the IPC_CREAT flag as part of the third argument (*shmflg*). For example, to create a shared memory segment whose identifier is **myshm**, whose size is 4096 bytes, and that can be read and written by the owner and group, the code might be:

```
myshm = sgmget (ftok("/usr4/mypro",42) | 0,4096,0660|IPC_CREAT))
if(shmid == 1)
        printf("\nshmget failed with error number = %d\n", errno);
else
        printf("\ncall to shmget successful, shmid = %d\n", shmid);
exit(0);
```

If the **shmget** call is successful, it returns the shared memory identifier and creates a shared memory region with an associated shared memory structure (in this case, myshm_ds) that can be attached with **shmat** or accessed with **shmctl** for status information or to change permissions for the shared memory segment.

4. Allocate the semaphore, binary semaphore, or message that will be used to control access to the shared memory region.

5. After the shared memory segment has been allocated, issue the **setpri** call to give the process a real-time execute priority, if desired. Non-real-time

processes can use shared memory, but typically processes that require the speed of shared memory also require real-time execute priorities.

6. If desired, issue the **plock** and **resident** calls to lock the process' text data, and stack segments in memory.

7. After completing step 6, lock the shared memory segment in memory with the **shmctl** call. If the shared memory segment is not locked, it can be paged out of main memory when the system requires more memory. For example, the following code locks the shared memory segment created above:

```
shmctl(mysem_ds,SHM_LOCK,0)
```

The SHM_UNLOCK *cmd* for the second argument to **shmctl** can be used to reverse the effect of SHM_LOCK. Most applications do not need SHM_UNLOCK.

4.5.3 Allocating a Physical Shared Memory Segment

The standard **shmget** call lets the operating system choose the location of the shared memory segment. Some real-time processes need to specify the physical address at which the shared memory will be allocated. If the process creating the shared memory segment has real-time or superuser privileges, it can specify the physical address at which the shared memory region will be created by using the optional fourth argument. The IPC_PHYS flag tells the system that this is a physical shared memory segment.

The synopsis for the **shmget** call is as follows:

```
#include <sys/types.h>
#include <sys/ipc.h>
#include <sys/shm.h>

int shmget (key, size, shmflg)
key_t key;
int size, shmflg;
```

All these include files are located in the **/usr/include/sys** directory of the operating system.

The **shmget** is a function with three formal arguments that returns an integer type value on successful completion, which is the shared memory identifier **shmid**.

For instance, to create a shared memory region at physical address the call is:

```
myshm2=shmget(ftok("/usr4/mypro",42),
```

```
4096,0660|IPC_CREAT|IPC_PHYS,XX)
```

The following guidelines should be used to determine the physical address:

- Do not use locations from the kernel's general memory pool.
- Physical shared memory segments must be aligned on a page boundary.
- The address range (determined by the beginning address and the size) must not overlap any other shared memory segments.

4.5.3.1 Example Program Using the **shmget** System Call

The example program shown in Figure 4.7, is a menu-driven program which allows all possible combinations of using the **shmget** system call to be exercised. From studying this program, the reader can observe the method of passing arguments and receiving return values. The user-written program requirements are pointed out. This program begins (lines 4-7) by including the required header files as specified by the **shmget** entry. Although the **errno.h** header file is included, declaring **errno** as an external variable will also work.

Variable names have been chosen to be as close as possible to those in the synopsis for the system call. Their declarations are self-explanatory. The variables declared for this program and their purposes are as follows:

- **key** - used to pass the value for the desired **key.**

- **opperm** - used to store the desired operation permissions.

- **opperm_flags** - used to store the combination from the logical ORing of the **opperm** and **flags** variables; it is then used in the system call to pass the **shmflg** argument.

- **shmid** - used for returning the message queue identification number for a successful system call or the error code (-1) for an unsuccessful one.

- **size** - used to specify the shared memory segment size.

The program begins by prompting for a hexadecimal **key**, an octal operation permissions code, and finally for the control command combinations (flags) which are selected from a menu (lines 14-31). All possible combinations are allowed even though they might not be valid. This allows observing the errors for illegal combinations.

Next, the menu selection for the flags is combined with the operation permissions, and the result is stored at the address of the **opperm_flags** variable (lines 35-50).

A display then prompts for the **size** of the shared memory segment, and it is stored at the address of the size variable (lines 51-54).

The system call is made next, and the result is stored at the address of the **shmid** variable (line 56).

Since the **shmid** variable now contains a valid message queue identifier or the error code (-1), it is tested to see if an error occurred (line 58). If **shmid** equals -1, a message indicates that an error resulted and the external **errno** variable is displayed (lines 60, 61).

If no error occurred, the returned shared memory segment identifier is displayed (line 65).

```
/*This is a program to illustrate
**the shared memory get, shmget(),
**system call capabilities.*/

#include    <sys/types.h>
#include    <sys/ipc.h>

#include    <sys/shm.h>
#include    <errno.h>

/*Start of main C language program*/
main()
{
    key_t key;              /*declare as long integer*/
    int opperm, flags;
    int shmid, size, opperm_flags;
    /*Enter the desired key*/
    printf("Enter the desired key in hex = ");
    scanf("%x", &key);

    /*Enter the desired octal operation
      permissions.*/
    printf("\nEnter the operation\n");
    printf("permissions in octal = ");
    scanf("%o", &opperm);

    /*Set the desired flags.*/
    printf("\nEnter corresponding number to\n");
    printf("set the desired flags:\n");
    printf("No flags                  = 0\n");
    printf("IPC_CREAT                 = 1\n");
    printf("IPC_EXCL                  = 2\n");
    printf("IPC_CREAT and IPC_EXCL    = 3\n");
    printf("            Flags         = ");
    /*Get the flag(s) to be set.*/
    scanf("%d", &flags);

    /*Check the values.*/
    printf ("\nkey =0x%x, opperm = 0%o, flags = 0%o\n",
        key, opperm, flags);

    /*Incorporate the control fields (flags) with
      the operation permissions*/
    switch (flags)
    {
    case 0:    /*No flags are to be set.*/
        opperm_flags = (opperm | 0);
        break;
    case 1:    /*Set the IPC_CREAT flag.*/
        opperm_flags = (opperm | IPC_CREAT);
        break;
    case 2:    /*Set the IPC_EXCL flag.*/
        opperm_flags = (opperm | IPC_EXCL);
        break;
```

Figure 4.7 - Example program: Allocating shared memory by using **shmget** system call

```
        case 3:    /*Set the IPC_CREAT and IPC_EXCL flags.*/
            opperm_flags = (opperm | IPC_CREAT | IPC_EXCL);
        }

        /*Get the size of the segment in bytes.*/
        printf ("\nEnter the segment");
        printf ("\nsize in bytes = ");
        scanf ("%d", &size);

        /*Call the shmget system call.*/
        shmid = shmget (key, size, opperm_flags);

        /*Perform the following if the call is unsuccessful.*/
        if(shmid ==  1)
        {
            printf ("\nThe shmget system call failed!\n");
            printf ("The error number = %d\n", errno);
        }
        /*Return the shmid on successful completion.*/
        else
            printf ("\nThe shmid = %d\n", shmid);
        exit(0);
    }
```

Figure 4.7 - cont'd

4.5.4 Controlling Shared Memory

This section gives a detailed description of using the **shmctl** system call for controlling shared memory operations.

The synopsis for the **shmctl** system call is as follows:

```
#include <sys/types.h>
#include <sys/ipc.h>
#include <sys/shm.h>

int shmctl (shmid, cmd, buf)
int shmid, cmd;
struct shmid_ds *buf;
```

The **shmctl** system call requires three arguments to be passed to it, and **shmctl** returns an integer value.

On successful completion, a zero value is returned; and when unsuccessful, **shmctl** returns a -1.

The **shmid** variable must be a valid, non-negative, integer value. In other words, it must have already been created by using the **shmget** system call.

The **cmd** argument can be replaced by one of the following control commands (flags):

- IPC_STAT - return the status information contained in the associated data structure for the specified **shmid** and place it in the data structure pointed to by the ***buf** pointer in the user memory area.

- IPC_SET - for the specified **shmid**, set the effective user and group identification, and operation permissions.

- IPC_RMID - remove the specified **shmid** along with its associated shared memory segment data structure.

- SHM_LOCK - lock the specified shared memory segment in memory; must be superuser.

- SHM_UNLOCK - unlock the shared memory segment from memory; must be superuser.

A process must have an effective user identification of OWNER/CREATOR or superuser to perform an IPC_SET or IPC_RMID control command. Only the superuser can perform a SHM_LOCK or SHM_UNLOCK control command. A process must have read permission to perform the IPC_STAT control command.

4.5.4.1 Example Program: Using the **shmctl** System Call

The example program, given in Figure 4.8 is a menu-driven program that allows all possible combinations of using the **shmctl** system call to be exercised. From studying this program, the reader can observe the method of passing arguments and receiving return values. The user-written program requirements are pointed out.

This program begins by including the required header files as specified by the **shmctl** entry. Note in this program that **errno** is declared as an external variable, and therefore, the **errno.h** header file does not have to be included.

The variables declared for this program and their purposes are as follows:

- **uid** - used to store the IPC_SET value for the effective user identification.

- **gid** - used to store the IPC_SET value for the effective group identification.

- **mode** - used to store the IPC_SET value for the operation permissions.

- **rtrn** - used to store the return integer value from the system call.

- **shmid** - used to store and pass the shared memory identifier to the system call.

- **command** - used to store the code for the desired control command so that subsequent processing can be performed on it.

- **choice** - used to determine which member for the IPC_SET control command is to be changed.

- **shmid_ds** - used to receive the specified shared memory segment identifier's data structure when an IPC_STAT control command is performed.

- ***buf** - a pointer passed to the system call which locates the data structure in the user memory area where the IPC_STAT control command is to place its return values or where the IPC_SET command gets the values to set.

Note that the **shmid_ds** data structure in this program (line 16) uses the data structure located in the **shm.h** header file of the same name as a template for its declaration. This is a perfect example of the advantage of local variables.

The next important thing to observe is that although the ***buf** pointer is declared to be a pointer to a data structure of the **shmid_ds** type, it must also be initialized to contain the address of the user memory area data structure (line 17).

Now that all the required declarations have been explained for this program, this is how it works.

First, the program prompts for a valid shared memory segment identifier which is stored at the address of the **shmid** variable (lines 18-20). This is required for every **shmctl** system call.

Then, the code for the desired control command must be entered (lines 21-29), and it is stored at the address of the command variable. The code is tested to determine the control command for subsequent processing.

If the IPC_STAT control command is selected (code 1), the system call is performed (lines 39, 40) and the status information returned is printed out (lines 41-71). Note that if the system call is unsuccessful (line 146), the status information of the last successful call is printed out. In addition, an error message is displayed and the **errno** variable is printed out (lines 148, 149). If the system call is successful, a message indicates this along with the shared memory segment identifier used (lines 151-154).

If the IPC_SET control command is selected the first step is to get the current status information for the specified message queue identifier (lines 90-92). This is necessary because this program provides for changing only one member at a time, and the system call changes all of them. Also, if an invalid value happened to be stored in the user memory area for one of these members, it would cause repetitive failures for this control command until corrected. The program then prompts for a code corresponding to the member to be changed (lines 93-98). This code is stored at the address of the choice variable (line 99). Then, depending on the member picked, the program prompts for the new value (lines 105-127). The value is placed at the address of the appropriate member in the user memory area data structure, and the system call is made (lines 128-130). The program returns the same messages as for IPC_STAT above, indicating success or failure.

If the IPC_RMID control command (Code 3) is selected, the system call is performed (lines 132-135), and the **shmid** along with its associated message queue and data structure are removed from the operating system. Note that the ***buf** pointer is not required as an argument to perform this control command and its value can be zero or NULL. The program returns the same messages as for the other control commands.

If the SHM_LOCK control command (Code 4) is selected, the system call is performed (lines 137, 138). The program returns the same messages as for the other control commands.

If the SHM_UNLOCK control command (Code 5) is selected, the system call is performed (lines 140-142). The program returns the same messages as for the other control commands.

It is suggested that the source program file be named **shmctl.c** and that the executable file be named **shmctl**.

```
/*This is a program to illustrate
**the shared memory control, shmctl(),
**system call capabilities.
*/

/*Include necessary header files.*/
#include    <stdio.h>
#include    <sys/types.h>
#include    <sys/ipc.h>
#include    <sys/shm.h>

/*Start of main C language program*/
main()
{
    extern int errno;
    int uid, gid, mode;
    int rtrn, shmid, command, choice;
    struct shmid_ds shmid_ds, *buf;
    buf = &shmid_ds;

    /*Get the shmid, and command.*/
    printf("Enter the shmid = ");
    scanf("%d", &shmid);

    printf("\nEnter the number for\n");
    printf("the desired command:\n");

    printf("IPC_STAT     =  1\n");
    printf("IPC_SET      =  2\n");
    printf("IPC_RMID     =  3\n");
    printf("SHM_LOCK     =  4\n");
    printf("SHM_UNLOCK   =  5\n");
    printf("Entry        =  ");
    scanf("%d", &command);

    /*Check the values.*/
    printf ("\nshmid =%d, command = %d\n",
        shmid, command);
    switch (command)
    {
    case 1:    /*Use shmctl() to duplicate
          the data structure for
                  shmid in the shmid_ds area pointed
                  to by buf and then print it out.*/
        rtrn = shmctl(shmid, IPC_STAT,
            buf);
        printf ("\nThe USER ID = %d\n",
            buf >shm_perm.uid);
        printf ("The GROUP ID = %d\n",
            buf >shm_perm.gid);
        printf ("The creator's ID = %d\n",
            buf >shm_perm.cuid);
        printf ("The creator's group ID = %d\n",
            buf >shm_perm.cgid);
        printf ("The operation permissions = 0%o\n",
```

Figure 4.8 - Example program: Controlling shared memory with **shmctl** system call

```
                buf >shm_perm.mode);
            printf ("The slot usage sequence\n");

            printf ("number = 0%x\n",
                buf >shm_perm.seq);
            printf ("The key= 0%x\n",
                buf >shm_perm.key);
            printf ("The segment size = %d\n",
                buf >shm_segsz);
            printf ("The pid of last shmop = %d\n",
                buf >shm_lpid);
            printf ("The pid of creator = %d\n",
                buf >shm_cpid);
            printf ("The current # attached = %d\n",
                buf >shm_nattch);
            printf("The in memory # attached = %d\n",
                buf->shm_cnattach);
            printf("The last shmat time = %d\n",
                buf->shm_atime);
            printf("The last shmdt time = %d\n",
                buf->shm_dtime);
            printf("The last change time = %d\n",
                buf->shm_ctime);
            break;


            /* Lines 73 - 87 deleted */

        case 2:    /*Select and change the desired
                     member(s) of the data structure.*/

            /*Get the original data for this shmid
                  data structure first.*/
            rtrn = shmctl(shmid, IPC_STAT, buf);

            printf("\nEnter the number for the\n");
            printf("member to be changed:\n");
            printf("shm_perm.uid   = 1\n");
            printf("shm_perm.gid   = 2\n");
            printf("shm_perm.mode  = 3\n");
            printf("Entry          = ");
            scanf("%d", &choice);
            /*Only one choice is allowed per
              pass as an illegal entry will
                  cause repetitive failures until
              shmid_ds is updated with
                  IPC_STAT.*/

            switch(choice){
            case 1:
                printf("\nEnter USER ID = ");
                scanf ("%d", &uid);
                buf >shm_perm.uid = uid;
                printf("\nUSER ID = %d\n",
                    buf >shm_perm.uid);
                break;
```

Figure 4.8 - cont'd

```
          case 2:
              printf("\nEnter GROUP ID = ");
              scanf("%d", &gid);
              buf >shm_perm.gid = gid;
              printf("\nGROUP ID = %d\n",
                  buf >shm_perm.gid);
              break;

          case 3:
              printf("\nEnter MODE = ");
              scanf("%o", &mode);
              buf >shm_perm.mode = mode;
              printf("\nMODE = 0%o\n",
                  buf >shm_perm.mode);
              break;
          }
          /*Do the change.*/
          rtrn = shmctl(shmid, IPC_SET,
              buf);
          break;

      case 3:    /*Remove the shmid along with its
                     associated
                     data structure.*/


          rtrn = shmctl(shmid, IPC_RMID, NULL);
          break;

      case 4: /*Lock the shared memory segment*/
          rtrn = shmctl(shmid, SHM_LOCK, NULL);
          break;
      case 5: /*Unlock the shared memory
                     segment.*/
          rtrn = shmctl(shmid, SHM_UNLOCK, NULL);
          break;
      }
      /*Perform the following if the call is unsuccessful.*/
      if(rtrn ==  1)
      {
          printf ("\nThe shmctl system call failed!\n");
          printf ("The error number = %d\n", errno);
      }
      /*Return the shmid on successful completion.*/
      else
          printf ("\nShmctl was successful for shmid = %d\n",
              shmid);
      exit (0);
  }
```

Figure 4.8 - cont'd

4.5.5 Attaching and Detaching a Shared Memory Segment

After the shared memory segment has been allocated, all processes that will access it (including the process that created it) must attach to the shared memory segment with the **shmat** call. Any process that attaches a shared memory segment should also include code to explicitly detach the segment using the **shmdt** call, when the process exits.

The synopsis for the **shmat** and **shmdt** system calls is as follows:

```
#include <sys/types.h>
#include <sys/ipc.h>
#include <sys/shm.h>

char *shmat (shmid, shmaddr, shmflg)
int shmid;
char *shmaddr;
int shmflg;

int shmdt (shmaddr)
char *shmaddr;
```

Attaching a Shared Memory Segment

The **shmat** system call requires three arguments to be passed to it, and it returns a character pointer value.

The system call can be cast to return an integer value. On successful completion, this value will be the address in core memory where the process is attached to the shared memory segment and when unsuccessful it will be a -1.

The **shmid** argument must be a valid, non-negative, integer value. It must have already been created by using the **shmget** system call.

The shm**addr** argument can be zero or user supplied when passed to the **shmat** system call. If it is zero, the operating system selects the address of where the shared memory segment will be attached. If it is user supplied, the address must be a valid address that the operating system would have selected.

The **shmflg** argument is used to pass the SHM_RND and SHM_RDONLY flags to the **shmat** system call.

Detaching Shared Memory Segments

The **shmdt** system call requires one argument to be passed to it. **shmdt** returns an integer value.

On successful completion, a value of zero is returned. When unsuccessful, **shmdt** returns a -1.

4.5.5.1 Example program: Using the **shmat** and **shmdt** System Calls

The example program in Figure 4.9 is a menu-driven program which allows all possible combinations of using the **shmat** and **shmdt** system calls to be exercised.

From studying this program, the reader can observe the method of passing arguments and receiving return values. The user-written program requirements are pointed out.

The variables declared for this program and their purposes are as follows:

- **flags** - used to store the codes of SHM_RND or SHM_RDONLY for the **shmat** system call.
- **addr** - used to store the address of the shared memory segment for the **shmat** and **shmdt** system calls.
- **i** - used as a loop counter for attaching and detaching.
- **shmid** - used to store and pass the desired shared memory segment identifier.
- **shmflg** - used to pass the value of flags to the **shmat** system call.
- **retrn** - used to store the return values from both system calls.
- **detach** - used to store the desired number of detach operations.

This example program combines both the **shmat** and **shmdt** system calls. The program prompts for the number of attachments and enters a loop until they are done for the specified shared memory identifiers. Then, the program prompts for the number of detachments to be performed and enters a loop until they are completed for all of the specified shared memory segment addresses.

shmat

The program prompts for the number of attachments to be performed, and the value is stored at the address of the attach variable (lines 17-21).

To perform the specified number of attachments, a loop is entered using the attach variable and the **i** counter (lines 23-70).

In this loop, the program prompts for a shared memory segment identifier (lines 24-27) and stores the identifier at the address of the **shmid** variable (line 28). Next, the program prompts for the address where the segment is to be attached (lines 30-34), and stores the address at the address of the **addr** variable (line 35). Then, the program prompts for the desired flags to be used for the attachment (lines 37-44). The code representing the flags is stored at the address of the flags variable (line 45). The flags variable is tested to determine the code to be stored for the **shmflg** variable which is used to pass them to the **shmat** system call (lines 46-57). The system call is made (line 60). If successful, a message to that effect is displayed along with the attach address (lines 66-68). If unsuccessful, a message to that effect and the error code are displayed (lines 62, 63). The loop then continues until it finishes.

shmdt

After the attach loop completes, the program prompts for the number of detach operations to be performed (lines 71-75). This value is stored at the address of the detach variable (line 76).

To perform the specified number of detachments a loop is entered using the detach variable and the **i** counter (lines 78-95). In this loop, the program prompts for the address of the shared memory segment to be detached (lines 79-83), and stores the value at the address of the **addr** variable (line 84). Then, the **shmdt** system call is performed (line 87). If successful, a message to that effect is displayed along with the address from which the segment was detached (lines 92, 93). If unsuccessful, the error number is displayed (line 89). The loop continues until it finishes.

```
/*This is a program to illustrate
**the shared memory operations, shmop(),
**system call capabilities.
*/
/*Include necessary header files.*/
#include    <stdio.h>
#include    <sys/types.h>
#include    <sys/ipc.h>
#include    <sys/shm.h>
/*Start of main C language program*/
main()
{
    extern int errno;
    int flags, addr, i, attach;

    int shmid, shmflg, retrn, detach;
    /*Loop for attachments by this process.*/
    printf("Enter the number of\n");
    printf("attachments for this\n");
    printf("process (1-4).\n");
    printf("       Attachments = ");

    scanf("%d", &attach);
    printf("Number of attaches = %d\n", attach);

    for(i = 1; i <= attach; i++) {
        /*Enter the shared memory ID.*/
        printf("\nEnter the shmid of\n");
        printf("the shared memory segment to\n");
        printf("be operated on = ");
        scanf("%d", &shmid);
        printf("\nshmid = %d\n", shmid);

        /*Enter the value for shmaddr.*/
        printf("\nEnter the value for\n");
        printf("the shared memory address\n");
        printf("in hexadecimal:\n");
        printf("          Shmaddr = ");
        scanf("%x", &addr);
        printf("The desired address = 0x%x\n", addr);

        /*Specify the desired flags.*/
        printf("\nEnter the corresponding\n");
        printf("number for the desired\n");
        printf("flags:\n");
        printf("SHM_RND                = 1\n");
        printf("SHM_RDONLY             = 2\n");
        printf("SHM_RND and SHM_RDONLY = 3\n");
        printf("          Flags        = ");
        scanf("%d", &flags);
        switch(flags)

        {
```

Figure 4.9 - Example program: Attaching and detaching shared memory segment with **shmat** and **shmdt** system calls

```
        case 1:
            shmflg = SHM_RND;
            break;
        case 2:
            shmflg = SHM_RDONLY;
            break;
        case 3:
            shmflg = SHM_RND | SHM_RDONLY;
            break;
        }
        printf("\nFlags = 0%o\n", shmflg);

        /*Do the shmat system call.*/
        retrn = (int)shmat(shmid, addr, shmflg);
        if(retrn ==  1)  {
            printf("\nShmat failed.  ");
            printf("Error = %d\n", errno);

        }
        else {
            printf ("\nShmat was successful\n");
            printf("for shmid = %d\n", shmid);
            printf("The address = 0x%x\n", retrn);
        }
    }

    /*Loop for detachments by this process.*/
    printf("Enter the number of\n");
    printf("detachments for this\n");
    printf("process (1-4).\n");
    printf("        Detachments = ");

    scanf("%d", &detach);
    printf("Number of attaches = %d\n", detach);
    for(i = 1; i <= detach; i++) {

        /*Enter the value for shmaddr.*/
        printf("\nEnter the value for\n");
        printf("the shared memory address\n");
        printf("in hexadecimal:\n");
        printf("            Shmaddr = ");
        scanf("%x", &addr);
        printf("The desired address = 0x%x\n", addr);

        /*Do the shmdt system call.*/
        retrn = (int)shmdt(addr);
        if(retrn == -1)  {
            printf("Error = %d\n", errno);
        }
        else {
            printf ("\nShmdt was successful\n");
            printf("for address  = 0%x\n", addr);
        }
    }
}
```

Figure 4.9 - cont'd

4.5.6 Getting Physical Shared Memory Segment

This section explains how the **smget** system call can be used to map a specified physical address to a process' virtual space.

The synopsis for **shmget** when used for physical shared memory is:

```
#include  <sys/types.h>
#include  <sys/ipc.h>
#include  <sys/shm.h>

int shmdt (key, size, shmflg, physadr)
key_t key;
int size, shmflg;
int physadr;
```

The request for physical shared memory is made by setting IPC_PHYS in **shmflg**. This causes **shmget** to access the fourth argument, **physadr**. This is the physical address to be mapped into the process. Two other flags apply for physical shared memory. If (**shmflg** & IPC_CI) is true, the memory will be cache inhibited. If (**shmflg** & IPC_NOCLEAR) is true, the memory will not be cleared on the first attach.

It is necessary that any areas to be used as physical shared memory not be in the kernel's general memory pool. Only superuser or users with real-time privileges can use physical shared memory.

4.5.6.1 Example Program: Using the **shmget** System Call for Attaching Physical Shared Memory Segments

The example program, given in Figure 4.10, illustrates the use of the **shmget** system call to allocate the physical shared memory into the process' virtual space.

```
/*This is a program to illustrate
**the use of shmget(2) using
**physical shared memory capabilities.*/
#include    <sys/types.h>
#include    <sys/ipc.h>
#include    <sys/shm.h>
#include    <errno.h>
/*Start of main C language program*/
main()
{
    key_t key;              /*declare as long integer*/
    int opperm, flags, paddr;
    int shmid, size, opperm_flags;
    /*Enter the desired key*/
    printf("Enter the desired key in hex = ");
    scanf("%x", &key);
    /*Enter the desired octal operation
      permissions.*/
    printf("\nEnter the operation\n");
    printf("permissions in octal = ");
    scanf("%o", &opperm);
    /*Set the desired flags.*/
    printf("\nEnter corresponding number to\n");
    printf("set the desired flags:\n");
    printf("No flags                    = 0\n");
    printf("IPC_CREAT                   = 1\n");
    printf("IPC_EXCL                    = 2\n");
    printf("IPC_CREAT and IPC_EXCL      = 3\n");
    printf("            Flags           = ");
    /*Get the flag(s) to be set.*/
    scanf("%d", &flags);
    /*Check the values.*/
    printf ("\nkey =0x%x, opperm = 0%o, flags = 0%o\n",
 key, opperm, flags);
    /*Incorporate the control fields (flags) with
      the operation permissions*/
    switch (flags)
    {
    case 0:    /*No flags are to be set.*/
 opperm_flags = (opperm | 0);
 break;
    case 1:    /*Set the IPC_CREAT flag.*/
 opperm_flags = (opperm | IPC_CREAT);
 break;
    case 2:    /*Set the IPC_EXCL flag.*/
 opperm_flags = (opperm | IPC_EXCL);
 break;
    case 3:    /*Set the IPC_CREAT and IPC_EXCL flags.*/
 opperm_flags = (opperm | IPC_CREAT | IPC_EXCL);
    }
    /*Set the physical shared memory flag */
    opperm_flags |= IPC_PHYS;
    /*Get the size of the segment in bytes.*/
    printf ("\nEnter the segment");
    printf ("\nsize in bytes = ");
```

Figure 4.10 - Example program: Allocating physical shared memory with the **shmget** system call

```
    scanf ("%d", &size);
    /*Get the physical address of the segment */
    printf ("\nEnter the physical address in hex = ");
    scanf ("%x", &paddr);
    /*Call the shmget system call.*/
    shmid = shmget (key, size, opperm_flags, paddr);
    /*Perform the following if the call is unsuccessful.*/
    if(shmid == -1)
    {
printf ("\nThe shmget system call failed!\n");
printf ("The error number = %d\n", errno);
    }
    /*Return the shmid on successful completion.*/
    else
printf ("\nThe shmid = %d\n", shmid);
    exit(0);
}
```

Figure 4.10 - cont'd

4.5.7 Checking the Status of a Shared Memory Segment

The **shmctl** call with the IPC_STAT command for the second value is used to check the current status of a shared memory segment. This is accomplished by writing the current value of each member of the controlling structure into another structure which the process can then access. Note that the shared memory control structure includes a structure that shows access permissions for the shared memory structure. Consequently, these values are also available through IPC_STAT.

For instance, the following call writes the current value of each member of the system_ds structure into the check_shm structure and then reads some of the information from check_shm:

```
shmctl(myshm_ds,IPC_STAT,check_shm);

printf ("/nUser ID = %d\n", check_shm>shm_perm.uid);
printf ("/nThe number of processes attached = \%d\n", check_shm>shm_nattch;
```

Table 4.13 shows the shared memory state information.

The implied states of Table 4.13 are as follows:

- **Unallocated Segment** - the segment associated with this segment descriptor has not been allocated for use.
- **Incore** - the shared segment associated with this descriptor has been allocated for use. Therefore, the segment exists and is currently resident in memory.
- **On Disk** - the shared segment associated with this segment descriptor is currently resident on the swap device.
- **Locked Incore** - the shared segment associated with this segment descriptor is currently locked in memory and will not be a candidate for swapping until the segment is unlocked. Only a superuser may lock and unlock a shared segment.
- **Unused** - this state is currently unused and should never be encountered by the normal user in shared memory handling.

Table 4.13
Shared Memory State Information

Lock Bit	Swap Bit	Allocated Bit	Implied State
0	0	0	Unallocated Segment
0	0	1	Incore
0	1	0	Unused
0	1	1	On Disk
1	0	1	Locked Incore
1	1	0	Unused
1	0	0	Unused
1	1	1	Unused

4.6 INTERPROCESS COMMUNICATIONS USING SEMAPHORES

The semaphore system calls provide a powerful synchronization method of controlling access to resources that are shared among processes. They are used to arbitrate the use of resources among processes and to synchronize processes with external events.

Each semaphore includes a counter that describes the number of resources available for use. If no resources are available, the counter may indicate how many processes are currently blocked waiting on the resources. When the value of the semaphore is 0, the resource is unavailable. In this case, the process can either wait for the value of the semaphore to be incremented (indicating that the resource has become available) or return without accessing the resource.

A semaphore represents a data structure (**sem**) that contains four members:

semval — Value of the semaphore, representing a count of resources for which the semaphore is responsible.

sempid — Process identifier (PID) of the last process to access the semaphore.

semncnta — Number of processes waiting for the semaphore value to become greater than its current value.

semzcnt Number of processes waiting for the semaphore value to be equal to zero.

The array of semaphores is identified by semid; each semaphore in the array is identified by an integral number, beginning with 0, and has a sem structure associated with it. Each process creates a local structure (*sops*) that is tied to the semaphore number, and uses this structure with the **semop** call to increment and decrement the semaphore. Figure 4.11 illustrates the relationship of the structures used with semaphores.

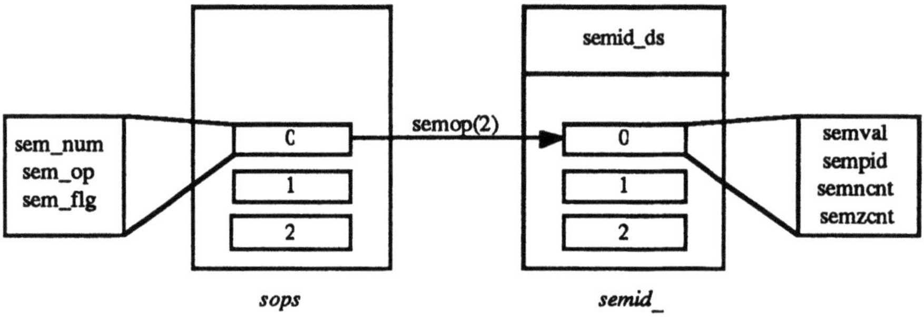

Figure 4.11 - Data structures for semaphores

The system calls and routines for handling semaphores are listed in Table 4.14.

Table 4.14
System Calls for Semaphores

System Call	Description
semget (key, nsems, semflg)	create/get a semaphore
semctl (semid, semnum, cmd, arg)	control a semaphore
semop (semid, sops, nsops)	modify a semaphore

Semaphore sets are created by using the **semget** system call.

The process performing the **semget** system call becomes the owner/creator and determines how many semaphores are in the set. The process also sets the operation permissions for the set, including itself. Additionally, this process can relinquish ownership of the set or change the operation permissions using the **semctl**, semaphore control system call. The creating process always remains the creator as long as the facility exists. Other processes with permission can use **semctl** to perform other control functions.

Provided a process has alter permission, it can manipulate the semaphore(s). Each semaphore within a set can be manipulated in two ways with the **semop** system call: a) incremented, and b) decremented.

To increment a semaphore, an integer value of the desired magnitude is passed to the **semop** system call. To decrement a semaphore, a minus (-) value of the desired magnitude is passed.

The operating system ensures that only one process can manipulate a semaphore set at any given time. Simultaneous requests are performed sequentially in an arbitrary order.

A process can test for a semaphore value to be greater than a certain value by attempting to decrement the semaphore by one more than that value. If the process is successful, then the semaphore value is greater than that certain value. Otherwise, the semaphore value is not. While doing this, the process can have its execution suspended (IPC_NOWAIT flag not set) until the semaphore value permits the operation (other processes increment the semaphore), or the semaphore facility is removed.

The ability to suspend execution is called a "blocking semaphore operation." This ability is also available for a process which is testing for a semaphore to become zero or equal to zero. Only read permission is required for this test and it is accomplished by passing a value of zero to the **semop** system call.

On the other hand, if the process is not successful and the process does not request to have its execution suspended, it is called a "nonblocking semaphore operation". In this case, the process is returned a known error code (-1) and the external **errno** variable is set accordingly.

The blocking semaphore operation allows processes to communicate based on the values of semaphores at different points in time. Remember also that IPC facilities remain in the operating system until removed by a permitted process or until the system is reinitialized.

Operating on a semaphore set is done by using the **semop**, semaphore operation system call.

When a set of semaphores is created, the first semaphore in the set is semaphore zero. The last semaphore in the set is one less than the total in the set.

An array of these "blocking/nonblocking operations" can be performed on a set containing more than one semaphore. When performing an array of operations, the "blocking/nonblocking operations" can be applied to any or all of the semaphores in the set. Also, the operations can be applied in any order of semaphore number. However, no operations are done until they can all be done successfully. This requirement means that preceding changes made to semaphore values in the set must be undone with a "blocking semaphore operation" or all of the semaphore operations in the set cannot be completed successfully. No changes are made until they can all be made. For example, if a process has successfully completed three of six operations on a set of ten semaphores but is "blocked" from performing the fourth operation, no changes are made to the set until the fourth and remaining operations (fifth and sixth) are successfully performed. Consequently, any operation preceding or succeeding the "blocked" operation, including the blocked operation itself, can specify that the operation be cancelled (undone). Otherwise, the operations are performed and the semaphores are changed or one "nonblocking operation" is unsuccessful and none are changed.

The ability to undo operations requires the operating system to maintain an array of "undo structures" corresponding to the array of semaphore operations to be performed. Each semaphore operation which is to be undone has an associated adjust variable used for undoing the operation, if necessary.

Any unsuccessful nonblocking operation for a single semaphore or a set of semaphores causes immediate return with no operations performed at all. When this occurs, a known error code (-1) is returned to the process, and the external variable **errno** is set accordingly.

System calls make these semaphore capabilities available to processes. The calling process passes arguments to a system call and the system call either successfully or unsuccessfully performs its function. If the system call is successful, it performs its function and returns the appropriate information. Otherwise, a known error code (-1) is returned to the process and the external variable **errno** is set accordingly.

4.6.1 Creating a Semaphore Structure and Array

Before semaphores can be used (operated on or controlled) a uniquely identified **data structure** and **semaphore set** (array) must be created. The unique identifier is called the semaphore identifier (**semid**). **semid** is used to identify or reference a particular data structure and semaphore set.

The semaphore set contains a predefined number of structures in an array, one structure for each semaphore in the set. The number of semaphores (**nsems**) in a semaphore set is user selectable. The following members are included in each structure within a semaphore set:

- semaphore text map address,
- process identification (PID) performing last operation,
- number of processes awaiting the semaphore value to become greater than its current value, and
- number of processes awaiting the semaphore value to equal zero.

There is one associated data structure for the uniquely identified semaphore set. This data structure contains information related to the semaphore set as follows:

- operation permissions data (operation permissions structure),
- pointer to first semaphore in the set (array),
- number of semaphores in the set,
- last semaphore operation time, and
- last semaphore change time.

The C language data structure definition for the semaphore set (array member) is as follows:

```
struct sem
{
        ushort      semval;         /* semaphore text map address*/
        short       sempid          /* pid of last operation */
        ushort      semncnt;        /* # awaiting semval > cval */
        ushort      semzcnt;        /* # awaiting semval = 0 */
};
```

Likewise, the structure definition for the associated semaphore data structure is as follows:

```
struct semid_ds
{
        struct ipc_perm sem_perm;       /* operation permission struct */
        struct sem      *sem_base;      /* ptr to first semaphore in set */
        ushort          sem_nsems;      /* # of semaphores in set */
        time_t          sem_otime;      /* last semop time */
        time_t          sem_ctime;      /* last change time */
};
```

The synopsis for the **semget** system call is as follows:

```
#include    <sys/types.h>
#include    <sys/ipc.h>
#include    <sys/sem.h>

int semget (key, nsems, semflg)
key_t key;
int nsems, semg;
```

semget is a function of three formal arguments and returns an integer type value on successful completion (**semid**).

When the IPC_CREAT flag is set in the **semflg** argument, as received by **semget**, two tasks are performed by **semget**.

(1) to get a new **semid** and create an associated data structure and semaphore set for it, and

(2) to return an existing **semid** that already has an associated data structure and semaphore set.

The task performed is determined by the value of the **key** argument passed to the **semget** system call. For the first task, if the **key** is not already in use for an existing **semid**, a new **semid** is returned. The **semid** includes an associated data structure and semaphore set created for it, provided no system tunable parameter would be exceeded.

There is also a provision for specifying a **key** of value zero (0) which is known as the private **key** (IPC_PRIVATE = 0). When specified, a new **semid** is always returned with an associated data structure and semaphore set created for it unless a system tunable parameter would be exceeded. When the **ipcs** command is performed the KEY field for the **semid** is all zeros.

When performing the first task, the process which calls **semget** becomes the owner/creator and the associated data structure is initialized accordingly. The creator of the semaphore set also determines the initial operation permissions for the facility.

For the second task, if **semid** exists for the key specified, the value of the existing **semid** is returned. If it is not desired to have an existing **semid** returned, a control command (IPC_EXCL) can be specified (set) in the **semflg** argument passed to the system call. The system call will fail if it is passed a value for the number of semaphores (**nsems**) that is greater than the number actually in the set. If the number of semaphores in the set is not known, use 0 for **nsems**.

Once a uniquely identified semaphore set and data structure are created, semaphore operations [**semop**] and semaphore control [**semctl**)] can be used.

4.6.1.1 Example Program: Using the semget System Call

The example program given in Figure 4.12, is a menu-driven program which allows all possible combinations of using the **semget** system call to be exercised.

This program begins (lines 4-8) by including the required header files as specified by the **semget** entry.

The variables declared for this program and their purpose are as follows:

- **key** - used to pass the value for the desired key.
- **opperm** - used to store the desired operation permissions.
- **flags** - used to store the desired control commands (flags).

- **opperm_flags** - used to store the combination from the logical ORing of the opperm and flags variables. It is then used in the system call to pass the semflg argument.

- **semid** - used for returning the semaphore set identification number for a successful system call or the error code (-1) for an unsuccessful one.

The program begins by prompting for a hexadecimal **key**, an octal operation permissions code, and the control command combinations (flags) which are selected from a menu (lines 15-32). All possible combinations are allowed even though they might not be valid. This allows observing for illegal combinations.

Next, the menu selection for the flags is combined with the operation permissions, and the result is stored at the address of the **opperm_flags** variable (lines 36-52).

Then, the number of semaphores for the set is requested (lines 53-57), and its value is stored at the address of **nsems**.

The system call is made next. The result is stored at the address of the **semid** variable (lines 60, 61).

Since the **semid** variable now contains a valid semaphore set identifier or the error code (-1), it is tested to see if an error occurred (line 63). If **semid** equals -1, a message indicates that an error resulted and the external **errno** variable is displayed (lines 65, 66). Note that the external **errno** variable is only set when a system call fails. It should be tested immediately following system calls.

If no error occurred, the returned semaphore set identifier is displayed (line 70).

It is suggested the the source program file be named **semget.c** and that the executable file be named **semget**.

```
/*This is a program to illustrate
**the semaphore get, semget(),
**system call capabilities.*/

#include    <stdio.h>
#include    <sys/types.h>
#include    <sys/ipc.h>
#include    <sys/sem.h>
#include    <errno.h>

/*Start of main C language program*/
main()
{
    key_t key;      /*declare as long integer*/
    int opperm, flags, nsems;
    int semid, opperm_flags;

    /*Enter the desired key*/
    printf("\nEnter the desired key in hex = ");
    scanf("%x", &key);

    /*Enter the desired octal operation
         permissions.*/
    printf("\nEnter the operation\n");
    printf("permissions in octal = ");
    scanf("%o", &opperm);

    /*Set the desired flags.*/
    printf("\nEnter corresponding number to\n");
    printf("set the desired flags:\n");
    printf("No flags                     = 0\n");

    printf("IPC_CREAT                    = 1\n");
    printf("IPC_EXCL                     = 2\n");
    printf("IPC_CREAT and IPC_EXCL       = 3\n");
    printf("             Flags           = ");
    /*Get the flags to be set.*/
    scanf("%d", &flags);

    /*Error checking (debugging)*/
    printf ("\nkey =0x%x, opperm = 0%o, flags = 0%o\n",
        key, opperm, flags);
    /*Incorporate the control fields (flags) with
         the operation permissions.*/
    switch (flags)
    {
    case 0:    /*No flags are to be set.*/
        opperm_flags = (opperm | 0);
        break;
    case 1:    /*Set the IPC_CREAT flag.*/
        opperm_flags = (opperm | IPC_CREAT);
        break;
    case 2:    /*Set the IPC_EXCL flag.*/
        opperm_flags = (opperm | IPC_EXCL);
        break;
```

Figure 4.12 - Example program: Creating/getting a semaphore using the **semget** system call

```
        case 3: /*Set the IPC_CREAT and IPC_EXCL
                      flags.*/
            opperm_flags = (opperm | IPC_CREAT | IPC_EXCL);
        }

        /*Get the number of semaphores for this set.*/
        printf("\nEnter the number of\n");
        printf("desired semaphores for\n");
        printf("this set (25 max) = ");
        scanf("%d", &nsems);

        /*Check the entry.*/
        printf("\nNsems = %d\n", nsems);

        /*Call the semget system call.*/
        semid = semget(key, nsems, opperm_flags);

        /*Perform the following if the call is unsuccessful.*/
        if(semid ==  1)
        {
            printf("The semget system call failed!\n");
            printf("The error number = %d\n", errno);
        }
        /*Return the semid on successful completion.*/
        else
            printf("\nThe semid = %d\n", semid);
        exit(0);
    }
```

Figure 4.12 - cont'd

4.6.2 Controlling Semaphores

Semaphore control is done by using the **semctl** system call. These control operations permit the programmer to control the semaphore facility in the following ways:

1. to return the value of a semaphore.
2. to set the value of a semaphore.
3. to return the process identification (PID) of the last process performing an operation on a semaphore set.
4. to return the number of processes waiting for a semaphore value to become greater than its current value.
5. to return the number of processes waiting for a semaphore value to equal zero.
6. to get all semaphore values in a set and place them in an array in user memory.
7. to set all semaphore values in a semaphore set from an array of values in user memory.
8. to place all data structure member values and status of a semaphore set into user memory area.
9. to change operation permissions for a semaphore set.
10. to remove a particular **semid** from the operating system along with its associated data structure and semaphore set.

The synopsis for the **semctl** system call is as follows:

```
#include   <sys/types.h>
#include   <sys/ipc.h>
#include   <sys/sem.h>

int semctl (semid, semnum, cmd, arg)
int semid, cmd;
int semnum;
union semun
{
        int val;
        struct semid_ds *bu;
        ushort array[];
} arg;
```

The **semctl** system call requires four arguments to be passed to it. It returns an integer value.

The **semid** argument must be a valid, non-negative integer value that has already been created by using the **semget** system call.

The **semnum** argument is used to select a semaphore by its number. This relates to array (atomically performed) operations on the set. When a set of semaphores is created, the first semaphore is 0 and the last semaphore is one less than the total in the set.

The **cmd** argument can be replaced by one of the following control commands (flags):

- GETVAL - return the value of a single semaphore within a semaphore set.
- SETVAL - set the value of a single semaphore within a semaphore set.
- GETPID - return the Process Identifier (PID) of the process that performed the last operation on the semaphore within a semaphore set.
- GETNCNT - return the number of processes waiting for the value of a particular semaphore to become greater than its current value.
- GETZCNT - return the number of processes waiting for the value of a particular semaphore to be equal to zero.
- GETALL - return the values for all semaphores in a semaphore set.
- SETALL - set all semaphore values in a semaphore set.
- IPC_STAT - return the status information contained in the associated data structure for the specified **semid** and place it in the data structure pointed to by the buf pointer in the user memory area. **arg.buf** is the union member that contains the value of buf.
- IPC_SET - for the specified semaphore set (**semid**) set the effective user/group identification and operation permissions.
- IPC_RMID - remove the specified (**semid**) semaphore set along with its associated data structure.

A process must have an effective user identification of OWNER/CREATOR or superuser to perform an IPC_SET or IPC_RMID control command. Read/alter permission is required as applicable for the other control commands.

4.6.2.1 Example Program: Using the **semctl** System Call

This section gives a menu-driven program (Figure 4.13) which illustrates using the **semctl** system call to control semaphores.

The variables declared for this program and their purpose are as follows:

- **semid_ds** - used to receive the specified semaphore set identifier's data structure when an IPC_STAT control command is performed.

- **c** - used to receive the input values from the **scanf** function (line 117), when performing a SETALL control command.

- **i** - used as a counter to increment through the union **arg.array** when displaying the semaphore values for a GETALL (lines 97-99) control command and when initializing the **arg.array** to perform a SETALL (lines 115-119) control command.

- **length** - used as a variable to test for the number of semaphores in a set against the **i** counter variable (lines 97, 115).

- **uid** - used to store the IPC_SET value for the effective user identification.

- **gid** - used to store the IPC_SET value for the effective group identification.

- **mode** - used to store the IPC_SET value for the operation's permissions.

- **rtrn** - used to store the return integer from the system call which depends on the control command or to store a -1 when unsuccessful.

- **semid** - used to store and pass the semaphore set identifier to the system call.

- **semnum** - used to store and pass the semaphore number to the system call.

- **cmd** - used to store the code for the desired control command so that subsequent processing can be performed on it.

- **choice** - used to determine which member (**uid, gid, mode**) is to be changed for the IPC_SET control command.

- **arg.val** - used to pass the system call a value to set (SETVAL) or store (GETVAL) a value returned from the system call for a single semaphore (union member).

- **arg.buf** - a pointer passed to the system call which locates the data structure in the user memory area where the IPC_STAT control command is to place its return values, or where the IPC_SET command gets the values to set (union member).

- **arg.array** - used to store the set of semaphore values when getting (GETALL) or initializing (SETALL) (union member).

Note that the **semid_ds** data structure in this program (line 14) uses the data structure located in the **sem.h** header file of the same name as a template for its declaration. This is an excellent example of the advantage of local variables.

The **arg** union (lines 18-22) serves three purposes. The compiler allocates enough storage to hold its largest member. The program can then use the union by referencing union members as if they were regular structure members. Note that the array is declared to have 25 elements (0 through 24). This number corresponds to the maximum number of semaphores allowed per set (SEMMSL), which is a system tunable parameter.

An important program aspect to note is that although the ***buf** pointer member (**arg.buf**) of the union is declared to be a pointer to a data structure of the **semid_ds** type, it must also be initialized to contain the address of the user memory area data structure (line 24). Because of the way this program is written, the pointer does not need to be reinitialized later. If used to increment through the array though, it needs to be reinitialized just before calling the system call.

Now that all the required declarations have been presented for this program, the program works as follows.

First, the program prompts for a valid semaphore set identifier, which is stored at the address of the **semid** variable (lines 25-27). This is required for all **semctl** system calls.

Then, the code for the desired control command must be entered (lines 28-42) and the code is stored at the address of the **cmd** variable. The code is tested to determine the control command for subsequent processing.

If the GETVAL control command is selected, a message prompting for a semaphore number is displayed (lines 49, 50). When it is entered, it is stored at the address of the **semnum** variable (line 51). Then, the system call is performed and the semaphore value is displayed (lines 52-55). If the system call is successful, a message indicates this along with the semaphore set identifier used (lines 195, 196). If the system call is unsuccessful, an error message is displayed along with the value of the external **errno** variable (lines 191-193).

If the SETVAL control command is selected, a message prompting for a semaphore number is displayed (lines 56, 57). When it is entered it is stored at the address of the **semnum** variable (line 58). Next, a message prompts for the value to which the semaphore is to be set. The value is stored as the **arg.val** member of the union (lines 59, 60). Then, the system call is performed (lines 61, 63). The program returns the same messages as for GETVAL above.

If the GETPID control command is selected, the system call is made immediately since all required arguments are known (lines 64-67) and the PID of the process performing the last operation is displayed. The program returns the same messages as for GETVAL above.

If the GETNCNT control command is selected, a message prompting for a semaphore number is displayed (lines 68-72). When entered, it is stored at the address of the **semnum** variable (line 73). Then, the system call is performed and the number of processes waiting for the semaphore to become greater than its current value is displayed (lines 74-77). The program returns the same messages as for GETVAL above.

If the GETZCNT control command is selected, a message prompting for a semaphore number is displayed (lines 78-81). When it is entered, it is stored at the address of the **semnum** variable (line 82). Then the system call is performed and the number of processes waiting for the semaphore value to become equal to zero is displayed (lines 83, 86). The program returns the same messages as for GETVAL above.

If the GETALL control command is selected, the program first performs an IPC_STAT control command to determine the number of semaphores in the set (lines 88-93). The length variable is set to the number of semaphores in the set (line 91). Next, the system call is made and, upon success, the **arg.array** union member contains the values of the semaphore set (line 96). Now, a loop is entered which displays each element of the **arg.array** from zero to one less than the value of length (lines 97-103). The semaphores in the set are displayed on a single line, separated by a space. The program returns the same messages as for GETVAL above.

If the SETALL control command is selected the program first performs an IPC_STAT control command to determine the number of semaphores in the set (lines 106-108). The length variable is set to the number of semaphores in the set (line 109). Next, the program prompts for the values to be set and enters a loop which takes values from the keyboard and initializes the **arg.array** union member to contain the desired values of the semaphore set (lines 113-119). The loop puts the first entry into the array position for semaphore number zero and ends when the semaphore number that is filled in the array equals one less than the value of length. The system call is then made (lines 120-122). The program returns the same messages as for GETVAL above.

If the IPC_STAT control command is selected (code 8), the system call is performed (line 127) and the status information returned is printed out (lines 128-139). Only the members that can be set are printed out in this program. Note that if the system call is unsuccessful, the status information of the last successful one is printed out. In addition, an error message is displayed and the **errno** variable is printed out (lines 191, 192).

If the IPC_SET control command is selected the program gets the current status information for the semaphore set identifier specified (lines 143-146). This is necessary because this example program provides for changing only one member at a time and the **semctl** system call changes all of them. Also, if an invalid value happened to be stored in the user memory area for one of these members, it would cause repetitive failures for this control command until the condition was corrected. The next step is to prompt for a code corresponding to the member to be changed (lines 147-153). This code is stored at the address of the choice variable (line 154). Now, depending on the member picked, the program prompts for the new value (lines 155-178). The value is placed at the address of the appropriate member in the user memory area data structure and the system call is made (line 181). The program returns the same messages as for GETVAL above.

If the IPC_RMID control command (code 10) is selected, the system call is performed (lines 183-185). The **semid** along with its associated data structure and semaphore set is removed from the operating system. The program returns the same messages as for the other control commands.

```
/*This is a program to illustrate
**the semaphore control, semctl(),
**system call capabilities.
*/

/*Include necessary header files.*/
#include    <stdio.h>
#include    <sys/types.h>
#include    <sys/ipc.h>
#include    <sys/sem.h>

/*Start of main C language program*/
main()
{
    extern int errno;
    struct semid_ds semid_ds;
    int c, i, length;
    int uid, gid, mode;
    int retrn, semid, semnum, cmd, choice;
    union semun  {
        int val;
        struct semid_ds *buf;
        ushort array[25];
    } arg;
    /*Initialize the data structure pointer.*/
    arg.buf = &semid_ds;

    /*Enter the semaphore ID.*/
    printf("Enter the semid = ");
    scanf("%d", &semid);
    /*Choose the desired command.*/
    printf("\nEnter the number for\n");
    printf("the desired cmd:\n");
    printf("GETVAL      =  1\n");
    printf("SETVAL      =  2\n");
    printf("GETPID      =  3\n");
    printf("GETNCNT     =  4\n");
    printf("GETZCNT     =  5\n");
    printf("GETALL      =  6\n");
    printf("SETALL      =  7\n");
    printf("IPC_STAT    =  8\n");
    printf("IPC_SET     =  9\n");
    printf("IPC_RMID    =  10\n");
    printf("Entry       =  ");
    scanf("%d", &cmd);
    /*Check entries.*/

    printf ("\nsemid =%d, cmd = %d\n\n",
        semid, cmd);

    /*Set the command and do the call.*/
    switch (cmd)
    {
```

Figure 4.13 - Example program: Controlling semaphores by using **semctl** system call

```
        case 1: /*Get a specified value.*/
            printf("\nEnter the semnum = ");
            scanf("%d", &semnum);
            /*Do the system call.*/
            retrn = semctl(semid, semnum, GETVAL, 0);
            printf("\nThe semval = %d\n", retrn);
            break;
        case 2: /*Set a specified value.*/
            printf("\nEnter the semnum = ");
            scanf("%d", &semnum);
            printf("\nEnter the value = ");
            scanf("%d", &arg.val);
            /*Do the system call.*/
            retrn = semctl(semid, semnum, SETVAL, arg.val);
            break;
        case 3: /*Get the process ID.*/
            retrn = semctl(semid, 0, GETPID, 0);
            printf("\nThe sempid = %d\n", retrn);
            break;
        case 4: /*Get the number of processes
              waiting for the semaphore to
              become greater than its current
                      value.*/
            printf("\nEnter the semnum = ");
            scanf("%d", &semnum);
            /*Do the system call.*/
            retrn = semctl(semid, semnum, GETNCNT, 0);
            printf("\nThe semncnt = %d", retrn);
            break;
        case 5: /*Get the number of processes
              waiting for the semaphore
                      value to become zero.*/
            printf("\nEnter the semnum = ");
            scanf("%d", &semnum);
            /*Do the system call.*/
            retrn = semctl(semid, semnum, GETZCNT, 0);
            printf("\nThe semzcnt = %d", retrn);
            break;

        case 6: /*Get all the semaphores.*/
            /*Get the number of semaphores in
              the semaphore set.*/
            retrn = semctl(semid, 0, IPC_STAT, arg.buf);
            length = arg.buf >sem_nsems;
            if(retrn == -1)
                goto ERROR;
            /*Get and print all semaphores in the

              specified set.*/
            retrn = semctl(semid, 0, GETALL, arg.array);
            for (i = 0; i < length; i++)
            {
                printf("%d", arg.array[i]);
                /*Separate each
                  semaphore.*/
                printf("%c", ' ');
```

Figure 4.13 - cont'd

```
            }
            break;

        case 7: /*Set all semaphores in the set.*/
            /*Get the number of semaphores in
              the set.*/
            retrn = semctl(semid, 0, IPC_STAT, arg.buf);
            length = arg.buf >sem_nsems;
            printf("Length = %d\n", length);
            if(retrn ==  1)
                goto ERROR;
            /*Set the semaphore set values.*/
            printf("\nEnter each value:\n");
            for(i = 0; i < length ; i++)
            {
                scanf("%d", &c);
                arg.array[i] = c;
            }
            /*Do the system call.*/
            retrn = semctl(semid, 0, SETALL, arg array);
            break;
        case 8: /*Get the status for the semaphore set.*/
            /*Get and print the current status values.*/
            retrn = semctl(semid, 0, IPC_STAT, arg.buf);
            printf ("\nThe USER ID = %d\n",
                arg.buf >sem_perm.uid);
            printf ("The GROUP ID = %d\n",
                arg.buf >sem_perm.gid);
            printf ("The operation permissions = 0%o\n",
                arg.buf >sem_perm.mode);
            printf ("The number of semaphores in set = %d\n",
                arg.buf >sem_nsems);
            printf ("The last semop time = %d\n",
                arg.buf >sem_otime);

            printf ("The last change time  = %d\n",
                arg.buf >sem_ctime);
            break;

        case 9:    /*Select and change the desired
                       member of the data structure.*/
            /*Get the current status values.*/
            retrn = semctl(semid, 0, IPC_STAT, arg.buf);
            if(retrn ==  1)
                goto ERROR;

            /*Select the member to change.*/
            printf("\nEnter the number for the\n");
            printf("member to be changed:\n");
            printf("sem_perm.uid   = 1\n");
            printf("sem_perm.gid   = 2\n");
            printf("sem_perm.mode  = 3\n");
            printf("Entry          = ");
            scanf("%d", &choice);
            switch(choice){
```

Figure 4.13 - cont'd

```
            case 1: /*Change the user ID.*/
                printf("\nEnter USER ID = ");
                scanf ("%d", &uid);
                arg.buf >sem_perm.uid = uid;
                printf("\nUSER ID = %d\n",
                    arg.buf >sem_perm.uid);
                break;

            case 2: /*Change the group ID.*/
                printf("\nEnter GROUP ID = ");
                scanf("%d", &gid);
                arg.buf >sem_perm.gid = gid;
                printf("\nGROUP ID = %d\n",
                    arg.buf >sem_perm.gid);
                break;

            case 3: /*Change the mode portion of
                  the operation
                              permissions.*/
                printf("\nEnter MODE = ");
                scanf("%o", &mode);
                arg.buf >sem_perm.mode = mode;
                printf("\nMODE = 0%o\n",
                    arg.buf >sem_perm.mode);
                break;
            }
            /*Do the change.*/
            retrn = semctl(semid, 0, IPC_SET, arg.buf);
            break;
        case 10:    /*Remove the semid along with its
                      data structure.*/
            retrn = semctl(semid, 0, IPC_RMID, 0);
        }
        /*Perform the following if the call is unsuccessful.*/
        if(retrn ==  1)
        {
    ERROR:
            printf ("\n\nThe semctl system call failed!\n");
            printf ("The error number = %d\n", errno);
            exit(0);
        }
        printf ("\n\nThe semctl system call was successful\n");
        printf ("for semid = %d\n", semid);
        exit (0);
    }
```

Figure 4.13 - cont'd

4.6.3 Operations on Semaphores

Semaphore operations consist of incrementing, decrementing, and testing for zero. A single system call is used to perform these operations. It is called **semop**.

The synopsis for the **semop** system call is as follows:

```
#include <sys/types.h>
#include <sys/ipc.h>
#include <sys/sem.h>

int semop (semid, sops, nsops)
int semid;
struct sembuf **sops;
unsigned nsops;
```

The **semop** system call requires three arguments to be passed to it, and it returns an integer value. Upon successful completion, a zero value is returned. When unsuccessful a -1 is returned.

The **semid** argument must be a valid, non-negative integer value. It must have already been created by using the **semget** system call.

The **sops** argument is a pointer to an array of structures in the user memory area that contains the following for each semaphore to be changed:

- the semaphore number
- the operation to be performed
- the control command (flags)

The semaphore number determines the particular semaphore within the set on which the operation is to be performed.

The operation to be performed is determined by the following:

- A positive integer value means to increment the semaphore value by its value.

- A negative integer value means to decrement the semaphore value by its value.

- A value of zero means to test if the semaphore is equal to zero.

The following operation commands (flags) can be used:

(a) IPC_NOWAIT - This operation command can be set for any operation in the array. The system call will return unsuccessfully without changing any semaphore values if any operation for which IPC_NOWAIT is set cannot be performed successfully. The system call will be unsuccessful when trying to decrement a semaphore more than its current value or when testing for a semaphore to be equal to zero when it is not.

(b) SEM_UNDO - This operation command allows any operation in the array to be undone when any operation in the array is unsuccessful and the IPC_NOWAIT flag is not set. That is, the blocked operation waits until it can perform its operation. When it and all succeeding operations are successful, all operations with the SEM_UNDO flag set are undone. Remember, no operations are performed on any semaphores in a set until all operations are successful. When the blocked operation and all subsequent operations are successful, undoing is accomplished by using an array of adjust values for the operations that are to be undone.

4.6.3.1 Example Program: Using the **semop** System Call

The example program in Figure 4.14 illustrates the use of **semop** system call for semaphore operations.

The following structures and variables are used in the program:

- **sembuf** - used as an array buffer (line 14) to contain a maximum of ten **sembuf** type structures; ten equals SEMOPM, which is the maximum number of operations on a semaphore set for each **semop** system call.

- **sops** - used as a pointer (line 14) to **sembuf** for the system call and for accessing the structure members within the array.

- **rtrn** - used to store the return values from the system call.

- **flags** - used to store the code of the IPC_NOWAIT or SEM_UNDO flags for the **semop** system call (line 60).

- **i** - used as a counter (line 32) for initializing the structure members in the array and used to print out each structure in the array (line 79).

- **nsops** - used to specify the number of semaphore operations for the system call; must be less than or equal to SEMOPM.

- **semid** - used to store the desired semaphore set identifier for the system call.

First, the program prompts for the semaphore set identifier on which the system call is to perform its operations (lines 19-22). **Semid** is stored at the address of the **semid** variable (line 23).

A message is displayed requesting the number of operations to be performed on this set (lines 25-27). The number of operations is stored at the address of the **nsops** variable (line 28).

Next, a loop is entered to initialize the array of structures (lines 30-77). The semaphore number, operation, and operation command (flags) are entered for each structure in the array. The number of structures equals the number of semaphore operations (**nsops**) to be performed for the system call. Thus, **nsops** is tested against the **i** counter for loop control. Note that **sops** is used as a pointer to each element (structure) in the array and **sops** is incremented just like **i. sops** is then used to point to each member in the structure for setting them.

After the array is initialized, all its elements are printed out for feedback (lines 78-85).

The **sops** pointer is set to the address of the array (lines 86, 87). **Sembuf** could be used directly, if desired, instead of **sops** in the system call.

The system call is made (line 89) and, depending on success or failure, a corresponding message is displayed. The result of the operation(s) can be viewed by using the **semctl** GETALL control command.

```
/*This is a program to illustrate
**the semaphore operations, semop(),
**system call capabilities.
*/

/*Include necessary header files.*/
#include    <stdio.h>
#include    <sys/types.h>
#include    <sys/ipc.h>
#include    <sys/sem.h>
/*Start of main C language program*/
main()
{
    extern int errno;
    struct sembuf sembuf[10], *sops;
    char string[];
    int retrn, flags, sem_num, i, semid;
    unsigned nsops;
    sops = sembuf; /*Pointer to array sembuf.*/

    /*Enter the semaphore ID.*/
    printf("\nEnter the semid of\n");
    printf("the semaphore set to\n");
    printf("be operated on = ");
    scanf("%d", &semid);
    printf("\nsemid = %d", semid);

    /*Enter the number of operations.*/
    printf("\nEnter the number of semaphore\n");
    printf("operations for this set = ");
    scanf("%d", &nsops);
    printf("\nnosops = %d", nsops);

    /*Initialize the array for the
      number of operations to be performed.*/
    for(i = 0; i < nsops; i++, sops++)
    {
        /*This determines the semaphore in
          the semaphore set.*/
        printf("\nEnter the semaphore\n");
        printf("number (sem_num) = ");
        scanf("%d", &sem_num);
        sops >sem_num = sem_num;
        printf("\nThe sem_num = %d", sops >sem_num);

        /*Enter a (-)number to decrement,
          an unsigned number (no +) to increment,
          or zero to test for zero.  These values
          are entered into a string and converted
          to integer values.*/
        printf("\nEnter the operation for\n");
        printf("the semaphore (sem_op) = ");
        scanf("%s", string);
        sops >sem_op = atoi(string);
```

Figure 4.14 - Example program: Operations on semaphores using **semop** system call

```
            printf("\nsem_op = %d\n", sops >sem_op);
            /*Specify the desired flags.*/
            printf("\nEnter the corresponding\n");
            printf("number for the desired\n");
            printf("flags:\n");
            printf("No flags                    = 0\n");
            printf("IPC_NOWAIT                  = 1\n");
            printf("SEM_UNDO                    = 2\n");
            printf("IPC_NOWAIT and SEM_UNDO     = 3\n");
            printf("            Flags           = ");
            scanf("%d", &flags);

            switch(flags)
            {
            case 0:
                sops >sem_flg = 0;
                break;
            case 1:
                sops >sem_flg = IPC_NOWAIT;
                break;
            case 2:
                sops >sem_flg = SEM_UNDO;
                break;
            case 3:
                sops >sem_flg = IPC_NOWAIT | SEM_UNDO;
                break;
            }
            printf("\nFlags = 0%o\n", sops >sem_flg);
        }

        /*Print out each structure in the array.*/
        for(i = 0; i < nsops; i++)
        {
            printf("\nsem_num = %d\n", sembuf[i].sem_num);
            printf("sem_op = %d\n", sembuf[i].sem_op);
            printf("sem_flg = %o\n", sembuf[i].sem_flg);
            printf("%c", ' ');
        }

        sops = sembuf; /*Reset the pointer to
                         sembuf[0].*/

        /*Do the semop system call.*/
        retrn = semop(semid, sops, nsops);
        if(retrn ==  1)  {
            printf("\nSemop failed.  ");
            printf("Error = %d\n", errno);
        }
        else {
            printf ("\nSemop was successful\n");
            printf("for semid = %d\n", semid);

            printf("Value returned = %d\n", retrn);
        }
    }
```

Figure 4.14 - cont'd

4.6.4 Using Binary Semaphores

The fastest method of interprocess communication is shared memory (Section 4.5), where cooperating processes map the same area of memory into their address space. When one process writes to a location in the shared area, the data is immediately available to any other process that has that location mapped in its address space. The time required to access this location is no more than a normal memory reference.

When using shared memory it is important to ensure that two processes do not access the same area of memory at the same time. In addition to the UNIX System V semaphore mechanism, the REAL/IX operating system provides a binary semaphore mechanism[1] to synchronize processes sharing memory. Unlike UNIX System V semaphores which can have a large number of states, binary semaphores have only two states: locked and unlocked.

Binary semaphore operations do not access the operating system directly. Instead, a combination of test and set instructions are used to determine if a binary semaphore is available. The operating system is called only when there is contention. Most binary semaphore operations can be accomplished in about 5 microseconds, resulting in a significant performance improvement.

The system calls and routines for using binary semaphores are listed in Table 4.15.

Table 4.15
System Calls for Binary Semaphores

System Call or Command	Description
bsget(*key, bsem, bsemflg*)	get a binary semaphore.
bsfree(*bid*)	free a binary semaphore.
bslk(*bsem, bid*)	lock a binary semaphore.
bslkc(*bsem*)	conditionally lock a binary semaphore.
bsunlk(*bsem, bid*)	unlock a binary semaphore.

Binary semaphores are implemented in the following way:

1. Begin execution of the code at a non-real-time priority. In other words, do not execute **setpri** call until after the binary semaphore, shared memory segment, and any other resources being used have been preallocated.

---

[1] Note that the semaphores discussed in this section are for user-level programs. They should not be confused with the kernel semaphores used in drivers.

2. Establish a shared memory region using the **shmget** system call. **shmget** returns a unique identifier (*key*) for the region. Each binary semaphore requires 4 bytes of shared memory for its functionality. You can either allocate a one-page shared memory region for the use of the binary semaphore, or use part of the shared memory region that the binary semaphore is protecting. If the binary semaphore is protecting a resource other than a shared memory region, you must allocate a shared memory region for the binary semaphore. Several binary semaphores can share one region as long as they specify different addresses.

3. Execute the **shmat** system call to attach to the shared memory region. **shmat** returns a unique virtual address for each attach that is performed. This virtual address is associated with the physical address of the shared memory region.

4. Execute a **bsget** call to get a binary semaphore for the shared memory region. **bsget** actually creates and initializes the user-supplied binary semaphore associated with the argument *key* (this is the same *key* you used to establish the shared memory region). The argument *bsem* contains a pointer to the binary semaphore itself. Upon creation, the binary semaphore is initialized to an unlocked condition and a binary semaphore identifier and associated data structure are created for *key*.

   Note that you must have real-time or superuser privileges in order to use this service.

5. At this point, you can set the process priority to a fixed real-time priority.

6. Before reading or writing the shared memory region, lock the binary semaphore with either the **bslk** or **bslkc** routine. This will prevent another process from accessing the region until the read or write operation is completed.

7. When finished accessing the region, unlock the binary semaphore with the **bsunlk** call. **bsfree** will free the binary semaphore when it is no longer needed.

4.6.4.1 Example of Using Shared Memory with Binary Semaphores

The example programs in this section show how binary semaphores can be used to control access to a shared memory region.

Example 1: The program given in Figure 4.15 creates a shared memory region and obtains two virtual addresses by executing **shmat** twice. The binary semaphore is established and data is written to shared memory and the success of this write is confirmed by reading the data back.

```
/* binary semaphore test for 'bsget' - get a binary semaphore */

#include <stdio.h>
#include <sys/types.h>
#include <sys/signal.h>
#include <sys/ipc.h>
#include <sys/binsem.h>
#include <sys/shm.h>
#include "err_code.g"

#define NOTREALTIME 2
#define K 1024
#define key 77          /* IPC_PRIVATE is a legitimate option */

extern int errno;
extern char *shmat();
int smid,i,*bsem;
void **p;

main(argc,argv)
int argc;
char **argv;
{
   int result=0;
   char *virtaddr, *virtaddr2;
   int bsid, *pint;
   extern cleanup();

   if (argc < 2)  /* if the program is activated with no options put */
   {              /* out the help message and exit */

      printf(" usage:    bs_get  [nort]\n");
      printf(" usage:    bs_get  [setrt]\n");
      exit(0);
   }
   else

      if (!strcmp(argv[1],"setrt"))    /* set realtime privileges */
      {
         if (setrt() == -1)
         {
            printf("Set realtime privilege - setrt failed.\n");
            printf("Error code is: %s\n",err_codes(errno));
         }
         else {
            if (setpri(0,188) == -1) {
               printf("setpri: can't get realtime privileges
                  - %s\n",err_codes(errno));
               exit(1);
            } else
               printf("YES - Realtime privileges\n");
         }
      }

   if (strcmp(argv[1],"nort") == 0)     /* set user id to non-realtime */
      setuid(NOTREALTIME);
```

Figure 4.15 - Example 1: Using binary semaphores

```
   /* when a signal is received from another process, do cleanup and quit */

   if ((smid=shmget(key,4096,0777|IPC_CREAT)) == -1)
   {
      printf(" call to shmget failed, smid = %d\n",smid);
      printf(" Error code is: %s\n",err_codes(errno));
   }
   else
      printf(" call to shmget successful, smid = %d\n",smid);

   if ((int)(virtaddr=shmat(smid,0,0)) <0)
   {
      printf(" call to shmat failed, virtaddr = %d\n",(int)virtaddr);

      printf(" Error code is: %s\n",err_codes(errno));
   }
   else
      printf(" call to shmat successful, virtaddr = %d\n",(int)virtaddr);

   if ((int)(virtaddr2=shmat(smid,0,0)) <0)
   {
      printf(" call to shmat failed, virtaddr2 = %d\n",(int)virtaddr2);
      printf(" Error code is: %s\n",err_codes(errno));
   }
   else
      printf(" call to shmat successful, virtaddr2 = %d\n",(int)virtaddr2);
   /* get a binary semaphore for the shared memory return id */
   if ((bsid=bsget(key,virtaddr,0777|IPC_CREAT)) <0)
   {
      printf(" call to bsget failed, bsid = %d\n",bsid);
      printf(" Error code is: %s\n",err_codes(errno));
                  exit(1);
   }
   else
      printf(" call to bsget successful, bsid = %d\n",bsid);

   pint = (int *)(virtaddr + 4);

   /* this is how binary semaphores protect a critical region:
    * by locking a binary semaphore for this process and
    * Then, to allow other users access, it must be unlocked.
    * Note: the bslk takes the first virtual address for its own use
    */

if ( bslkc(virtaddr) != 1)
   printf(" Error code is: %s\n",err_codes(errno));
else
   bsunlk((int *)virtaddr,bsid);

bslk((int *)virtaddr,bsid);
   for (i=0; i < 256; i++)
      *pint++ = i;
   pint = (int *)(virtaddr + 4);
   *pint = 256;
bsunlk((int *)virtaddr,bsid);
```

Figure 4.15 - cont'd

```
pint = (int *)(virtaddr2 + 4);
for (i=0; i<256;i++)
   printf("index:  %d,\tvalue:  %d\n",i,*pint++);

shmdt(virtaddr);
shmdt(virtaddr2);
if (bsfree(smid)== -1) {
   printf(" Call to bsfree failed <%d>\n",bsid);
   printf(" Error code is: %s\n",err_codes(errno));
}
else
   printf(" call to bsfree successful, bsid = %d\n",bsid);
/* the first process pauses to give the second process a chance
 * to execute.
 */


pause();
   cleanup();

}

cleanup()
{
   shmctl(smid, IPC_RMID, 0);
   puts("Cleanup completed.\n");
   exit();
}
```

Figure 4.15 - cont'd

Example 2: The program in Figure 4.16 shows how another process would use binary semaphores to access the region of shared memory owned by the previous program given in Figure 4.15.

```
/* binary semaphore test for 'bsget' - get a binary semaphore */

#include <stdio.h>
#include <sys/types.h>
#include <sys/signal.h>
#include <sys/ipc.h>
#include <sys/binsem.h>
#include <sys/shm.h>
#include "err_code.g"

#define NOTREALTIME 2
extern int errno;
extern char *shmat();

main(argc,argv)
int argc;
char **argv;
{
   int i, *pint, result=0;
   int smid;
   int key=77;
   char *virtaddr;
   int *i_addr;
   int bsid;

   if (setrt() == -1)
   {
      printf("Set realtime privilege - setrt failed.\n");
      printf("Error code is: %s\n",err_codes(errno));
   }
   else {
      if (setpri(0,188) == -1) {
         printf("setpri: can't get realtime privileges

            - %s\n",err_codes(errno));
         exit(1);
      } else
         printf("YES - Realtime privileges\n");
   }
   if ((smid=shmget(key,256,0777)) == -1)
   {
      printf(" call to shmget failed, smid = %d\n",smid);
      printf(" Error code is: %s\n",err_codes(errno));
   }
   else
      printf(" call to shmget successful, smid = %d\n",smid);


   if ((virtaddr=shmat(smid,0,0)) == NULL)
   {
      printf(" NULL POINTER: call to shmat failed, virtaddr
         = %d\n",(int)virtaddr);
```

Figure 4.16 - Example 2: Using binary semaphores

```
    printf(" Error code is: %s\n",err_codes(errno));
    exit(1);
}
else
    printf(" call to shmat successful, virtaddr = %d\n",(int)virtaddr);

if ((bsid=bsget(key,(int *)virtaddr,0777|IPC_CREAT)) == -1) {
    printf("Call to bsget failed, bsid = %d\n", bsid);
    printf("Error code is: %s\n", err_codes(errno));
    exit(1);
} else
    printf("Call to bsget successful, bsid = %d\n", bsid);

/* addr to start at */
pint = (int *)(virtaddr + 4);

while (*pint == 0)
    ;
bslk((int *)virtaddr,bsid);
puts("Begin reading.\n");
for (i=0; i < 256; i++)
    printf("%d\n", *pint++);
bsunlk((int *)virtaddr,bsid);
```

Figure 4.16 - cont'd

4.7 INTERPROCESS COMMUNICATIONS USING MESSAGES

Messages are one method of coordinating access to a shared resource. They are most commonly used with shared memory but can be used for other resources as well. While binary semaphores and semaphores are faster ways of coordinating access to shared memory, messages are often easier then semaphores to implement and easier to port to other systems.

The message facility uses a message queue into which messages are sent and from which messages are received, as illustrated in Figure 4.17.

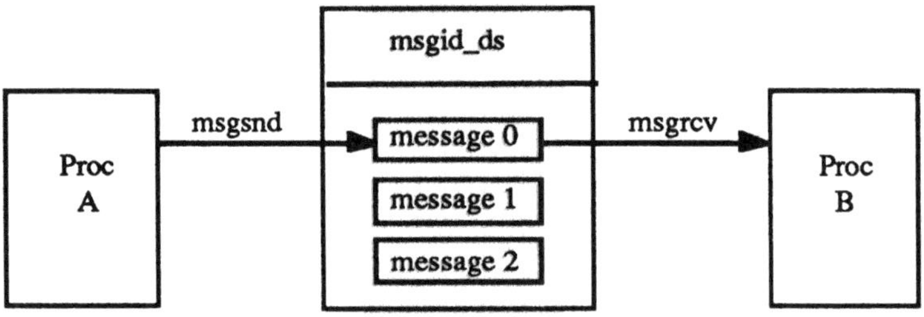

Figure 4.17 - Sending and receiving messages

The msgid_ds data structure serves as a sort of the header to the shared memory region. It contains control information (such as the number of processes attached to this region, the PID of the owner and the last operation, and the time of the last attach, detach, and control operation) as well as a structure that defines access permissions for the shared memory region.

The system calls and routines for using messages are listed in Table 4.16.

Table 4.16
System Calls for Messages

System Call	Description
msgget(*key, msgflg*)	create/get a message
msgctl(*msgid, cmd, buf*)	controlling a message
msgsnd(*msgid, msgp, msgsz, msgflg*)	send a message
msgrcv(*msgid, msgp, msgsz, msgtyp, msgflg*))	receive a message

Processes using messages can perform two operations: (a) sending, and (b) receiving a message.

Before a message can be sent or received by a process, a process must have the operating system generate the necessary software mechanisms to handle these operations. A process does this by using the **msgget** system call. While doing this, the process becomes the owner/creator of the message facility and specifies the initial operation permissions for all other processes, including itself. Subsequently, the owner/creator can relinquish ownership or change the operation permissions using the **msgctl** system call. However, the creator remains the creator as long as the facility exists. Other processes with permission can use **msgctl** to perform various other control functions.

Processes that have permission and are attempting to send or receive messages can suspend execution if they are unsuccessful at performing their operation. That is, a process attempting to send a message can wait until the process which is to receive it is ready and vice versa. A process which specifies that execution is to be suspended is performing a "blocking message operation." A process which does not allow its execution to be suspended is performing a "non-blocking message operation".

A process performing a blocking message operation can be suspended until one of three conditions occurs:

(a) It is successful.
(b) It receives a signal.
(c) The facility is removed.

System calls make these message capabilities available to processes. The calling process passes arguments to a system call and the system call either successfully or unsuccessfully performs its function. If the system call is successful, it performs its function and returns applicable information. Otherwise, a known error code (-1) is returned to the process and an external error number variable **errno** is set accordingly.

Before a message can be sent or received, a uniquely identified message queue and data structure must be created. The unique identifier created is called the message queue identifier. It is used to identify or reference the associated message queue and data structure.

4.7.1 Creating Message Queues

The **msgget** system call is used to perform two tasks when only the IPC_CREAT flag is set in the **msgflg** argument that it receives:

(1) to get a new **msgid** and create an associated message queue and data structure for it, and

(2) to return an existing **msgid** that already has an associated message queue and data structure.

The synopsis for the **msgget** system call is given as follows:

```
#include <sys/types.h>
#include <sys/ipc.h>
#include <sys/msg.h>

int msgget (key, msgflg)
key_t key;
int msgflg;
```

The **msgget** call is a function with two formal arguments that returns an integer type value on successful completion (**msgid**). The next two lines declare the types of formal arguments. **key_t** is declared by a **typedef** in the **types.h** header file to be an integer.

The task performed is determined by the value of the **key** argument passed to the **msgget** system call. For the first task, if the **key** is not already in use for an existing **msgid**, a new **msgid** is returned with an associated message queue and data structure created for the **key**. This occurs provided no system tunable parameters would be exceeded.

There is also a provision for specifying a **key** of value zero which is known as the private **key** (IPC_PRIVATE = 0). When this is specified, a new **msgid** is always returned with an associated message queue and data structure created for it unless a system tunable parameter would be exceeded. For security reasons the KEY field for the **msgid** is all zeros, when the **ipcs** command is performed.

The value passed to the **msgflg** argument must be an integer type octal value and it will specify the following:

(a) access permissions,
(b) execution modes, and
(c) control fields (commands).

Access permissions determine the read/write attributes and execution modes determine the user/group/other attributes of the **msgflg** argument. Control commands are predefined constants.

4.7.1.1 Example Program: Using the msgget System Call

The program given in Figure 4.18, illustrates the use of the **msgget** system call in creating message queues and getting messages.

Variable names have been chosen to be as close as possible to those in the synopsis for the system call. Their declarations are self-explanatory. The variable declared for this program and their purposes are as follows:

- **key** - used to pass the value for the desired **key.**
- **opperm** - used to store the desired operation permissions.
- **flags** - used to store the desired control commands (flags).
- **opperm_flags** - used to store the combination from the logical ORing of the **opperm** and **flags** variables. It is then used in the system call to pass the **msgflg** argument.
- **msgid** - used for returning the message queue identification number for a successful system call or the error code (-1) for an unsuccessful one.

The program begins by prompting for a hexadecimal **key**, an octal operation permissions code, and finally for the control command combinations (flags) which are selected from a menu (lines 15-32). All possible combinations are allowed even though they might not be valid. This allows observing for illegal combinations.

Next, the menu selection for the flags is combined with the operation permissions and the result is stored at the address of the **opperm_flags** variable (lines 36-51).

The system call is made next, and the result is stored at the address of the **msgid** variable (line 53).

Since the **msgid** variable now contains a valid message queue identifier or the error code (-1), it is tested to see if an error occurred (line 44). If **msgid** equals -1, a message indicates that an error resulted and the external **errno** variable is displayed (lines 57, 58).

If no error occurred, the returned message queue identifier is displayed (line 62).

```
/*This is a program to illustrate
**the message get, msgget(),
**system call capabilities.*/

#include    <stdio.h>
#include    <sys/types.h>
#include    <sys/ipc.h>
#include    <sys/msg.h>
#include    <errno.h>

/*Start of main C language program*/
main()

{
    key_t key;              /*declare as long integer*/
    int opperm, flags;
    int msqid, opperm_flags;
    /*Enter the desired key*/
    printf("Enter the desired key in hex = ");
    scanf("%x", &key);

    /*Enter the desired octal operation
      permissions.*/
    printf("\nEnter the operation\n");
    printf("permissions in octal = ");
    scanf("%o", &opperm);

    /*Set the desired flags.*/
    printf("\nEnter corresponding number to\n");
    printf("set the desired flags:\n");
    printf("No flags                     = 0\n");
    printf("IPC_CREAT                    = 1\n");
    printf("IPC_EXCL                     = 2\n");
    printf("IPC_CREAT and IPC_EXCL       = 3\n");
    printf("            Flags            = ");

    /*Get the flag(s) to be set.*/
    scanf("%d", &flags);
    /*Check the values.*/
    printf ("\nkey =0x%x, opperm = 0%o, flags = 0%o\n",
        key, opperm, flags);

    /*Incorporate the control fields (flags) with
      the operation permissions*/
    switch (flags)
    {
    case 0:    /*No flags are to be set.*/
        opperm_flags = (opperm | 0);
        break;
    case 1:    /*Set the IPC_CREAT flag.*/
        opperm_flags = (opperm | IPC_CREAT);
        break;
    case 2:    /*Set the IPC_EXCL flag.*/
        opperm_flags = (opperm | IPC_EXCL);
        break;
```

Figure 4.18 - Example program: Creating message queue with the **msgget** system call

```
        case 3:    /*Set the IPC_CREAT and IPC_EXCL flags.*/
            opperm_flags = (opperm | IPC_CREAT | IPC_EXCL);
        }

        /*Call the msgget system call.*/
        msqid = msgget (key, opperm_flags);

        /*Perform the following if the call is unsuccessful.*/
        if(msqid ==  1)
        {
            printf ("\nThe msgget system call failed!\n");
            printf ("The error number = %d\n", errno);
        }

        /*Return the msqid on successful completion.*/
        else
            printf ("\nThe msqid = %d\n", msqid);
        exit(0);
    }
```

Figure 4.18 - cont'd

4.7.2 Controlling Message Queues

Message control is done by using the **msgctl** system call. It permits you to control the message facility in the following ways:

(a) to determine the associated data structure status for a message queue identifier (**msgid**),

(b) to change operation permissions for a message queue,

(c) to change the size (**msg_qbytes**) of the message queue for a particular **msgid**, and

(d) to remove a particular **msgid** from the operating system along with its associated message queue and data structure.

The synopsis for the **msgctl** system call is as follows:

```
#include <sys/types.h>
#include <sys/ipc.h>
#include <sys/msg.h>

int msgctl (msgid, cmd, buf
int msgid, cmd;
struct msgid_ds *buf;
```

The **msgctl** system call requires three arguments to be passed to it, then it returns an integer value.

On successful completion, a zero value is returned. When unsuccessful, a -1 is returned.

The **msgid** variable must be a valid, non-negative integer value. In other words, it must have already been created by using the **msgget** system call.

The **cmd** argument can be replaced by one of the following control commands (flags):

IPC_STAT return the status information contained in the associated data structure for the specified **msgid** and place it in the data structure pointed to by the ***buf** pointer in the user memory area.

IPC_SET for the specified **msgid**, set the effective user and group identification, operation permissions, and the number of bytes for the message queue.

IPC_RMID — remove the specified **msgid** along with its associated message queue and data structure.

A process must have an effective user identification of OWNER/CREATOR or superuser to perform an IPC_SET or IPC_RMID control command. Read permission is required to perform the IPC_STAT control command.

4.7.2.1 Example Program: Using the msgctl System Call

The program shown in Figure 4.19 illustrates the use of the **msgctl** system call in controlling message queues.

uid — used to store the IPC_SET value for the effective user identification.

gid — used to store the IPC_SET value for the effective group identification.

mode — used to store the IPC_SET value for the operation permissions.

bytes — used to store the IPC_SET value for the number of bytes in the message queue (msg_qbytes).

rtrn — used to store the return integer value from the system call.

msgid — used to store and pass the message queue identifier to the system call.

command — used to store the code for the desired control command so that subsequent processing can be performed on it.

choice — used to determine which member is to be changed for the IPCS_SET control command.

msgid_ds — used to receive the specified message queue identifier's data structure when an IPC_STAT control command is performed.

buf — a pointer passed to the system call which locates the data structure in the user memory area where the IPC_STAT control command is to place its return values or where the IPC_SET command gets the values to set.

First, the program prompts for a valid message queue identifier which is stored at the address of the **msgid** variable (lines 19, 20). This is required for every **msgctl** system call.

Then the code for the desired control command must be entered (lines 21-27) and stored at the address of the command variable. The code is tested to determine the control command for subsequent processing.

If the IPC_STAT control command is selected (code 1), the system call is performed (lines 37, 38) and the status information returned is printed out (lines 39-46). Only the members that can be set are printed out in this program. Note that if the system call is unsuccessful (line 106), the status information of the last successful call is printed out. In addition, an error message is displayed and the **errno** variable is printed out (lines 108, 109). If the system call is successful, a message indicates this along with the message queue identifier used (lines 111-114).

If the IPC_SET control command is selected (code 2), the first step is to get the current status information for the message queue identifier specified (lines 50-52). This is necessary because this example program provides for changing only one member at a time and the system call changes all of them. Also, if an invalid value happened to be stored in the user memory area for one of these members, it would cause repetitive failures for this control command until the condition was corrected. The next thing the program does is to prompt for a code corresponding to the member to be changed (lines 53-59). This code is stored at the address of the choice variable (line 60).

Now, depending on the member picked, the program prompts for the new value (lines 66-95). The value is placed at the address of the appropriate member in the user memory area data structure, and the system call is made (lines 96-98). The program returns the same messages as for IPC_STAT above.

If the IPC_RMID control command (code 3) is selected, the system call is performed (lines 100-103) and the **msgid** along with its associated message queue and data structure are removed from the operating system. Note that the *buf pointer is not required as an argument to perform this control command and its value can be zero or NULL. The program returns the same messages as for the other control commands.

```
/*This is a program to illustrate
**the message control, msgctl(),
**system call capabilities.
*/

/*Include necessary header files.*/
#include    <stdio.h>
#include    <sys/types.h>
#include    <sys/ipc.h>
#include    <sys/msg.h>

/*Start of main C language program*/
main()
{
    extern int errno;
    int uid, gid, mode, bytes;
    int rtrn, msqid, command, choice;
    struct msqid_ds msqid_ds, *buf;
    buf = &msqid_ds;

    /*Get the msqid, and command.*/
    printf("Enter the msqid = ");
    scanf("%d", &msqid);
    printf("\nEnter the number for\n");
    printf("the desired command:\n");
    printf("IPC_STAT    =  1\n");
    printf("IPC_SET     =  2\n");
    printf("IPC_RMID    =  3\n");
    printf("Entry       =  ");
    scanf("%d", &command);

    /*Check the values.*/
    printf ("\nmsqid =%d, command = %d\n",
        msqid, command);
    switch (command)
    {
    case 1:    /*Use msgctl() to duplicate
          the data structure for
                   msqid  in the msqid_ds area pointed
                  to by buf and then print it out.*/
        rtrn = msgctl(msqid, IPC_STAT,
            buf);
        printf ("\nThe USER ID = %d\n",
            buf >msg_perm.uid);
        printf ("The GROUP ID = %d\n",
            buf >msg_perm.gid);
        printf ("The operation permissions = 0%o\n",
            buf >msg_perm.mode);
        printf ("The msg_qbytes = %d\n",
            buf >msg_qbytes);
        break;
    case 2:    /*Select and change the desired
                  member(s) of the data structure.*/
        /*Get the original data for this msqid
             data structure first.*/
```

Figure 4.19 - Example program: Controlling message queues using the msgctl system call

```
        rtrn =  msgctl (msqid, IPC_STAT, buf);
        printf("\nEnter the number for the\n");
        printf("member to be changed:\n");
        printf("msg_perm.uid   = 1\n");
        printf("msg_perm.gid   = 2\n");
        printf("msg_perm.mode  = 3\n");
        printf("msg_qbytes     = 4\n");
        printf("Entry          = ");

        scanf("%d", &choice);
        /*Only one choice is allowed per
          pass as an illegal entry will
              cause repetitive failures until
          msqid_ds is updated with
              IPC_STAT.*/
        switch(choice){
        case 1:
            printf("\nEnter USER ID = ");
            scanf ("%d", &uid);
            buf >msg_perm.uid = uid;
            printf("\nUSER ID = %d\n",
                buf >msg_perm.uid);
            break;
        case 2:
            printf("\nEnter GROUP ID = ");
            scanf("%d", &gid);
            buf >msg_perm.gid = gid;
            printf("\nGROUP ID = %d\n",
                buf >msg_perm.gid);
            break;
        case 3:
            printf("\nEnter MODE = ");
            scanf("%o", &mode);
            buf >msg_perm.mode = mode;
            printf("\nMODE = 0%o\n",
                buf >msg_perm.mode);
            break;

        case 4:
            printf("\nEnter msq_bytes = ");
            scanf("%d", &bytes);
            buf >msg_qbytes = bytes;
            printf("\nmsg_qbytes = %d\n",
                buf >msg_qbytes);
            break;
        }
        /*Do the change.*/
        rtrn = msgctl(msqid, IPC_SET,
            buf);
        break;

    case 3:    /*Remove the msqid along with its
                   associated message queue
                   and data structure.*/
        rtrn = msgctl(msqid, IPC_RMID, NULL);
```

Figure 4.19 - cont'd

```
        }
        /*Perform the following if the call is unsuccessful.*/
        if(rtrn ==  1)
        {
            printf ("\nThe msgctl system call failed!\n");
            printf ("The error number = %d\n", errno);
        }
        /*Return the msqid on successful completion.*/
        else
            printf ("\nMsgctl was successful for msqid = %d\n",
                msqid);
        exit (0);
    }
```

Figure 4.19 - cont'd

4.7.3 Message Operations

Message operations consist of sending and receiving messages. System calls for these operations are **msgsnd** and **msgrcv**.

The synopses for these two operations are given as follows:

```
#include <sys/types.h>
#include <sys/ipc.h>
#include <sys/msg.h>

int msgsnd (msgid, msgp, msgsz, msgflg)
int msgid;
struct msgbuf *msgp;
int msgsz, msgflg;

int msgrcv (msgid, msgp, msgsz, msgtyp, msgflg)
int msgid;
struct msgbuf *msgp;
int msgsz;
long msgtyp;
int msgflg;
```

Sending a Message

The **msgsnd** system call requires four arguments to be passed to it. It returns an integer value.

Upon successful completion, a zero value is returned. When unsuccessful, **msgsnd** returns a -1.

The **msgid** argument is a pointer to a structure in the user memory area that contains the type of the message and the message to be sent.

The **msgp** argument is a pointer to a structure in the user memory area that will receive the message type and the message text.

The **msgsz** argument specifies the length of the message to be received. If its value is less than the message in the array, an error can be returned if desired. See the **msgflg** argument for details.

The **msgtyp** argument is used to pick the first message on the message queue of the particular type specified. If it is equal to zero, the first message on the queue is received. If it is greater than zero, the first message of the same type is received. If it is less than zero, the lowest type that is less than or equal to its absolute value is received.

The **msgflg** argument allows the "blocking message operation" to be performed if the IPC_NOWAIT flag is not set (**msgflg** & IPC_NOWAIT = 0). This condition would occur if there were no messages on the message queue of the desired type (**msgtyp**) to be received. If the IPC_NOWAIT flag is set and there is no message of the desired type on the queue, the system call will fail immediately. **msgflg** can also specify that the system call fail if the message is longer than the size to be received. This can be accomplished by not setting the MSG_NOERROR flag in the **msgflg** argument (**msgflg** & MSG_NOERROR = 0). If the MSG_NOERROR flag is set, the message is truncated to the length specified by the **msgsz** argument of **msgrcv**.

4.7.3.1 Example Program: Using the **msgsnd** and **msgrcv** System Calls

The example program in Figure 4.20 in this section is a menu-driven program which allows all possible combinations of using the **msgsnd** and **msgrcv** system calls to be exercised.

sndbuf — used as a buffer to contain a message to be sent (line 13). It uses the **msgbuf1** data structure as a template (lines 10-13). The **msgbuf1** structure (lines 10-13) is almost an exact duplicate of the **msgbuf** structure contained in the **msg.h** header file. The only difference is that the character array for **msgbuf1** contains the maximum message size (MSGMAX) for the computer where in **msgbuf** it is set to one (1) to satisfy the compiler. For this reason **msgbuf** cannot be used directly as a template for the user-written program. It is there to enable the user to determine its members.

rcvbuf — used as a buffer to receive a message (line 13). It uses the **msgbuf1** data structure as a template (lines 10-13).

***msgp** — used as a pointer (line 13) to both the **sndbuf** and **rcvbuf** buffers.

i — used as a counter for inputting characters from the keyboard, storing them in the array, and keeping track of the message length for the **msgsnd** system call. It is also used as a counter to output the received message for the **msgrcv** system call.

c — used to receive the input character from the **getchar** function (line 50).

flag — used to store the code of IPC_NOWAIT for the **msgsnd** system call (line 61).

flags used to store the code of the IPC_NOWAIT or MSG_NOERROR flags for the **msgrcv** system call (line 117).

choice used to store the code for sending or receiving (line 30).

rtrn used to store the return values from all system calls.

msgud used to store and pass the desired message queue identifier for both system calls.

msgsx used to store and pass the size of the message to be sent or received.

msgflg used to pass the value of flags for sending or the value of flags for receiving.

msgtyp used for specifying the message type for sending, or used to pick a message type for receiving.

Note that a **msgid_ds** data structure is set up in the program (line 21) with a pointer which is initialized to point to it (line 22). This will allow the data structure members that are affected by message operations to be observed. They are observed by using the **msgctl** (IPC_STAT) system call to get them for the program and to print them out (lines 80-92 and lines 161-168).

The first thing the program prompts for is whether to send or receive a message. A corresponding code must be entered for the desired operation. This code is stored at the address of the choice variable (lines 23-30). Depending on the code, the program proceeds as in the following **msgsnd** or **msgrcv** sections.

msgsnd

When the code is to send a message, the **msgp** pointer is initialized (line 33) to the address of the send data structure, **sndbuf**. Next, a message type must be entered for the message. It is stored at the address of the variable **msgtyp** (line 42) and is then (line 43) put into the **mtype** member of the data structure pointed to by **msgp**.

The program now prompts for a message to be entered from the keyboard and enters a loop of getting and storing into the **mtext** array of the data structure (lines 48-51). This will continue until an end of file is recognized, which for the **getchar** function is a control-d (CTRL-D) immediately following a carriage return (<CR>). When this happens, the size of the message is determined by adding one to the i counter (lines 52, 53). This is required since the message was stored beginning in the zero array element of **mtext**. The message as defined by **msgsz** also contains the terminating characters and the size defined here will appear to be three characters short of **msgsz**.

The message is immediately echoed from the **mtext** array of the **sndbuf** data structure to provide feedback (lines 54-56).

The final issue to be decided is whether to set the IPC_NOWAIT flag. The program does this by requesting that a code of 1 be entered for yes or any other value for no (lines 57-65). It is stored at the address of the flag variable. If a 1 is entered, IPC_NOWAIT is logically OR'd with **msgflg**. Otherwise, **msgflg** is set to zero.

The **msgsnd** system call is performed (69). If it is unsuccessful, a failure message is displayed along with the error number (lines 70-72). If it is successful, the returned value (which should be zero) is printed (lines 73-76).

Every time a message is successfully set, there are three members of the associated data structure which are updated. They are described as follows:

msg_qnum represents the total number of messages on the message queue. It is incremented by one.

msg_lspid contains the Process Identification (PID) number of the last process sending a message. It is set accordingly.

msg_stime contains the time in seconds since January 1, 1970, Greenwich Mean Time (GMT) of the last message sent. It is set accordingly.

These members are displayed after every successful message send operation (lines 79-92).

msgrcv

If the code specifies that a message is to be received, the program continues execution as in the following paragraphs. The **msgp** pointer is initialized to the **rcvbuf** data structure (line 99).

Next, the message queue identifier of the message queue from which to receive the message is requested and it is stored at the address of **msquid** (lines 100-103).

The message type is requested and is stored at the address of **msgtyp** (lines 104-107).

The code for the desired combination of control flags is requested next and is stored at the address of flags (lines 108-117). Depending on the selected combination, **msgflg** is set accordingly (lines 118-133).

Finally, the number of bytes to be received is requested and is stored at the address of **msgsz** (lines 134-137).

The **msgrcv** system call is performed (line 144). If it is unsuccessful, a message and error number is displayed (lines 145-148). If successful, a message so indicates and the number of bytes returned is displayed followed by the received message (lines 153-159).

When a message is successfully received, three members of the associated data structure are updated as follows:

msg_qnum contains the number of messages on the message queue. It is decremented by one.

msg_lrpid contains the process identification (PID) of the last process receiving a message. It is set accordingly.

msg_rtime contains the time in seconds since January 1, 1970, Greenwich Mean Time (GMT) that the last process received a message. It is set accordingly.

```
/*This is a program to illustrate
**the message operations, msgop(),
**system call capabilities..
*/

/*Include necessary header files.*/
#include    <stdio.h>
#include    <sys/types.h>
#include    <sys/ipc.h>
#include    <sys/msg.h>

struct msgbuf1 {
    long    mtype;
    char    mtext[8192];
} sndbuf, rcvbuf, *msgp;

/*Start of main C language program*/
main()
{
    extern int errno;
    int i, c, flag, flags, choice;
    int rtrn, msqid, msgsz, msgflg;
    long mtype, msgtyp;
    struct msqid_ds msqid_ds, *buf;
    buf = &msqid_ds;

    /*Select the desired operation.*/
    printf("Enter the corresponding\n");
    printf("code to send or\n");

    printf("receive a message:\n");
    printf("Send            =  1\n");
    printf("Receive         =  2\n");
    printf("Entry           =  ");
    scanf("%d", &choice);
    if(choice == 1) /*Send a message.*/
    {
        msgp = &sndbuf; /*Point to user send structure.*/

        printf("\nEnter the msqid of\n");
        printf("the message queue to\n");
        printf("handle the message = ");
        scanf("%d", &msqid);

        /*Set the message type.*/
        printf("\nEnter a positive integer\n");
        printf("message type (long) for the\n");
        printf("message = ");
        scanf("%d", &msgtyp);
        msgp >mtype = msgtyp;

        /*Enter the message to send.*/
        printf("\nEnter a message: \n");

        /*A control-d (^d) terminates as
          EOF.*/
```

Figure 4.20 - Example program: Message operations using the **msgsnd** and **msgrcv** system calls

```
        /*Get each character of the message
          and put it in the mtext array.*/
        for(i = 0; ((c = getchar()) != EOF); i++)
            sndbuf.mtext[i] = c;

        /*Determine the message size.*/
        msgsz = i + 1;

        /*Echo the message to send.*/
        for(i = 0; i < msgsz; i++)
            putchar(sndbuf.mtext[i]);

        /*Set the IPC_NOWAIT flag if
          desired.*/
        printf("\nEnter a 1 if you want the\n");
        printf("the IPC_NOWAIT flag set:  ");
        scanf("%d", &flag);
        if(flag == 1)
            msgflg |= IPC_NOWAIT;
        else
            msgflg = 0;
        /*Check the msgflg.*/
        printf("\nmsgflg = 0%o\n", msgflg);

        /*Send the message.*/
        rtrn = msgsnd(msqid, msgp, msgsz, msgflg);
        if(rtrn ==  1)
        printf("\nMsgsnd failed.  Error = %d\n",
                errno);
        else {
            /*Print the value of test which
                  should be zero for successful.*/
            printf("\nValue returned = %d\n", rtrn);

            /*Print the size of the message
              sent.*/
            printf("\nMsgsz = %d\n", msgsz);

            /*Check the data structure update.*/
            msgctl(msqid, IPC_STAT, buf);

            /*Print out the affected members.*/

            /*Print the incremented number of
              messages on the queue.*/
            printf("\nThe msg_qnum = %d\n",
                buf >msg_qnum);
            /*Print the process id of the last sender.*/
            printf("The msg_lspid = %d\n",
                buf >msg_lspid);
            /*Print the last send time.*/
            printf("The msg_stime = %d\n",
                buf >msg_stime);
        }
    }
```

Figure 4.20 - cont'd

```
        if(choice == 2)  /*Receive a message.*/
        {
            /*Initialize the message pointer
              to the receive buffer.*/
            msgp = &rcvbuf;
            /*Specify the message queue which contains
                   the desired message.*/
            printf("\nEnter the msqid = ");
            scanf("%d", &msqid);

            /*Specify the specific message on the queue
                  by using its type.*/
            printf("\nEnter the msgtyp = ");
            scanf("%d", &msgtyp);

            /*Configure the control flags for the
                  desired actions.*/
            printf("\nEnter the corresponding code\n");
            printf("to select the desired flags: \n");
            printf("No flags                       =  0\n");
            printf("MSG_NOERROR                    =  1\n");
            printf("IPC_NOWAIT                     =  2\n");
            printf("MSG_NOERROR and IPC_NOWAIT     =  3\n");
            printf("                    Flags      =  ");
            scanf("%d", &flags);
            switch(flags) {
                /*Set msgflg by ORing it with the appropriate
                          flags (constants).*/
            case 0:
                msgflg = 0;
                break;
            case 1:
                msgflg |= MSG_NOERROR;
                break;
            case 2:
                msgflg |= IPC_NOWAIT;
                break;
            case 3:
                msgflg |= MSG_NOERROR | IPC_NOWAIT;
                break;
            }

            /*Specify the number of bytes to receive.*/
            printf("\nEnter the number of bytes\n");
            printf("to receive (msgsz) = ");
            scanf("%d", &msgsz);

            /*Check the values for the arguments.*/
            printf("\nmsqid =%d\n", msqid);
            printf("\nmsgtyp = %d\n", msgtyp);
            printf("\nmsgsz = %d\n", msgsz);
            printf("\nmsgflg = 0%o\n", msgflg);

            /*Call msgrcv to receive the message.*/
            rtrn = msgrcv(msqid, msgp, msgsz, msgtyp, msgflg);
```

Figure 4.20 - cont'd

```
            if(rtrn ==  1)  {
                printf("\nMsgrcv failed.  ");
                printf("Error = %d\n", errno);
            }
            else {
                printf ("\nMsgctl was successful\n");
                printf("for msqid = %d\n",
                    msqid);

                /*Print the number of bytes received,
                  it is equal to the return
                  value.*/
                printf("Bytes received = %d\n", rtrn);

                /*Print the received message.*/
                for(i = 0; i<=rtrn; i++)
                    putchar(rcvbuf.mtext[i]);
            }
            /*Check the associated data structure.*/
            msgctl(msqid, IPC_STAT, buf);
            /*Print the decremented number of messages.*/
            printf("\nThe msg_qnum = %d\n", buf >msg_qnum);
            /*Print the process id of the last receiver.*/
            printf("The msg_lrpid = %d\n", buf >msg_lrpid);

            /*Print the last message receive time*/
            printf("The msg_rtime = %d\n", buf >msg_rtime);
        }
    }
```

Figure 4.20 - cont'd

4.8 USING FILES

As discussed in Section 3.6, on file subsystems, the REAL/IX operating system provides enhancements to the UNIX System V file system which increases the performance of applications.

This section describes how to use these enhancements in real-time applications. The following topics are presented: (a) the REAL/IX fast file system (F5), (b) preallocation of file space and contiguous files, (c) bypassing the buffer cache and increasing performance of individual I/O operations, and (d) asynchronous file I/O.

4.8.1 Fast File System

UNIX operating systems organize data into file systems. Each file system has a superblock, which describes the file system to the operating system. Internally, the file system is held together by a series of inodes, one for each file in the file system. Inodes contain information such as access permissions for the file and pointers to the data blocks for the files. All allocated inodes are stored together in a list following the superblock in the file system.

User-level programs access files through system calls (which may be accessed through library routines). These calls go through the file system and (if so programmed) the system buffer cache. Below the buffer cache, the I/O subsystem handles the interaction with the disk device where the file data is stored.

The REAL/IX operating system supports two file system architectures, referred to as S5 and F5 (see Section 3.6). The S5 architecture is the same as the file system structure in UNIX System V and can be used with applications that depend on that file system structure. The F5 file system contains internal enhancements to reduce file access times for both real-time and time-sharing programs that do not depend on the internal structure of the file system. In addition, the F5 file system provides the following features:

(a) The ability to preallocate contiguous file space, called extents,
(b) Support for I/O operations that bypass the buffer cache, and
(c) Support for asynchronous I/O operations.

To access a file, the program issues either an **open** or **creat** system call, each of which takes a file pathname as an argument. If successful, these system calls return a file descriptor which represents a slot in the system's file descriptor table. All subsequent I/O operations use the file descriptor (fildes) to identify the file. The file descriptor remains associated with the file until the process terminates or explicitly closes the file. More than one process can open the same file. Each process will have a different file descriptor associated with the file.

4.8.2 Creating Files and File Systems

Real-time applications that have file access requirements should use dedicated file systems that can be optimized for the needs of the application. The following steps are recommended in creating file systems for a real-time application:

(1) Use the F5 file system architecture unless the application depends on the internal S5 architecture.

(2) Select a logical block size for the file system that is ideal for the most critical files. REAL/IX file systems can use logical block sizes ranging from 1K to 128K, with corresponding buffers in the system buffer cache. The operating system transfers data one logical block at a time. Consequently, an 8000 byte file requires 8 I/O operations to perform a read or write operation if the file system uses 1K logical blocks, but only one operation if the file system uses 8K or larger logical blocks. Since disk and memory resources are wasted, using unnecessarily large logical blocks may hurt system performance.

(3) Configure the buffer cache to have an adequate number of buffers the same size or larger than the logical block size of the file system.

(4) While file system data blocks and physical disk blocks can be preallocated for the specific application, buffers cannot be preallocated. The buffer cache should be configured to prevent contention with less critical processes. For instance, if the critical application uses an 8K file system and a less critical application uses 4K logical blocks, be sure to configure an adequate number of 4K buffers. Otherwise, I/O operations on the 4K file system may use the 8K buffers.

(5) The partitions in the center of the disks provide the most efficient access. File systems dedicated to real-time applications should be located here.

4.8.3 Preallocating File Space

UNIX operating systems do not require that files be created with an initial allocation. In fact, on most UNIX systems, initial file allocation is not possible. Rather, a file is created when opened for writing for the first time and space for the data is allocated one block at a time as writes are done to the file. As a file expands, free blocks are allocated for the file and associated with the file's inode. As the file shrinks, data blocks that are no longer needed are deallocated from the file and made available to other files in the file system. This conserves space in the file system, since the maximum waste for each file is less than the size of one logical block.

The drawback of the standard scheme is that executing processes must absorb the overhead of allocating and deallocating data storage blocks for their files. Further, blocks associated with a file may be scattered around the disk resulting in increased file access times. This overhead is not excessive for most standard applications, but may be unacceptable for critical real-time processes. For this reason, the F5 file system architecture allows up to four *extents* to be allocated for each file. An extent is a chunk of contiguous data blocks that are preallocated when the file is created.

In addition to the data block address array discussed above, inodes for files in F5 file systems have an extent list. An extent is a set of preallocated, contiguous data blocks. The operating system does not impose a limit on the number of data blocks that can be allocated to one extent beyond the limit of the size of the file system. In other words, the operating system will allow the creation of a file system that contains one file with one extent that contains all the data storage blocks allocated for the file system.

Contiguous file space is preallocated using the **prealloc** command or **prealloc** system call.

For F5 file systems, a bitmap of all free data blocks in the file system is stored outside the super block. To allocate data blocks for a file, the operating system can quickly search this bitmap to identify free data blocks. This speeds data block allocation for all files and enables the operating system to quickly identify contiguous blocks available to be allocated for extents.

Statistical information about files in the F5 file system is returned by the **estat** and **efstat** system calls (similar to that returned by the **stat** and **fstat** system calls for S5 file systems). This information includes file size and number of links, as well as information on the extents.

Files in an F5 file system can be truncated using the **trunc** system call. This call writes zeros (unless otherwise stated) to all physical space remaining after the newly specified logical end of file. The file must be open for writing or **trunc** will fail.

4.8.4 Bypassing the Buffer Cache

Unless otherwise specified, file I/O operations use the system buffer cache as an intermediate storage area between user address space and the device itself. For instance, when writing a file, the data is actually written to the buffer cache. The operating system periodically flushes the contents of the buffer cache to the disk. Each buffer has a buffer header associated with it that holds the control information about the buffer such as the block and file system for this data. This buffering scheme is defined in the *buf.h* header file. The system buffer cache has a tunable number of buffers and buffer headers and a tunable number of hash slots for the buffer cache.

Use of the buffer cache has significant advantages for general applications but it also has disadvantages for some real-time applications. Consequently, the REAL/IX operating system provides the capability of bypassing the buffer cache by setting a file control (**fcntl**) command on the file descriptor. I/O operations that bypass the buffer cache transfer information between user address space and the device without leaving the data in the buffer cache.

There are two cases in which a bypass of the buffer cache may be useful:

(a) when the order of the actual writes to disk is important, and

(b) when asynchronous I/O is used on the file. In this case the buffer cache must be bypassed.

The latter case also reduces the chance of inconsistent results if both synchronous and asynchronous requests are used simultaneously on the same file.

4.8.5 Asynchronous File I/O

Most UNIX kernels support only synchronous I/O operations, meaning that any I/O operation issued by a process causes that process to block until the I/O operation is complete. A real-time application needs the capability of overlapping I/O operations with process execution. The REAL/IX operating system supports asynchronous I/O operations for files and devices. This capability enables the process that initiated the I/O operation to continue the process execution stream once the I/O operation is queued to the device. When the I/O operation completes (either successfully or unsuccessfully), the initiating process is notified with either the common event notification mechanism or by polling a control block. This polling option saves the overhead of a system call.

The ability to overlap application processing and I/O operations initiated by the application program and the ability to allow one process to simultaneously perform several separate I/O operations is required by a number of real-time applications. For instance, journalizing functions must be able to queue logging records for output without blocking the initiating process. Often, data acquisition processes have two or more channels delivering intermittent data that must be read within a certain time. The process issues one asynchronous read on each channel. When one of the channels needs data collection, the process reads the data and posts it to secondary memory with an asynchronous write.

The REAL/IX system provides facilities for asynchronous read and write operations, and the ability to cancel an asynchronous I/O request. There are also option initialization services that speed I/O throughput by preallocating and initializing various data structures.

The REAL/IX implementation of asynchronous I/O provides the following capabilities:

- Asynchronous I/O requests can be issued for both regular files and I/O devices.

- Multiple asynchronous read and write operations can be simultaneously queued to one file descriptor.

- One process can queue asynchronous read and write operations to several open file descriptors.

- Asynchronous I/O operations to the extended portion of extent-based files can bypass the buffer cache, which further improves I/O throughput. Unbuffered I/O functionality is implemented in the inode associated with a file descriptor, using **fcntl** requests. Unbuffered I/O can be emulated when required.

- Pending asynchronous I/O requests can be canceled.

- Notification of asynchronous I/O completion is optional. If used, notification can be obtained through either polling or the common event notification method.

- Asynchronous I/O operations can be used with both sequential and random access devices.

- One driver and its associated devices can support both synchronous and asynchronous read and write operations.

When a user process wishes to issue a request that will generate notification of completion, an asynchronous I/O control block (aiocb) structure must be established. This structure contains information to control the I/O operation, such as where to position the file pointer in a file and whether to post an event to the sending process when the I/O operation completes. When the I/O operation completes, the aiocb structure is updated, indicating either that the operation was successful or to pass the appropriate error code.

To code an asynchronous I/O operation in a user-level application program, the following steps are required.

1. Use the **open** system call to open the file and get a file descriptor (*fildes*):

```
desc1 = int open (/fsys/stats, O_RDWR | O_CREAT)
```

2. Use the **evget** system call to initialize an event identifier (eid) if you want to be notified when the asynchronous I/O operation completes. Completion events can be received either synchronously or asynchronously:

- To receive the event synchronously:

```
eid1=evget(EVT_QUEUE,0,0,0)
evrcv(0,eid1)
```

Alternately, **evrcvl** can be used, to receive the events only from the specified *evl* list.

- To receive the event asynchronously:

```
func {
      [code event-handling function]
}
void sigset(SIGTERM, func)
eid2=evget(EVT_QUEUE,0,SIGTERM,0)
```

3. Populate an aiocb structure:

```
struct aiocb aiocb;

     aiocb1.offset=0;
     aiocb1.whence=1;
     aiocb1.rt_errno=0;
     aiocb1.nobytes=0;
     aiocb1.aioflag=0;
     aiocb1.eid=1;
```

4. Issue the **arinit** or **awinit** system call to preallocate internal resources for the asynchronous I/O operation. This step is optional, but will significantly improve the speed of subsequent read or write operations:

```
arinit(desc1, , ,&aiocb1)
```

5. If you want requests that cannot be done asynchronously to be done in emulation mode (rather than fail) or to bypass the buffer cache, use **fcntl**.

```
fcntl(desc1,F_SETAIOEMUL,1)        /* set AIO emulation */
fcntl(desc1,F_SETBYBCACHE, 1)      /* bypass buffer cache */
```

6. Issue the **aread** or **awrite** call to request the asynchronous I/O transfer:

```
aread(fildes1, , ,&aiocb1)
```

4.8.6 Using Both Synchronous and Asynchronous I/O on a File

It is possible for both synchronous and asynchronous operations to be requested on the same file. However, the system does not guarantee consistency in these cases. For example, a synchronous read operation might request data to be read from blocks 4 and 5 of a particular file. Block 4 is read from the disk, but before block 5 is read, an asynchronous write operation updates both blocks 4 and 5. The end result is that the read operation collects a mixture of old and new data.

Synchronous reads and writes are atomic with respect to other synchronous reads and writes. Likewise, asynchronous reads and writes are atomic with respect to other asynchronous operations. However, synchronous and asynchronous operations are not atomic with respect to each other. This discussion leads to some practical advice: avoid mixing synchronous and asynchronous operations on the same file.

It is a property (undocumented and not guaranteed) of UNIX System V that reads and writes are atomic. That is, once an operation which requires access to several disk blocks has started, other reads or writes to the file are delayed until the first one finishes. Very few programs should know or care about the atomic nature of I/O operations.

4.8.7 Synchronizing Disk Access

The file subsystem must be able to handle several simultaneous processes that access different files. To do this, the system keeps a cache of free blocks and inodes in memory along with the super block. When the user writes a file, he actually writes to these blocks. Synchronization is the process by which the contents of these blocks are written to the actual device.

For most file systems, these disk buffers (along with super blocks and updated inodes) are flushed to the disk devices by the **sync** command every 30 seconds (the time between synchronizations is determined by the NAUTOUP kernel parameter). This synchronization process is not related directly to any reads or writes of user processes. Note that, if the system crashes in that small interval before **sync** executes, the data may be lost even though the write operations appeared to complete successfully. As long as the value of the NAUTOUP parameter is kept so that **sync** runs frequently, the odds of actually losing data in this way are quite small. Note, however, that a high-priority real-time process may prevent **sync** from running.

The REAL/IX operating system also allows the programmer to mount some file systems as "synchronous file systems". For synchronous file systems, each write operation writes to the cache, then immediately writes the data blocks and the updated inode to the device. Synchronous file systems should be used only for applications in which the immediate updating of the file is critical. An example is a process control data acquisition system that gathers statistics and has some real-time processes that use data to run/change the actions of the system. While an individual write operation to a synchronous file system is faster than a write operation to a non-synchronous file system, the use of synchronous file systems can degrade overall system performance.

4.9 INTERFACING DEVICES

This section discusses how the REAL/IX real-time facilities can be used for writing user-level programs that interface to devices. These facilities are related to capabilities included in the device driver, so the driver implementation of these facilities is also discussed. The following topics are covered: (a) asynchronous I/O operations, (b) coding the user-level programs and writing drivers for asynchronous operations, (c) handling traditional UNIX system device interrupts, (d) using the REAL/IX connected interrupts, and (e) using the direct I/O mechanism.

4.9.1 Asynchronous I/O Operations

The REAL/IX operating system supports all UNIX System V I/O system calls (**read**, **write**, and so on). These calls always perform synchronous or blocking, I/O. After issuing the I/O request in synchronous I/O operations, the process blocks execution until the driver returns indicating that the data transfer is completed.

Some real-time applications also need to do asynchronous, or non-blocking, I/O operations. When transferring small amounts of data, this can be done using input/output control commands. For transferring larger amounts of data asynchronously, the REAL/IX operating system supports the asynchronous I/O interface. Asynchronous I/O operations are most efficient for cases where the driver needs to do a small number of similar I/O operations repeatedly, as is needed by many real-time applications.

Asynchronous I/O operations are initiated using the **aread** and **awrite** system calls. The data structures that control asynchronous operations can be preallocated using the **arinit** and **awinit** system calls. The structures can be freed explicitly using the **arwfree** system call. Operations can be canceled using the **acancel** system call.

Asynchronous I/O operations are initiated by a set of user-level system calls:

- **arinit** and **awinit** initialize data structures for the I/O transfer (optional)
- **aread** and **awrite** initiate the I/O transfer. If **arinit** or **awinit** did not initialize data structures, these calls will.
- **arwfree** frees the internal resources used for the transfer. If **arwfree** is not issued, the internal resources remain mapped into the process until the process exits or execs.

- **acancel** cancels one or more asynchronous I/O requests outstanding against a file descriptor.

These system calls can be associated with the file descriptor of either a data file accessed through the file subsystem or a special device file.

All asynchronous system calls activate the **sio**(D2X) driver entry point routine through the cdevsw(D4X) table. The **aio** routine is usually coded as a switch statement with four **case** statements providing the appropriate functionality for the system calls, as illustrated in Figure 4.21.

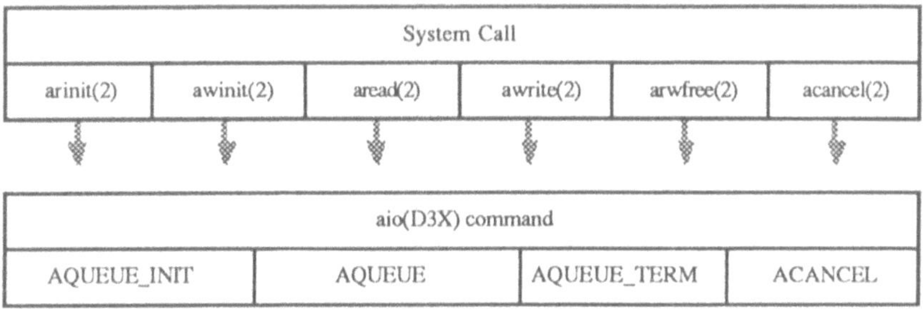

Figure 4.21 - System calls and aio

Asynchronous I/O operations are controlled through a set of data structures at the user-level and kernel-level. The user-level structure is known as an aiocb structure. This structure must be set up by the user process before initiating an asynchronous operation. Typically, there should be one aiocb structure for each type of asynchronous operation that will be requested (one for reading from a device, one for writing, etc.). The main purpose of an aiocb is to return status information upon completion of an asynchronous operation. The *aioflag* parameter in the structure determines whether or not an event is to be posted when status has been updated. In addition, certain parameters within the aiocb are used to control an implicit seek operation within the open file.

When a user process initiates an **aread** or **awrite** instruction on an open file, a pointer argument specifies a particular aiocb structure (previously set up for the read or write operation) to be used. Before data can be transferred, the kernel must validate certain parameters within the request. Example parameter information includes whether the file is open for reading or writing, or if the kernel needs to deliver an event at completion. The kernel then locks the buffer and the portion of the aiocb being used for status information into memory. This is important so that critical information is not lost in case the user process is ever paged out of memory. An areq(D4X) kernel structure is then allocated for the operation. The areq structure is responsible for transferring information from the aiocb structure to the device driver. Additionally, the areq structure updates the aiocb with status once the operation is complete.

Once the asynchronous operation has completed, the user process can check status by reading parameters within the aiocb structure. If the aiocb was set to post an event upon completion then an event will be delivered notifying the user process that status is available. Without the event mechanism, it is up to the user process to poll the aiocb location for updated status.

4.9.2 Traditional UNIX System Interrupts

An interrupt is a hardware-activated context switch that is generated when the central processing unit (CPU) needs the peripheral itself to perform some action, or is generated by the peripheral when the CPU must perform an action. For example, when a disk drive is ready to transfer information to the host to satisfy a read request, the disk drive generates an interrupt. The CPU acknowledges the interrupt and calls the appropriate driver's interrupt routine. The driver interrupt routine then wakes up the process waiting for data.

Interrupts are generated by (a) hardware devices, (b) instructions that cause software interrupts, and (c) exceptions such as page faults. Hardware interrupts are most often generated to notify the driver that a job has completed or an error has occurred.

Interrupts cause the processor to stop its current execution stream and to execute an instruction stream that services the interrupt. The system identifies the device causing the interrupt and accesses a table of interrupt vectors to transfer control to the interrupt handling routine for the device.

The interrupt handler typically does one of the following:

1. issues a wakeup call to the appropriate base-level routine of the driver, which in turn resumes execution. The base-level routine will eventually issue a return code that notifies the user-level process that the I/O is complete.

2. sends a signal to the appropriate user process(es) associated with this device.

3. updates the u_error member of the user structure to notify the user-level process that an error occurred.

Interrupts are always asynchronous events, in that they can arrive in the driver at any time. If an interrupt occurs that is at a higher priority than whatever is executing at the time, control switches to the interrupt handler to service the interrupt and then returns to whatever process was executing before. However, user-level programs are usually notified of the results of the interrupt synchronously, through return codes that the driver writes to the user.

4.9.3 Connected Interrupts

The traditional interrupt interface described in 4.9.2 works well in a general-purpose computing environment where the devices involved are traditional computer peripherals (such as disk drives, tape drives, terminals, and printers) and the design goal is to see that the system resources are distributed equitably among a number of users. Many real-time applications, however, involve devices whose interrupts need to be serviced as fast as possible, even if it means some other system processes are delayed. For instance, a device that is monitoring the calibration of a robotics arm posts an interrupt when the calibration goes out of acceptable range. The computer processes that can recalibrate the arm (or stop the flow of materials to that arm) need to react within a predictable time frame, usually within a few hundred microseconds.

The connected interrupt mechanism provides a consistent interface for such applications. To use this mechanism, the user-level process populates a cintrio structure that establishes the method by which it will be notified of device interrupts (polling or using common event notification mechanism) and whether it will be notified of every interrupt or only one interrupt at a time. The user-level program then uses the IOCTLs defined on the cintrio page to initiate an I/O operation.

The interrupt-handling routine of the driver is coded to notify the user-level process of interrupts using the connected interrupt mechanism. Drivers that use connected interrupts do not use signals or return codes to notify the user-level process that an interrupt has occurred. Rather these drivers use one of the following methods:

(1) post either a synchronous or an asynchronous event to the user-level process, or

(2) pass a device-specific data item to the location pointed to by the cintrio structure to indicate that the interrupt has been received. The user-level process polls this memory location, thus avoiding the overhead of the system call and operating system code required for any of the other methods.

Real-time applications that benefit from the connected interrupt mechanism are characterized by user-level processes that are waiting to be notified of an interrupt that is not directly associated with an I/O operation initiated by the user-level process. Connected interrupts are useful for monitoring devices that need to inform the user-level process of some external event. They cannot though be used for devices using block access. In general, devices that do standard read and write operations are better served by the traditional UNIX system interrupt mechanism.

4.9.3.1 Interfacing Connected Interrupts

This section explains what a user-level program does to use the connected interrupt mechanism. This requires that the driver for the device being interfaced be coded to define the IOCTL commands used with connected interrupts. The user-level program does the following:

1. Establishes access to the device with **open**

2. Sets up notification mechanism(s):

   - If the connected interrupt will use the event mechanism to communicate with the user process, use **evget** to set up an eid for this connected interrupt. Specify how these events are to be handled with evget (handle events asynchronously) or with **evrcv/evrcvl** (handle events synchronously).

   - If the user process will poll a memory location to detect a connected interrupt, set up the polling location in the cintrio structure in #3.

3. Populates the cintrio structure associated with a connected interrupt and uses this routine to connect a file descriptor to a cintrio structure.

4. Uses CI_CONNECT **ioctl** command to connect to the device's interrupt.

5. If only one interrupt is to be handled at a time, uses the CI_ACK ioctl command to acknowledge the interrupt so that subsequent interrupts can be received.

6. Uses the CI_UCONNECT **ioctl** command to disconnect interrupt notification.

The CI_SETMODE **ioctl** command can be used to switch notification methods. This is useful for applications that require event notification for some types of interrupts and polling notification for others.

4.9.3.2 Connected Interrupt Examples

Three example programs, presented in this section, illustrate the different methods of connecting to interrupt notification. The fourth program shows how semaphores can be used with the following option to synchronize with interrupts. All the programs listed in this section are receiving interrupts from the */dev/m147_clk* device.

Example 1: Connected interrupt notification using semaphores

The first example program, in Figure 4.22, shows how to use the connected interrupt method CINTR_SEMA to receive notification of connected interrupts.

```
#include <stdio.h>
#include <fcntl.h>

#include <sys/types.h>
#include <sys/cintrio.h>
#include <sys/evt.h>
#include <sys/time.h>
#include <sys/signal.h>
#include <sys/errno.h>
#include <sys/ipc.h>
#include <sys/shm.h>
#include <sys/pccclk.h>

extern errno;

main(argc, argv)
char *argv[];
{
	int cid;
	int fd;
	int i;
	struct pccclk clk;
	struct cintrio intr;

	if ((fd = open("/dev/m147_clk", O_RDWR, 0)) < 0) {
		perror("open");
		return(-1);
	}

	/* initialize the clock to interrupt every 1/2 second */
	clk.c_clkcnt = 0xffff - 63036; /* intr at 1/64 of a second */
	clk.c_mode = CLK_INTR|2;
	clk.c_mult = 32;
	if (ioctl(fd, CLK_SETUP, &clk) == -1) {
		printf("Error on setup: %d\n", errno);
		exit(1);
	}

	/* connect to the clock interrupt via the connected intr mechanism */
	intr.ci_method = CINTR_SEMA;
	intr.ci_flags = CINTR_PERIODIC;      /* get every interrupt */
```

Figure 4.22 - Example program: Connected interrupt notification using semaphores

```
        }
        print("start loop\n");
        for (i = 0; i < 15; i++) {
                cisema(cid);
                printf("got an interrupt\n");
        }

        /* stop clock */
        if (ioctl(fd, CLK_STOP, 0) == -1) {
                printf("Error on stop clk: %d\n", errno);
                exit(1);
        }

        /* disconnect from clock interrupt */
        if (ioctl(fd, CI_UCONNECT, 0) == -1) {
                printf("Error on unconnect: %d\n", errno);
                exit(1);
        }

        close(fd);
}
```

Figure 4.22 - cont'd

Example 2: Connected interrupt notification using the event mechanism

This example program, shown in Figure 4.23, shows how to use the connected interrupt method CINTR_EVENTS to have the user-level process notified when the driver receives an interrupt from the */dev/m147_clk* device.

```
#include <stdio.h>
#include <fcntl.h>
#include "sys/param.h"
#include "sys/types.h"
#include "sys/pccclk.h"
#include "sys/cintrio.h"
#include "sys/evt.h"

#define QUEUE_SZ        10          /* max event queued */
extern int errno;

main()
{
        int    fd, i, eid, poll;
        struct pccclk  clk;
        struct cintrio intr;
        struct event   event;

        if ((fd = open("/dev/m147_clk", O_RDWR)) == -1) {
                printf("open failed: %d\n", fd);
                exit(1);
        }

        /* initialize clock to interrupt once every 1/64th of a second */
        clk.c_clkcnt = 0xffff - 63036;
        clk.c_mode = CLK_INTR;
        clk.c_mult = 32;
        if (ioctl(fd, CLK_SETUP, &clk) == -1) {
                printf("Error on setup: %d\n", errno);
                exit(1);
        }

        /* get event id */
        if ((eid = evget(EVT_QUEUE, QUEUE_SZ, 0, 0)) == -1) {
                printf("Error on evget: %d\n", errno);
                exit(1);
        }

        /* connect to the clock interrupt */
        intr.ci_method = CINTR_EVENTS;
        intr.ci_id = eid;
        intr.ci_flags = CINTR_PERIODIC;
        if (ioctl(fd, CI_CONNECT, &intr) == -1) {
                printf("Error on connect: %d\n", errno);
                exit(1);
        }

        /* start clock */
        if (ioctl(fd, CLK_START, 0) == -1) {
```

Figure 4.23 - Example program: Connected interrupt notification using the event mechanism

```
                printf("Error on start clk: %d\n", errno);
                exit(1);
        }

        for (i = 0; i < 15; i++) {
                poll = evrc(1, &event);      /* wait for an any event */
                printf("eid = %d, type = %d, dataitem = %d\n", event.ev_eid,
                event.ev_type, event.ev_dataitem);
                printf(" evrcv return val = %d\n", poll);
        }

        /* stop clock */
        if (ioctl(fd, CLK_STOP, 0) == -1) {
                printf("Error on stop clk: %d\n", errno);
                exit(1);
        }

        /* free the event id */
        if (evrel(eid) == -1) {
                printf("Error on evrel: %d\n", errno);
                exit(1);
        }

        /* disconnect from clock interrupt */
        if (ioctl(fd, CI_UCONNECT, 0) == -1) {
                printf("Error on unconnect: %d\n", errno);
                exit(1);
        }

        close(fd);
}
```

Figure 4.23 - cont'd

Example 3: Interrupt notification using the polling mechanism

This example program, shown in Figure 4.24, illustrates how the connected interrupt method, CINTR_POLL can be used to have the user-level process polled when the driver receives an interrupt from the */dev/m147_clk* device.

```
#include <stdio.h>
#include <fctl.h>

#include "sys/param.h"
#include "sys/types.h"
#include "sys/pccclk.h"
#include "sys/cintrio.h"

extern int errno;
int    dataitem;

main()
{
      int    fd;
      int    i;
      int    old_dataitem;
      struct pcclk   clk;
      struct cintrio intr;

      if ((fd = open("/dev/m147_clk", O_RDWR)) == -1) {
            printf("open failed: %d\n", fd);
            exit (1);
      }

      /* initialize clock to interrupt once every 1/2 second */
      clk.c_clkcnt = 0xffff - 63036;
      clk.c_mode = CLK_INTR;
      clk.c_mult = 32;
      if (ioctl(fd, CLK_SETUP, &clk) == -1) {
            printf("Error on setup: %d\n", errno);
            exit(1);
      }

      /* connect to the clock interrupt */
      intr.ci_method = CINTR_POLL;
      intr.ci_polloc = &dataitem;
      intr.ci_flags = CINTR_PERIODIC;
      if (ioctl(fd, CI_CONNECT, &intr) == -1) {
            printf("Error on connect: %d\n", errno);
            exit(1);
      }

      /* start clock */
      if (ioctl(fd, CLK_START, 0) == -1) {
            printf("Error on start clk: %d\n", errno);
            exit(1);
      }

      old_dataitem = dataitem;
      for (i = 0; i < 15; i++) {
```

Figure 4.24 - Example program: Interrupt notification using the polling mechanism

```
                while (old_dataitem == dataitem)
                        ;
                printf(" dataitem=%d\n", dataitem);
                old_dataitem = dataitem;
        }

        /* stop clock */
        if (ioctl(fd, CLK_STOP, 0) == -1) {
                printf("Error on stop clk: %d\n", errno);
                exit(1);
        }

        /* disconnect from clock interrupt */
        if (ioctl(fd, CI_UCONNECT, 0) == -1) {
                printf("Error on unconnect: %d\n", errno);
                exit(1);
        }

        close(fd);
}
```

Figure 4.24 - cont'd

Example 4: Connected interrupts using semaphores with polling

This example program, shown in Figure 4.25, demonstrates how to use the connected interrupts method CINTR_SEMA in combination with polling. This code is receiving an interrupt from the */dev/m147_clk* device.

```
#include <stdio.h>
#include <fctl.h>

#include <sys/types.h>
#include <sys/cintrio.h>
#include <sys/evt.h>
#include <sys/time.h>
#include <sys/signal.h>
#include <sys/errno.h>
#include <sys/ipc.h>
#include <sys/shm.h>
#include <sys/pccclk.h>

extern errno;

int     dataitem;       /* connected interrupt poll location */

main(argc, argv)
char *argv[];
{
      int cid, fd, i;
      struct pccclk clk;
      struct cintrio intr;

      if ((fd = open("/dev/m147_clk", O_RDWR, 0)) < 0) {
            perror("open");
            return(-1);
      }

      /* initialize the clock to interrupt every 1/2 second */
      clk.c_clkcnt = 0xffff - 63036; /* intr at 1/64 of a second */
      clk.c_mode = CLK_INTR;
      clk.c_mult = 32;
      if (ioctl(fd, CLK_SETUP, &clk) == -1) {
            printf("Error on setup: %d\n", errno);
            exit(1);
      }

      /* connect to the clock interrupt via the connected intr mechanism */
      intr.ci_method = CINTR_SEMA;
      intr.ci_polloc = &dataitem;
      intr.ci_flags = CINTR_PERIODIC;      /* get every interrupt */
      if (ioctl(fd, CI_CONNECT, &intr) == -1) {
            printf("Error on connect: %d\n", errno);
            exit(1);
      }
      cid = intr.ci_id;       /* connected interrupt id */
```

Figure 4.25 - Example program: Connected interrupts using semaphores with polling

```
        /* start the clock */
        if (ioctl(fd, CLK_START, 0) == -1) {
                printf("Error on start clk: %d\n", errno);
                exit(1);
        }
        printf("start loop\n");
        for (i = 0; i < 15; i++) {
                cisema(cid);
                printf("got an interrupt; poll loc = %d\n", dataitem);
        }

        /* stop clock */
        if (ioctl(fd, CLK_STP, 0) == -1) {
                printf("Error on stop clk: %d\n", errno);
                exit(1);
        }

        /* disconnect from clock interrupt */
        if (ioctl(fd, CI_UCONNECT, 0) == -1) {
                printf("Error on unconnect clock: %d\n", errno);
                exit(1);
        }

        close(fd);
}
```

Figure 4.25 - cont'd

4.9.4 Direct I/O

The direct I/O mechanism allows a user-level program to control devices directly, thus saving the system overhead associated with regular I/O such as system call entry and exit. This facility is not recommended for I/O with traditional computer devices such as disks, tapes, and printers, but is useful with certain real-time devices.

Direct I/O is implemented by mapping the device registers into the user process' address space with the shared memory system calls (**shmget, shmat, shmctl, shmop**). Once mapped in, the process can read and write these registers like any variables. The example program in Figure 4.26 demonstrates how to use direct I/O to establish mapping between user address space and physical address space.

```
#include <sys/types.h>
#include <sys/param.h>
#include <sys/sysmacro.h>
#include <sys/ipc.h>
#include <sys/shm.h>
#include <sys/fcntl.h>
#include <sys/pcc.h>

#include <stdio.h>

/*
 *  This program demonstrates "Direct I/O" showing one how
 *  to establish a mapping between user address space and
 *  physical address space.
 *
 *  For sake of demonstration we will map to the PCC.
 */

/*
 *  Real address of PCC
 */
#define PCCADDR 0xfffe1000

/*
 *  address must be on a page boundary
 */
#define PCCADDR8k       ctob(btoct(PCCADDR))

#define PCCDELTA        (PCCADDR - PCCADDR8K)

main()
{
    int shmid;           /* shared memory id returned from shmget() call */
    int shmflg;           /* flag bits */
    struct pcc *pccp;          /* pointer to pcc bank */
    char  *x;                  /* temp variable */
```

Figure 4.26 - Example program: Use direct I/O to establish mapping between user/address space and physical address space

```
    if (getuid() != 0) {
        fprintf(stderr, "You must be root to execute this program\n");
        exit(-1);
    }

    /*
     *  set up the shmflags as follows for Direct I/O
     *
     *  IPC_CI -            Cache Inhibit
     *  IPC_NOCLEAR -       Don't clear memory
     *  IPC_PHYS    -       Attach to physical memory
     *
     */
    shmflg = IPC_CI | IPC_NOCLEAR | IPC_PHYS;

    /*
     *  obtain a shared memory identifier
     */
    if ((shmid = shmget((key_t)IPC_PRIVATE, sizeof(struct pcc), shmflg,
        PCCADDR8K)) < 0) {
            perror("shmget");
            exit(-1);
    }

    /*
     *  attach to this physical address
     */
    if ((x - (char *)shmat(shmid, 0, 0)) < 0) {
        perror("shmat");
        exit(-1)
    }
    pccp - (struct pcc *)(x + PCCDELTA);

    /*
     *  WARNING:  If you write to the PCC you are apt to
     *  bring down your system very quickly unless you
     *  really know what you are doing!!!
     */
    /*
     *  We look at the tick 1 counter here to watch it change
     */
    printf("The register's contents is [%x]\n", pccp->tctrl);

    /*
     *  now detach from the physical address
     */
    if ((shmdt(x)) < 0) {
        perror("shmdt");
        exit(-1);
    }
    /*
     *  remove the id from the system
     */
    if ((shmctl(shmid, IPC_RMID)) < 0) {
        perror("shmctl");
        exit(-1);
    }
}
```

Figure 4.26 - cont'd

4.10 WRITING SYSTEM CALLS

A real-time operating system should enable the real-time programmer to write and install system calls without rewriting and rebuilding the operating system. This allows user-level applications to create and execute functions with the privileges and speed associated with kernel-level code. This section provides instructions for writing and installing these system calls under the REAL/IX operating system.

User-installed system calls should be used to add new features to the kernel, but not to extend existing features. For example, the user should use the existing system calls that access device drivers rather than write new system calls for this purpose. The user should also avoid accessing existing kernel data structures, although he/she may create and access kernel data structures defined for specific applications.

4.10.1 Overview of System Calls

System calls look like ordinary function calls in C programs. Whereas library routines execute at user-level, system calls execute at kernel-level and so are always resident in memory (no part of the kernel is ever paged out of memory).

All system calls implemented on the system are listed in the sysent table. The sysent table lists the system call number, function name and the number of arguments required by the function. Each system call is assigned a unique number, which is passed to the kernel in a particular register. This enables the kernel to determine the system call being invoked.

To install a system call in the REAL/IX kernel, the following steps are required:

1. Write and compile the system call code as a kernel function.

2. Write and compile a **usysinit** function that is called at system boot time. This function makes entries in the sysent table and initializes semaphores for all user-installed system calls on the system.

3. Relink the operating system with your object code and the **usysinit** object module.

4. Reboot the system with the new kernel.

5. At this point, the user can access the user-installed system calls by sysent number from any user-level program using the **syscall** system call. In most cases, the user should build a library so that the system calls can be called by name.

4.10.2 Guidelines for Writing System Calls

Code that executes at kernel-level requires some different coding practices than code that executes at user-level. There are two reasons for this: first, kernel-level code does not have access to all facilities that user-level processes use and second, kernel-level code is capable of damaging the integrity of the operating system in ways that user-level programs never can. When writing code to run at kernel-level, adhere to the following rules and restrictions:

1. Structurally, the kernel is a large process that has a **main** routine. Everything else, including system calls, is written as a function to that **main** routine.

2. Each function must be defined in source code that does not include a **main** routine. To ease future maintenance tasks we suggest that the user create a separate directory that contains one *.c* file for each system call the user defines. The user may, however, put the code for several system calls in one *.c* file and locate the source code for the system calls anywhere on the system.

3. Kernel-level code cannot use any floating-point operations.

4. Kernel-level code is multi-threaded and preemptible. Consequently, it may require spin and suspend locks to preserve the integrity of the kernel.

5. Error conditions should be handled by setting u.u_error to the appropriate error number as defined in the **<sys/errno.h>** header file. When using user-installed system calls, we recommend that the user rely on the standard error codes rather than defining new ones.

6. Messages to the console or the putbuf are coded using the **cmn_err** kernel function. **printf** can be used, but this is discouraged.

7. Each system call can have up to six arguments defined. These parameters are declared as members of a structure and are referenced by a pointer in the user area called u.u_ap. Return values are assigned to the u.u_rvall field in the user area.

4.10.3 Installing System Calls in the Kernel

To install the system call in the kernel, write the usysinit function with a usyscall for each system call to be installed, compile it, and relink the kernel with this module. In order to relink the kernel, the user must have superuser privileges.

After writing the system call, install it in the kernel as follows:

1. Create a usysinit function that calls the usyscall kernel function for each user-defined system call. as outlined below

```
int usyscall (nsyscall, func, nargs)

uint   nsyscall;      /* number of the system call in sysent table
*/
int    (*func) ;      /* name of the system call */
uint   nargs;         /* number of arguments for the system call
*/
{

}
```

The *nsyscall* parameter must fall in the range of system call numbers reserved for user-defined system calls. The system call numbers available for user-custom services are 150-199. In *sys/param.h*, constants are defined for the lowest value (USYSCALLOW) and highest value (USYSCALLHI) in this range. The value of *nsyscall* is usually given in terms of these constants.

As an example, consider the user-defined system call, **respages**, shown in Figure 4.27. The purpose of this system call is to return the number of maximum physical pages of memory or the number of available resident pages of memory as determined by the argument *flags*.

```
#include <sys/types.h>
#include <sys/param.h>
#include <sys/sysmacros.h>
#include <sys/ipc.h>
#include <sys/shm.h>
#include <sys/immu.h>
#include <sys/region.h>
#include <sys/proc.h>
#include <sys/lock.h>
#include <sys/signal.h>
#include <sys/fs/s5dir.h>
#include <sys/user.h>
#include <sys/errno.h>
#include <sys/tuneable.h>
int
respages
{
    /*
     *  Parameters to the system call are declared
     *  as members of the following structure.
     */
    struct a {
            int flags;
    }   *uap;
    /*
     *  u.u_ap is a pointer to the structure containing
     *  the parameters of the system call.
     */
    uap = (struct a *)u.u_ap;
    /*
     *  The following statement is only necessary
     *  if realtime or superuser privileges are needed
     *  to execute the system call.
     */
    if ( ! (rtuser || suser ) )
            return;
    switch (uap->flags) {
    case 0:
            u.u_rval1 = availrmem - tune.t_minpagmem;
            break;
    case 1:
            u.u_rval1 = maxmem;
    default:
            u.u_error = EINVAL;
            break;
    }
}
```

Figure 4.27 - Example program: The user-defined system call **respages**

To install **respages** into the kernel, the code of *usysinit.c* is:

```
#include      <sys/param.h>

extern int respages;

int
usysinit
{

    usyscall(150, respages, 1);
}
```

The usyscall routine will fail if the *nsyscall* value is already in use or is not within the valid range for user-defined system calls. The usyscall will also fail if no function name is provided or if the value of *nargs* is greater than 6.

2. Move the source code for *respages.c* and *usysinit.c* to the */usr/src/uts/m68k/custom* directory.

3. Edit the makefile for user-defined system calls.

4. Execute a standard kernel build procedure with the command sysgen -big.

4.10.4 Accessing User-Defined System Calls

The system call can be accessed from a user-level program in one of two ways:

1. Create an assembly language system interface stub routine that allows the user-level program to access the system call by name. This is the recommended method.

2. Access the system call by number using the **syscall** system call.

Each of these methods is described in the following sections.

4.10.4.1 Using an Assembly Language Stub Routine

An assembly language stub routine can be linked with a user program to allow access to the newly installed system call by name. A typical stub routine (suitable for the **respages** system call) is shown below. Note that the value 150 in the mov.1 instruction must be equal to the value of the *nsyscall* parameter in the usyscall function in *usysinit.c*. Similar routines may be created for each user-defined system call by changing only the system call name and number.

```
          global  respages
          global  cerror%
respages:
          mov.l   &150,%d0
          trap    &0
          bcc.b   noerror
          jmp     cerror%
noerror:
          rts
```

It is customary to create a library of these system call interface routines (using **ar**), so that they are easily accessible by all users.

The example given in Figure 4.28 demonstrates the use of the **respages** system call within a user program.

```
extern int respages ;

int
main
{
          int av_pages;
          int max_pages;

          if ((av_pages = respages) == -1) {
                    perror("respages");
                    exit;
          }
          if ((max_pages = respages) == -1) {
                    perror("respages");
                    exit;
          }

          printf("Available resident pages = %d\n", av_pages);
          printf("Maximum physical pages = %d\n", max_pages);

          /* Test the error return */
          if (respages == -1)
                    perror("respages");
}
```

Figure 4.28 - Example program: The use of the **respages** system call

4.10.4.2 Using syscall to Access a System Call

User-installed system calls can be accessed by the *nsyscall* number with the **syscall** system call. This is useful when testing a system call, but is not recommended for production programs.

For example, to access **respages** by the *nsyscall* number using the same example program from Figure 4.28, the code is given in Figure 4.29.

```
extern int respages;

int
main
{
    int av_pages;
    int max_pages;

    if ((av_pages = syscall(150, 0)) == -1) {
        perror("respage)");
        exit;
    }

        if ((max_pages = syscall(150, 1)) == -1) {
        perror("respages");
        exit;
    }

    printf("Available resident pages = %d\n", av_pages);
    printf("Maximum physical pages = %d\n", max_pages);

    /* Test the error return */
    if (syscall(150, 2) == -1)
        perror("respages ");
{
```

Figure 4.29 - Example program: Accessing **respages** by the *nsyscall* number

4.11 PORTING APPLICATIONS

This section discusses the general procedure for porting applications to a real-time UNIX operating system, specifically the REAL/IX system. Some of the common problems that the user might encounter when porting an application are identified.

This section discusses the following porting scenarios separately:

1. porting SVID-compatible applications from other UNIX operating systems.

2. porting applications from proprietary real-time operating systems.

While other languages are available for the REAL/IX operating system, the C language is generally the preferred programming language unless the user specifically needs features of other languages.

4.11.1 Porting SVID-Compatible Applications

Most SVID-compatible user-level application programs will port easily to the REAL/IX operating system. Once they are ported, the applications may be modified to utilize the system's real-time features. Most binary C code that executes on Motorola's System V/68 operating system can be ported without being recompiled. The binary C code from other operating systems will usually need to be recompiled to use the appropriate data structures and instruction set.

The discussion in this section mostly pertains to applications that do not include kernel-level code such as drivers. Kernel-level code is much more machine-specific and will require further conversion.

4.11.1.1 Compiling the Code

To recompile C source code that runs on other UNIX operating systems, we suggest the following sequence:

1. Run **lint** and correct any non-portable code it identifies.

2. Verify that the header files included in the code are supported on the REAL/IX operating system.

3. Verify that the **cc** options used in the makefile are supported and make any necessary modifications to the makefile.

4. Compile the code with the optimization option.

5. If compilation errors are obtained, use standard tools such as the symbolic debugger, **sdb** and the disassembler, **dis**, to analyze the problem and to correct the code.

6. Run a parallel test of the application on the REAL/IX operating system and the other operating system to verify that the results are the same.

4.11.1.2 Adding Real-Time Features

Once the C code has compiled successfully and passed basic parallel testing, the user may want to modify the application to utilize the real-time features discussed earlier in this book. In addition, you may want to modify the tunable parameters to values appropriate for the application.

As a general rule, we suggest that the user add the appropriate features one or two at a time, using roughly the order given below. In this way, if there are some problems, it is easier to isolate the source. The following procedure is recommended:

1. Initialize identifiers for the common event notification mechanism. This is implemented first because so many other features utilize it. If the application uses the **sigset** or **signal** mechanism with the SIGUSR1 or SIGUSR2 signals, the user may want to recode these to use asynchronous events.

2. Set up dedicated file systems and reconfigure the buffer cache to use larger logical block sizes if appropriate.

3. Application-specific, general purpose routines should be kept in appropriate, user-defined libraries. Routines that do not access system data structures should be rewritten as system calls installed in the sysent table.

4. Preallocate the necessary resources, such as contiguous data blocks (extents) for critical application files and memory for processes that will be resident in memory.

5. Assign real-time privileges to the login(s) from which the application will be run, and have critical processes assign real-time priority to themselves. It may be necessary to reorganize the code so that all initialization is done during the initialization phase of the program.

6. Implement process interval timers to control time-critical functionality.

See the earlier sections of this book for discussions of the features referred to here and for guidelines on when and how to implement them.

4.11.2 Porting from Proprietary Operating Systems

Porting from proprietary operating systems is a more complicated process. If the programs are written in C, the user can try to just recompile them. If the code does not include non-standard system calls and library routines, the user may be able to port the application fairly easily. In most cases, if the application is written in assembly language, FORTRAN, or some other high-level language, the user will need to go through a process of substantially re-writing the application.

The first step is to analyze all sections of the existing application and determine which functionality should be in which programs and the order in which they should execute. The result of this should be an understanding (and preferably a written specification) that defines all programs to be written, and the flow-of-control required for each program. Consider the following points:

- The programmer may end up with fewer individual programs than he/she had on the proprietary operating system because of the ability to call shell programs like subroutines.

- It is recommended to isolate functions that could run in parallel into separate programs. This takes advantage of multiprocessor configurations that may be available in the future. On a multiprocessor system, separate processes can execute in parallel, which will improve the performance of the application.

- Critical parts of the application should not be coded in the same program as less-critical parts of the application. This enables the user to assign run-time priorities that favor only the critical functionality, rather than having non-critical functions running at the same priority as critical functions.

Once the analysis is done, coding the application should begin. In general, it is a good idea to develop and test small pieces of the application. It is easier to isolate bugs in small sections than in entire application systems. If each small piece is debugged, the testing and debugging of the entire application will go much more smoothly.

The coding process will vary for each application, but the following guidelines are appropriate in most cases:

1. If the application includes support for a specific device (such as a process I/O control board or a robotics device), develop the driver before the user-level code. Be sure that structures and definitions that are used by both the driver and the user-level programs are defined in application -specific header files.

2. Create application specific libraries for general purpose routines used in the application and application-specific header files to define application-specific structures and variables. These will simplify maintenance tasks in the future and ensure that all parts of the application agree on critical matters.

3. Next, develop the administrative and user programs that are required to thoroughly test the driver.

4. During testing of the application, use the **crash**(1M) program to take snap shots of the kernel during execution. The user may need to modify the value of tunable sysgen parameters to provide an optimal environment for the application. If necessary, critical routines can be written in assembly language. While this can improve performance, we recommend

it be used very sparingly to avoid porting problems with future hardware platforms.

4.12 PERFORMANCE MANAGEMENT

There are a few fundamental concepts to be considered in order to manage performance of the system. These concepts are described below.

1. An operating system can be customized to serve the performance needs of the particular user's environment. Many system facilities use data structures that are always resident in memory. On some operating systems, the system always reserves a specified amount of memory for these structures, which may be too small for some environments yet waste memory on others. But on UNIX operating systems, the user can modify the sizes of these structures. This includes expanding those that are used heavily and shrinking or even eliminating those that are unused.

2. Performance management is a constant task for the administrator. Performance degrades if file systems become disorganized or are filled with unneeded files. Moreover, the activities of users will change over time: memory tables that were once quite adequate will overflow as new users and applications become active, or user file systems and swap space will likely need to be expanded as new users are added.

3. Performance management involves a number of tradeoffs which must be carefully weighed and balanced. For example, one must balance reliability needs with performance needs.

4. When real-time applications are involved, the philosophy of performance management changes. The general approach is to ensure that critical real-time processes get all the resources required to execute as quickly as possible. Often this includes preallocating resources and holding on to them for long periods of time even when they are not needed so that they are available when they are needed. This will sometimes mean that other processes perform very poorly. The alternative is to distribute resources equitably to all executing processes and thereby risk having indeterminate response for the critical real-time processes.

Successful performance management is an art and the REAL/IX system provides tools to measure system activity. In this section, we provide guidelines on how to use these tools, however, the user must use his/her own judgement to obtain optimum system efficiency for a particular real-time environment.

The philosophies of performance management are different for systems running time-sharing versus systems running real-time applications. In a time-sharing environment, performance management is usually a matter of ensuring that all executing processes get an equitable portion of system resources. In contrast, in a real-time environment, performance management may be a matter of ensuring that critical real-time processes get the resources they need to react rapidly to an external event, even if other executing processes get no system resources for a period of time.

4.12.1 Creating an Efficient Environment

The first performance task is to create an efficient environment. This includes the following activities:

a. selecting an appropriate hardware configuration for your computing needs

b. modifying the tunable parameters to values that are appropriate for your configuration

c. arranging file systems and paging areas on disk for optimal load distribution

d. utilizing an appropriate file system architecture

e. helping users establish efficient environments

Hardware Configuration

The first step in performance management is to ensure that the hardware configuration is adequate. The following issues should be considered:

- In general, it is best to have general users and development work executing on a system separate from the production machine on which real-time processes are executing.

- While many disk controllers can support several disk drives, performance is usually better if each disk drive is attached to a separate controller.

- For environments that require large amounts of file I/O operations, be sure to configure an adequate amount of disk storage. Small disks lead to file systems that fill up, which degrades performance in addition to causing general aggravation. Also, with adequate disk storage, backups can be run to a scratch disk partition which can then be backed up to tape. Since disk-to-disk copies are faster than disk to tape, you can minimize the time the file systems are unavailable to users.

- Select an expandable hardware platform. As system usage grows, there may be the need to add hardware components to maintain good performance.

File System Structure

The REAL/IX operating system offers two file system structures and a variety of logical block sizes. Selecting the appropriate structure for the file systems can significantly improve system performance.

- The fast file system architecture (F5) provides better performance than the S5 file system architecture because of the bitmask used to access free data blocks. In addition, applications accessing files in F5 file systems can preallocate contiguous data storage blocks (extents) that permit large multiple-block transfers directly to user space.

- For large files, file systems that use larger logical block sizes provide better performance than file systems that use smaller logical block sizes. File systems can use logical block sizes ranging from 512 bytes to 128K.

It is best to spread user directories over multiple file systems located on different disks provided they do not need to be able to link files. This reduces the performance degradation that can result from contention of everyone accessing the same file system.

Choosing the Size and Number of Buffers

The REAL/IX operating system allows the definition of a wide variety of buffer sizes to support the variety of file system logical block sizes available. The number of each size of buffer and the buffer sizes themselves should be adjusted over time as the system utilization and configuration changes. Use the **sar -b** and **crash bfree** commands to study buffer usage on your system.

Disk I/O Balancing

For optimal system performance, disk activity should be spread equally over all the disks and disk controllers. To check this, study the **sar -d** report, especially the **%busy** (percent of time the device was busy with I/O) field. These values should be roughly similar for all disk devices. If they are not, the administrator should adjust the locations of swap areas and heavily-used file systems until the values are similar. To determine whether the swap device or file systems are causing the imbalance, run **sar -w** and look at the **swpin** (transfers from *swap* to memory) and **swpot** (transfers from memory to *swap*) fields.

Partitions located toward the center of the disk are accessed fastest. For this reason, swapping areas and heavily-used file systems should ideally be located there.

Setting Text Bit (Sticky Bit)

Provided that it is not overused, setting the text bit (commonly called the sticky bit) on a select group of frequently-used commands can improve performance. Without the sticky bit, a region table entry is deallocated when the last process exists and frees the pregion entry that points to that region. If the sticky bit is set, the region table entry for text pages of "sticky" commands are kept resident in memory, even when the process terminates. This can reduce the setup time on an **exec** for the text pages of a process.

On systems that usually run a light workload and are seldom in a tight-memory situation, setting the text bit for frequently used commands (such as **vi** and **cc**) can cause a significant improvement in performance. On systems with limited memory or a heavy workload, however, the text bit should not be used. If too many files have the sticky bit set, there may not be enough physical memory for users to execute other programs.

Arranging the Multiple Swap Areas

In addition to the */dev/swap* area required for booting, the system allows creating up to ninety-nine additional swapping areas. Swap areas are disk memory regions used to store process pages that **vhand** pages out to disk. Proper utilization of this feature can improve system performance.

A good starting place for general purpose systems is to allocate at least 1000 blocks of swap space for each user on the system. The exact amount of swap space required varies according to the efficiency of the application programs and the degree of system usage by each user. If users report that programs are failing because of inadequate memory, the administrator should allocate more swap devices or increase the size of the existing swap devices.

Many real-time environments are configured with large amounts of memory relative to the needs of the applications, locked into preallocated memory. Consequently, the swap device is seldom used for this code. If these are the only processes executing on the system, smaller amounts of disk space are required for swapping. However, if non-real-time applications are also running on the system, it may be necessary to allocate larger amounts of swap space because so much physical memory is preallocated to real-time processes.

If there is a large amount of paging activity, it is better to allocate multiple swap areas than to allocate one large area. These swap areas should be spread across different disks and should be located in the portions of the disk that are accessed most rapidly.

4.12.2 Maintaining System Efficiency

To maintain a high-performance environment, the following activities are recommended:

1. reorganize file systems regularly,

2. schedule jobs for non-prime time whenever possible,

3. monitor disk usage regularly,

4. encourage programmers to write efficient application programs

5. monitor the **sar** reports constantly. This familiarizes the administrator with the information they give, shows what normal values are for the environment, and keeps him/her aware of performance trends. The **sar** reports are described in Section 4.11.4.

File System Organization

As file systems and areas with temporary work space (primarily */tmp* and */usr/tmp*) are used, they tend to become physically scattered around the disk and I/O becomes less efficient. File systems should be reorganized periodically to restore good file system organization.

Critical real-time processes that have predetermined file space needs can define extents for their files and thereby further improve access time.

Directory Organization

Directory organization also affects I/O performance. When a file is removed from a directory, the inode number is nulled out. This leaves an unused slot of 16 bytes in the directory.

Directory searches of very large directories are less efficient because of file system indirection. The **find** command can be used to identify directories with a large number of entries. For example, for a file system that uses 2K logical blocks, directories with more than 1280 entries (20480 bytes, or 40 physical blocks that are 512 bytes each) use indirection.

Directories identified as being this large should be broken up into smaller directories. Take care to notify users when moving executable files and data that are shared among a number of users.

<u>Free Blocks and Inodes</u>

When file systems have few free blocks or free inodes, an excessive amount of system time is devoted to finding available space for writing. As a general guideline, a file system should have 10% to 20% of its blocks free at the beginning of the day.

If any file system has fewer than 5000 free blocks, the system performance may be notably impaired. If a file system has fewer than 2000 free blocks, users may not be able to create new or expand existing files. If the *root* or */usr* file system (or separate file systems that contain */tmp, /usr/tmp,* or */spool*) go below 2000 free blocks you may be unable to run some processes. When one of these file systems goes below 500 free blocks, accounting shuts down.

4.12.3 Solving Performance Problems

Poor response time at terminals or recurring error messages at the console indicate that the system is not performing as well as it could. To define the problem more specifically, the tools discussed in Section 4.11.4 should be used, and then the appropriate action should be taken to resolve it.

Some of the major areas for action are:

a. improve disk utilization
b. improve system usage patterns
c. reallocate memory resources by modifying the tunable parameters

Changes to the tunable parameters and other major adjustments to the system should be made only if the system is performing unsatisfactorily.

Poor response for some processes may be attributable to higher-priority real-time processes that are preventing them from executing. This is one of the hazards of systems running real-time applications. It is advantageous to check that processes have appropriate priorities and to consider that some applications may need to be moved to auxiliary systems.

Table 4.17 gives an overview of the problems that can impair system performance, describes how to identify them, and presents some possible solutions.

4.12.4 Measuring Performance

The REAL/IX operating system supports a number of tools that can help measure performance. The tools discussed here are:

- **ps**
- sar and sar
- **timex**
- **crash**

Table 4.17
Overview of Performance Problems

Category	Symptoms	Corrective Action
System Paging	swpin/s > 1.00 and %idle > 0 on sar -wu report	Reduce size of buffer cache and other system tables Improve structure of application programs Adjust paging parameters Replace the memory configuration with a larger configuration Move some users to another system
Disk or Swapping Bottleneck	%wio > 10% on sar -u report %busy > 50% on sar -d report	Use larger logical block size on file systems Reorganize file systems Increase buffers Balance disk load Reorganize /tmp and /usr/tmp Create more or larger swap areas Move swap areas to the inside of disks Allocate swapping areas across all disks Add more disk controllers
Device Interrupts	mdmin > 0 on sar -y report	Repair modems, ports, terminals, and/or lines
Table Overflows	Warning message on console Table overflows show on sar -v report	Increase table sizes
System Usage	%idle < 10% on sar -u report swpin/s > 1 and %idle = 0 on sar -wu report	Reduce the number of users Reschedule large jobs to run at non-prime time Move some users to another system

These tools do not provide absolute answers, but are useful for spotting general performance trends and for identifying the source of the problem when system performance is unacceptable.

These performance tools were designed for time-sharing computers on which all executing processes should get an equitable share of system resources when the system is properly tuned and configured. When executing real-time processes on the system, the system should be configured to provide the performance required by the real-time processes. In some cases these configurations will severely degrade the performance of non-real-time processes.

ps: The **ps** command reports information about active processes. The command gives a "snapshot" picture of what is going on. This "snapshot" is useful when the administrator is trying to identify what processes are loading the system.

sar -y: The **-y** option monitors terminal device activities. Activities recorded are as follows:

rawch/s	Input characters (raw queue) per second.
canch/s	Input characters processed by canon (canonical queue) per second.
outch/s	Output characters (output queue) per second.
rcvin/s	Receiver hardware interrupts per second.
xmtin/s	Transmitter hardware interrupts per second.
mdmin/s	Modem interrupts per second.

The number of modem interrupts per second (mdmin/s) should be close to 0 and the receive and transmit interrupts per second (xmitin/s and rcvin/s) should be less than or equal to the number of incoming or outgoing characters, respectively. If this is not the case, check for bad lines.

An example of **sar -y** output is as follows:

modcomp modcomp V.3 A.0 A.0 M68030 07/31/89

07:45:00	rawch/s	canch/s	outch/s	rcvin/s	xmtin/s	mdmin/s
08:00:01	0	0	0	0	0	0
08:15:01	1	0	34	1	34	0
08:30:00	1	0	13	1	13	0
...	...	...	...	...	...	...
Average	0	0	3	0	3	0

sar -A: The **sar -A** option is a composite of all other sar reports that provides a view of overall system performance. It can be used to get a more global perspective. If data from more than one time slice is shown, the report includes averages.

timex: The **sar** reports reflect information gathered at regular times on the system. The **timex** command times a command and reports the system activities that occurred just during the time the command was executing. If no other programs are running, then **timex** can give a good idea of which resources a specific command uses during its execution. System consumption can be collected for each application program and used for tuning the heavily loaded resources.

crash: The crash program can be used to analyze either an active kernel or the core image saved (usually after a system panic) into the */dump* directory. There are many uses for **crash**. Two typical crash commands are:

- **icount**, which measures the size of I/O operations on each file system,
- **bfree**, which reports the cache hit rate (similar to **sar -b**) separately for each buffer size configured on the system.

4.12.5 Performance Evaluation of the REAL/IX System

All results, presented in this section were obtained by running both the REAL/IX operating system and the standard UNIX operating system on MODCOMP Tri-D 9730 machines, based on a 25 MHz MC68030 processor with 8 Mbytes of memory. Results for other real-time UNIX operating systems were obtained from the vendors' published data.

Figure 4.30 summarizes the comparative values of the worst case process dispatch latency times for four real-time UNIX operating systems. Besides the Tri-D 9730 machine, the other three systems were Harris Night Hawk 3400, Concurrent/ Masscomp 6300, and HP 9000/825. When compared to the other three real-time UNIX operating systems, the REAL/IX operating system has superior process dispatch latency time performance.

The Tri-Dimensional analyzer is used to compare real-time features of the REAL/IX operating system versus the standard UNIX operating system. The Tri-Dimensional analyzer measures three critical real-time performance features of a computer: (a) CPU computational speed, measured in Millions of Instructions Per Second (MIPS 1), (b) interrupt handling capability, measured in Millions of Interrupts Per Second (MIPS 2), and (c) I/O throughput, measured in Millions of I/O operations (Mbytes/sec) Per Second, as described in Section 1.4.3. The three dimensional representation and the three MIPS parameters, measured by the Tri-Dimensional analyzer, gives a graphical view of the real-time capabilities of a computer system.

OS	TOTAL TIME MIN µs	TOTAL TIME MAX µs
HP-UX	655	1991
CX/RT	90	430
RTU	1605	11605
REAL/IX	50	360

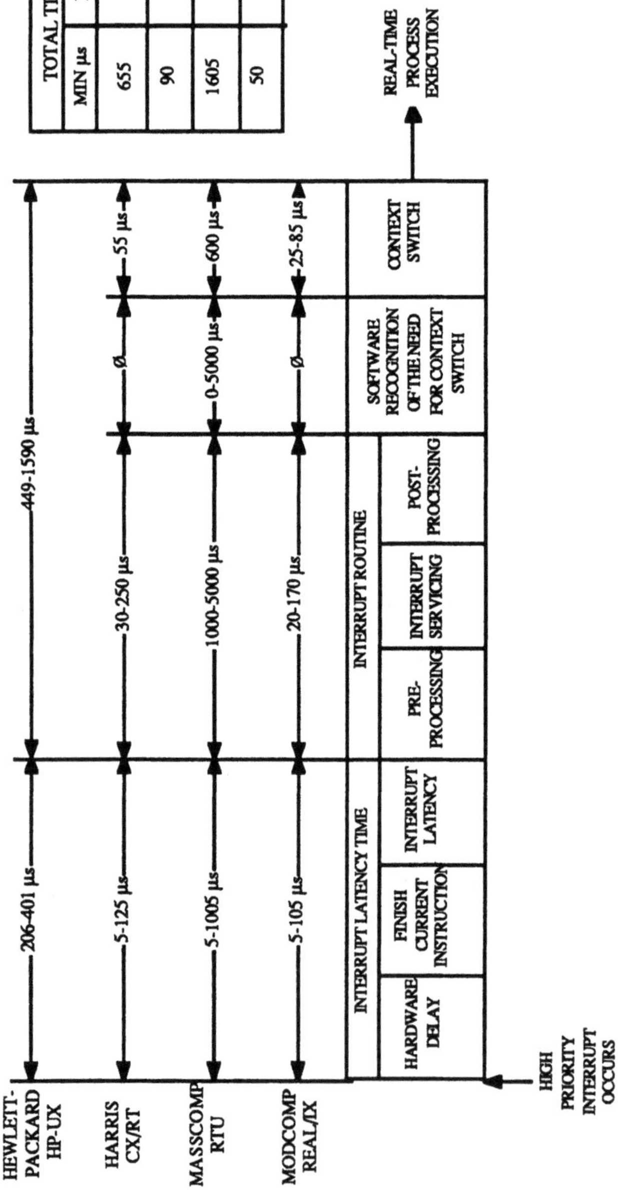

Figure 4.30 - Comparison of process dispatch latency times for four real-time UNIX operating systems

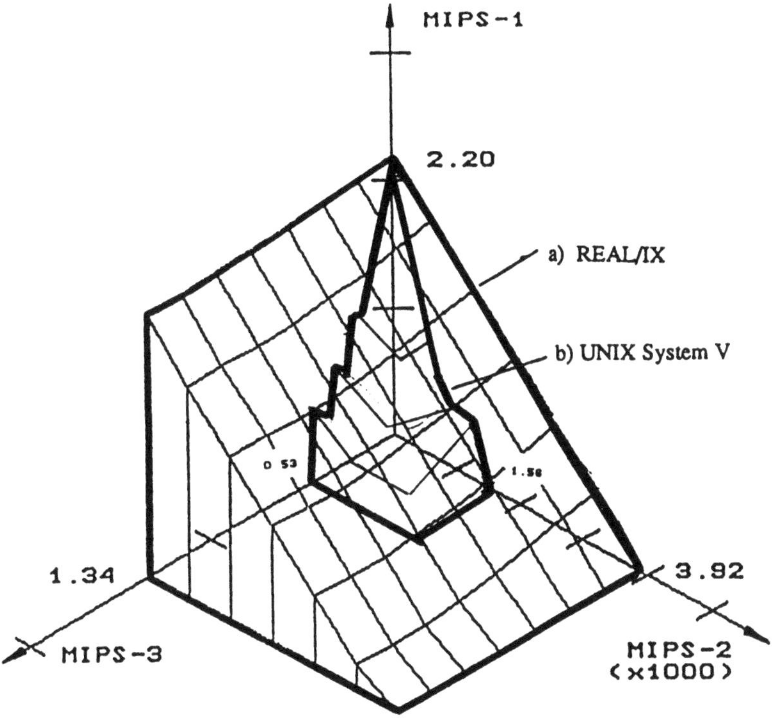

Figure 4.31 - Graphic results obtained from the Tri-Dimensional analyzer

The graphical results for the REAL/IX operating system and the standard UNIX System V operating systems are shown in Figure 4.31a and 4.31b, respectively. Note that in both cases, when the interrupt loading increases, the CPU power decreases. Note though that the performance degrades much faster in the case of the standard UNIX operating system, while in contrast, for the REAL/IX system the degradation of performance is much more gradual.

Also, in the case of the REAL/IX system, the CPU power remains almost constant when the I/O load increases, while for the standard UNIX system the CPU power decreases significantly when the I/O load increases. The reason for this is that the REAL/IX system supports asynchronous I/O. In asynchronous I/O the CPU execution and an I/O operation are performed concurrently. This is not the case in the standard UNIX operating system.

Furthermore, by analyzing the shapes of these two graphs, a general conclusion can be made that the REAL/IX system provides a deterministic response, because its graph is smooth. In the case of UNIX System V, the response is not deterministic, which is indicated by several turning points in the tri-dimensional graph.

The Tri-Dimensional analyzer has also calculated both the Volume and $MIPS_e$, defined in Section 1.4.3, for the REAL/IX system and standard UNIX operating system. For these measurements each operating system was executing on identical hardware, a Tri-Dimensional Model 9730 computer. Results are given below.

	REAL/IX	UNIX System V
Volume	5.27	0.46
$MIPS_e$	1.74	0.77

The volume of the REAL/IX curve is 10.1 times greater than that of the UNIX System V curve, and the REAL/IX system provides 2.15 higher equivalent $MIPS_e$ rating than the UNIX System V. In summary, this test indicates the significant superiority of the REAL/IX operating system over the UNIX System V in real-time, time-critical environments.

CHAPTER 5

Case Studies

In this chapter, two case studies are described:

(1) The Data Acquisition and Space Shuttle Launch Control System at NASA Kennedy Space Center, and

(2) The Communication Processor at Jet Propulsion Laboratory.

The first example includes a feasibility study and gives a step-by-step procedure of how to map a complex real-time application into a tightly-coupled real-time UNIX operating system based architecture.

The second example is a program example, which illustrates how to use the REAL/IX operating system in a time-critical application.

5.1 THE DATA ACQUISITION AND SPACE SHUTTLE LAUNCH CONTROL SYSTEM AT NASA KENNEDY SPACE CENTER

The Data Acquisition and Space Shuttle Launch Control System at NASA Kennedy Space Center performs launch control functions for the Space Shuttle from T-minus-72-hours until T-minus-31-seconds. At T-minus-31-seconds control is handed over to the space shuttle's on-board computers, but the launch control system continues to monitor all elements of the shuttle.

The current computer system consists of 400 MODCOMP 16-bit computers, however, there is an on-going project with the goal of replacing the system with a state-of-the-art real-time multiprocessor system. This study shows how a tightly-coupled multiprocessor system, described in Section 1.3, can be used to upgrade this data acquisition and launch control system.

The configuration of the core system for data acquisition and launch control is shown in Figure 5.1 [Luke89].

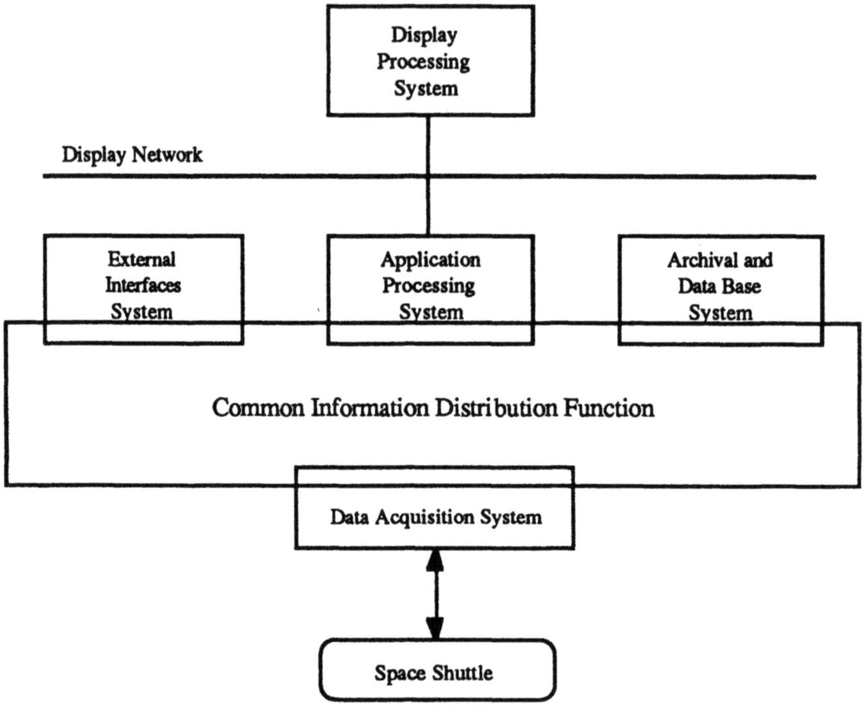

Figure 5.1. The configuration of the NASA core system for data acquisition and launch control

The core system is composed of five subsystems:

- Data Acquisition System,
- Application Processing System,
- Archival and Data Base System,
- External Interfaces System, and
- Display Processing System.

In this study we concentrate on the two most complicated subsystems: The Data Acquisition, and Application Processing Systems. First, the communication and processing requirements for these two systems are specified. Then, on the basis of the model of the system, the architecture is to meet these requirements.

5.1.1 The Data Acquisition System

The Data Acquisition System (DAS) performs data collection and distribution services. The core of the DAS is the Data Acquisition Processor (DAP), which receives data from the Data Acquisition Modules (DAMs) and passes this data to the Application Processing System (APS). The functional diagram of the DAP is shown in Figure 5.2.

As the number of DAMs in a particular set increases, the number of data packets to be distributed increases. This increase reaches the limit of a typical machine well before it reaches the bandwidth limit of the network. In order to reduce this traffic the DAP does a packet concentration function. Then, the DAP distributes data to the Application Processing System or just broadcasts all of the data for use by any Application Processor. This analysis assumes the later broadcast mode.

Front-end Data Traffic. The DAP system will pass out only significant changes of the front-end data. About 60,000 significant changes per second are expected, and they are evenly distributed across several data types, as shown in Table 5.1.

Table 5.1
Significant Changes Distributed Across Data Types

Data type	Change/sec	Kbytes/sec
Time Homogeneous	120	3
Analog Measurement	19980	280
Digital Pattern	8160	65
Discrete Measurement	29760	208
Single Precision FP	1680	17
Multi-Word Double Precision FP	240	4
Total	≈ 60,000	577

The total front-end traffic is 577,000 bytes/sec, which requires 400 Ethernet® packets/sec, with 1500 bytes per packet, as indicated in Figure 5.2.

Command Traffic. The application processor sends commands to the DAP system in order to change the value of an effector and/or to update front-end tables. An acknowledgement from the DAP system is expected for each command. These packets are small, 10 to 100 bytes (on average 64 bytes). The application processor generates 100 commands/sec and receives 100 acknowledgements/sec, as indicated in Figure 5.2.

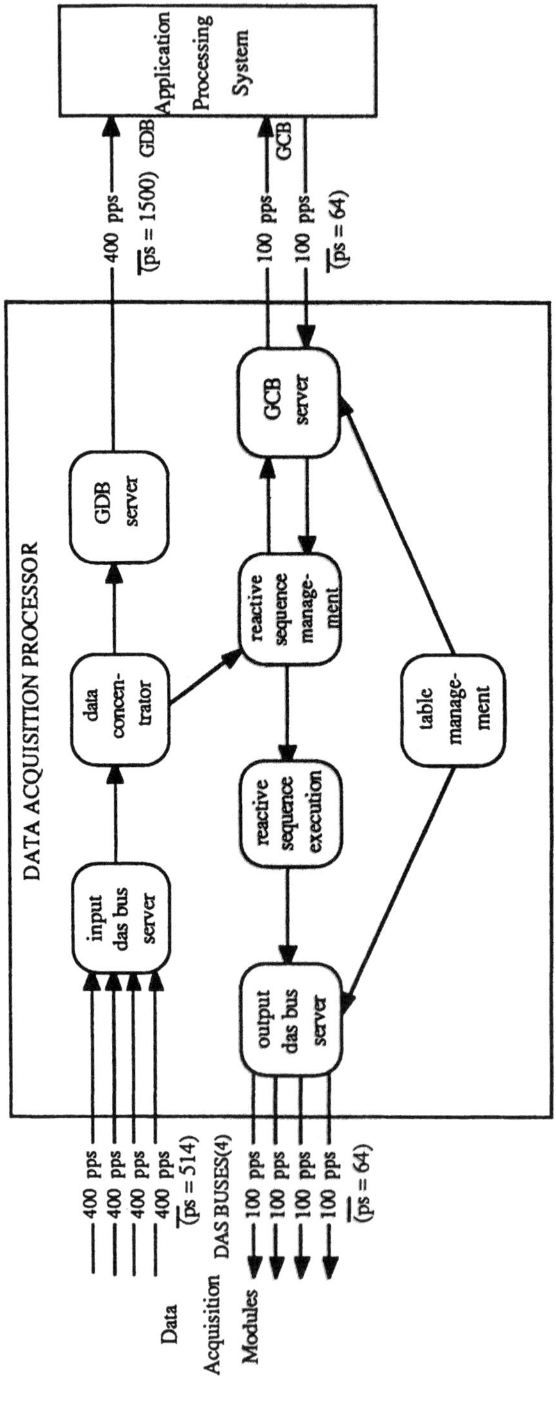

Figure 5.2 - The functional diagram of the Data Acquisition Processor

The DAP Model. The DAP model is derived [Luke89] in order to describe the worst case computational requirements for the DAP. The DAP system from Figure 5.2 is partitioned into eleven processing modules, as shown in Figure 5.3.

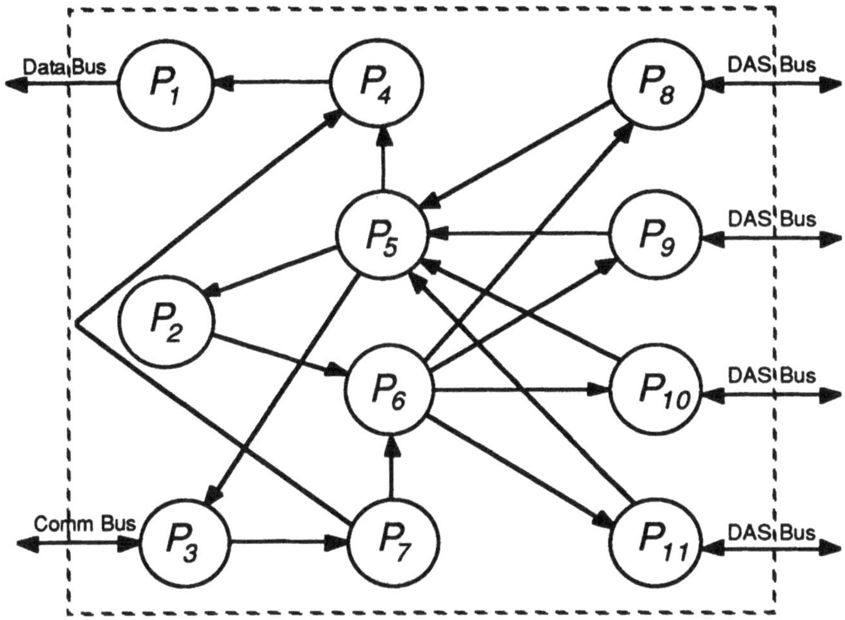

Figure 5.3 - The Data Acquisition Processor (DAP) Model

The eleven processing modules have the following functions:

P_1	-	Data Bus Handler
P_2	-	Reactive Control Logic
P_3	-	Command Bus Handler
P_4	-	Data Concentrator
P_5	-	Selector Module
P_6	-	Distributor Module
P_7	-	Security Module
P_8	-	DAS Bus Handler
P_9	-	DAS Bus Handler
P_{10}	-	DAS Bus Handler
P_{11}	-	DAS Bus Handler

In order to handle the worst case data rates, the Data Acquisition Processor must support the following:

a. Network Interfaces

- 1800 total packets received per second
- 500 packets received per second per DAS bus
- 100 packets sent per second per DAS bus
- 400 total packets broadcast per second on the Data Bus
- 200 total packets per second sent and received on the Command Bus

b. Processing Power

The required processing power of eleven processing modules can be decomposed into: (1) application instruction rate, (2) system call overhead, and (3) context switch overhead.

The total required instruction rate for processing module *i* is:

$$T_i = P_i + S_i + C_i$$

where:

T_i - total instruction rate for module *i*
P_i - application instruction rate for module *i*
S_i - system call overhead for module *i*
C_i - context switch overhead for module *i*

The application instruction rates (P_i) for the eleven processing elements are computed as follows:

$$P_1 = P_R \times N_I = 400 \times 30 = 12{,}000 \; inst/sec$$

$$P_2 = E_R \times N_I = 20 \times 500 = 10{,}000 \; inst/sec$$

$$P_3 = P_R \times N_I = 200 \times 50 = 10{,}000 \; inst/sec$$

$$P_4 = \frac{D_{PR}}{M_{length}} \times N_I = \frac{141{,}719}{8} \times 300 = 5{,}314{,}500 \; inst/sec$$

$$P_5 = N_B \times N_D \times P_R \times N_I = 4 \times 4 \times 125 \times 50 = 100{,}000 \; inst/sec$$

$$P_6 = N_B \times P_R \times N_I = 4 \times 100 \times 50 = 20{,}000 \; inst/sec$$

$$P_7 = \left(\frac{D_{PR}}{M_{length}}\right) \times N_I = \left(\frac{24{,}663}{8}\right) \times 100 = 308{,}288 \; inst/sec$$

$$P_8 = (N_D + 1) \times P_R \times N_I = (4 + 1) \times 100 \times 25 = 12{,}500 \; inst/sec$$

$$P_9 = (N_D + 1) \times P_R \times N_I = (4 + 1) \times 100 \times 25 = 12{,}500 \; inst/sec$$

$$P_{10} = (N_D + 1) \times P_R \times N_I = (4 + 1) \times 100 \times 25 = 12{,}500 \; inst/sec$$

$$P_{11} = (N_D + 1) \times P_R \times N_I = (4 + 1) \times 100 \times 25 = 12{,}500 \; inst/sec$$

where:

P_R = Packet Rate

D_{PR} = Practical Data Rate

M_{length} = Measurement length

N_I = Number of Instructions

N_D = Number of DAMs per DAS Bus

N_B = Number of DAS Buses

E_R = Reactive sequence exception rate

All the data is obtained experimentally [Luke89].

The total application instruction rate (P) is then given as:

$$P = \sum_{i=1}^{n} P_i = 5{,}824{,}788 \; inst/sec$$

The system call overheads (S_i) for eleven modules can be calculated as:

$$S_1 = P_R \times I_S = 400 \times 1200 = 480{,}000 \; inst/sec$$
$$S_2 = E_R \times I_S = 80 \times 1200 = 96{,}000 \; inst/sec$$
$$S_3 = P_R \times I_S = 500 \times 1200 = 240{,}000 \; inst/sec$$
$$S_4 = P_R \times I_S = 500 \times 1200 = 600{,}000 \; inst/sec$$
$$S_5 = N_B \times N_D \times P_R \times I_S = 4 \times 4 \times 200 \times 1200 = 3{,}840{,}000 \; inst/sec$$
$$S_6 = P_R \times I_S = 100 \times 1200 = 120{,}000 \; inst/sec$$
$$S_7 = P_R \times I_S = 100 \times 1200 = 120{,}000 \; inst/sec$$
$$S_8 = (N_D + 1) \times P_R \times I_S = (4 + 1) \times 100 \times 1200 = 600{,}000 \; inst/sec$$
$$S_9 = (N_D + 1) \times P_R \times I_S = (4 + 1) \times 100 \times 1200 = 600{,}000 \; inst/sec$$
$$S_{10} = (N_D + 1) \times P_R \times I_S = (4 + 1) \times 100 \times 1200 = 600{,}000 \; inst/sec$$
$$S_{11} = (N_D + 1) \times P_R \times I_S = (4 + 1) \times 100 \times 1200 = 600{,}000 \; inst/sec$$

where:

P_R = Packet Rate

D_{PR} = Practical Data Rate

M_{length} = Measurement length

I_S = Number of system instructions

N_D = Number of DAMs per DAS Bus

N_B = Number of DAS Buses

The total system call overhead (S) is then:

$$S = \sum_{i=1}^{n} S_i = 7{,}896{,}000 \ inst/sec$$

The context switch overheads (C_i) are calculated in the modules that perform communications with the DAMs and Application Processors. For these modules, (P_1, P_3, P_8, P_9, P_{10}, and P_{11} in Figure 5.3) the context switch overheads are computed as follows:

$$C_1 = P_R \times I_S = 400 \times 4000 = 1{,}600{,}000 \ inst/sec$$
$$C_3 = P_R \times I_S = 200 \times 4000 = 800{,}000 \ inst/sec$$
$$C_8 = P_R \times I_S = 400 \times 4000 = 1{,}600{,}000 \ inst/sec$$
$$C_9 = P_R \times I_S = 400 \times 4000 = 1{,}600{,}000 \ inst/sec$$
$$C_{10} = P_R \times I_S = 400 \times 4000 = 1{,}600{,}000 \ inst/sec$$
$$C_{11} = P_R \times I_S = 400 \times 4000 = 1{,}600{,}000 \ inst/sec$$

The total context switch overhead (C) is then calculated as:

$$C = \sum_{i=1}^{n} C_i = 8{,}800{,}000 \ inst/sec$$

The total processing power required by the DAP is summarized in Table 5.2

Tightly Coupled Multiprocessor as the Data Acquisition Processor. We will use the DAP model from Figure 5.3 in order to analyze the capabilities of the tightly coupled multiprocessor system, described in Section 1.3, in meeting the requirements for the DAP.

Table 5.2
Processing Power Required by the DAP

Process	Inst/sec
Application	5,824,788
System Calls	7,896,000
Context Switches	8,800,000
Total	22,520,788

Using the data for P_i, S_i , and C_i, the total instruction rate (T_i) for eleven processing modules becomes:

T_1 = 12,000 + 480,000 + 1,600,000 = 2,092,000 *inst/sec* ≈ 2.1 MIPS

T_2 = 10,000 + 96,000 + 0 = 106,000 *inst/sec* ≈ 0.1 MIPS

T_3 = 10,000 + 240,000 + 800,000 = 1,050,000 *inst/sec* ≈ 1.1 MIPS

T_4 = 5,314,500 + 600,000 + 0 = 5,914,500 *inst/sec* ≈ 6 MIPS

T_5 = 100,000 + 3,840,000 + 0 = 3,940,000 *inst/sec* ≈ 4 MIPS

T_6 = 20,000 + 120,000 + 0 = 140,000 *inst/sec* ≈ 0.2 MIPS

T_7 = 308,000 + 120,000 + 0 = 428,000 *inst/sec* ≈ 0.5 MIPS

T_8 = 12,000 + 600,000 + 1,600,000 = 2,212,000 *inst/sec* ≈ 2.25 MIPS

T_9 = 12,000 + 600,000 + 1,600,000 = 2,212,000 *inst/sec* ≈ 2.25 MIPS

T_{10} = 12,000 + 600,000 + 1,600,000 = 2,212,000 *inst/sec* ≈ 2.25 MIPS

T_{11} = 12,000 + 600,000 + 1,600,000 = 2,212,000 *inst/sec* ≈ 2.25 MIPS

Total ≈ 23 MIPS

Assuming the tightly coupled multiprocessor as the DAP system, with a 33 MHz MC68030 as the CPU or I/O processor each with 6.5 to 9.5 native machine inst/sec, the DAP model can be partitioned as shown in Figure 5.4.

The tightly coupled multiprocessor system consists of five processing elements: three I/O processors and two CPUs. These five processing elements require the following instruction rate:

$$IOP_1 = T_8 + T_9 = 2.25 + 2.25 = 4.5 \text{ Minst/sec}$$

$$IOP_2 = T_{10} + T_{11} = 2.25 + 2.25 = 4.5 \text{ Minst/sec}$$

$$IOP_3 = T_1 + T_3 = 2.1 + 1.1 = 3.2 \text{ Minst/sec}$$

$$CPU_1 = T_4 = 6 \text{ Minst/sec}$$

$$CPU_2 = T_2 + T_5 + T_6 + T_7 = 0.1 + 4 + 0.2 + 0.5 = 4.8 \text{ Minst/sec}$$

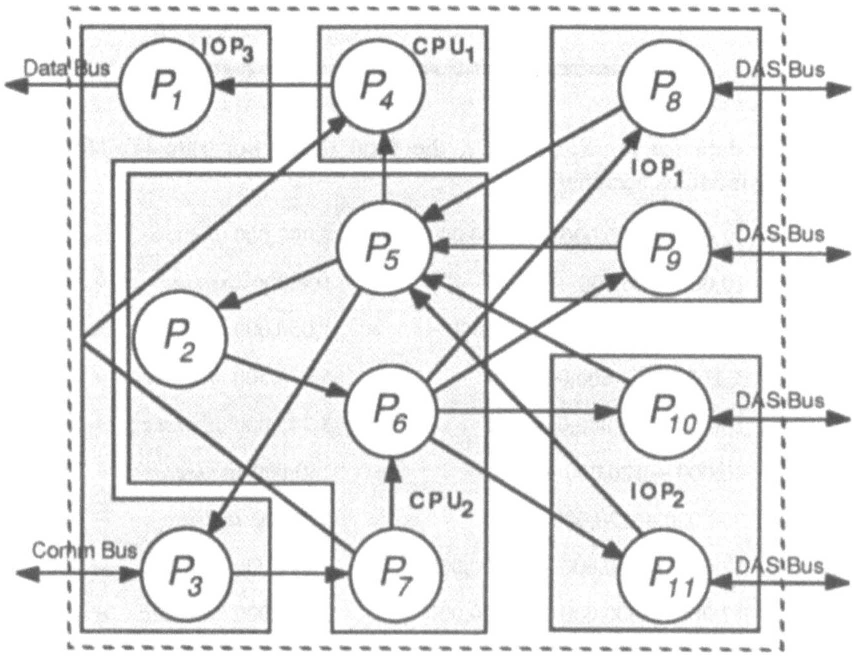

Figure 5.4 - Partitioning function of the DAP system into five processing elements: three I/O processors and two CPUs

The tightly coupled multiprocessor system, shown in Figure 5.5, consisting of five processing elements, three configured as I/O processors and two as CPU processors, meets these requirements.

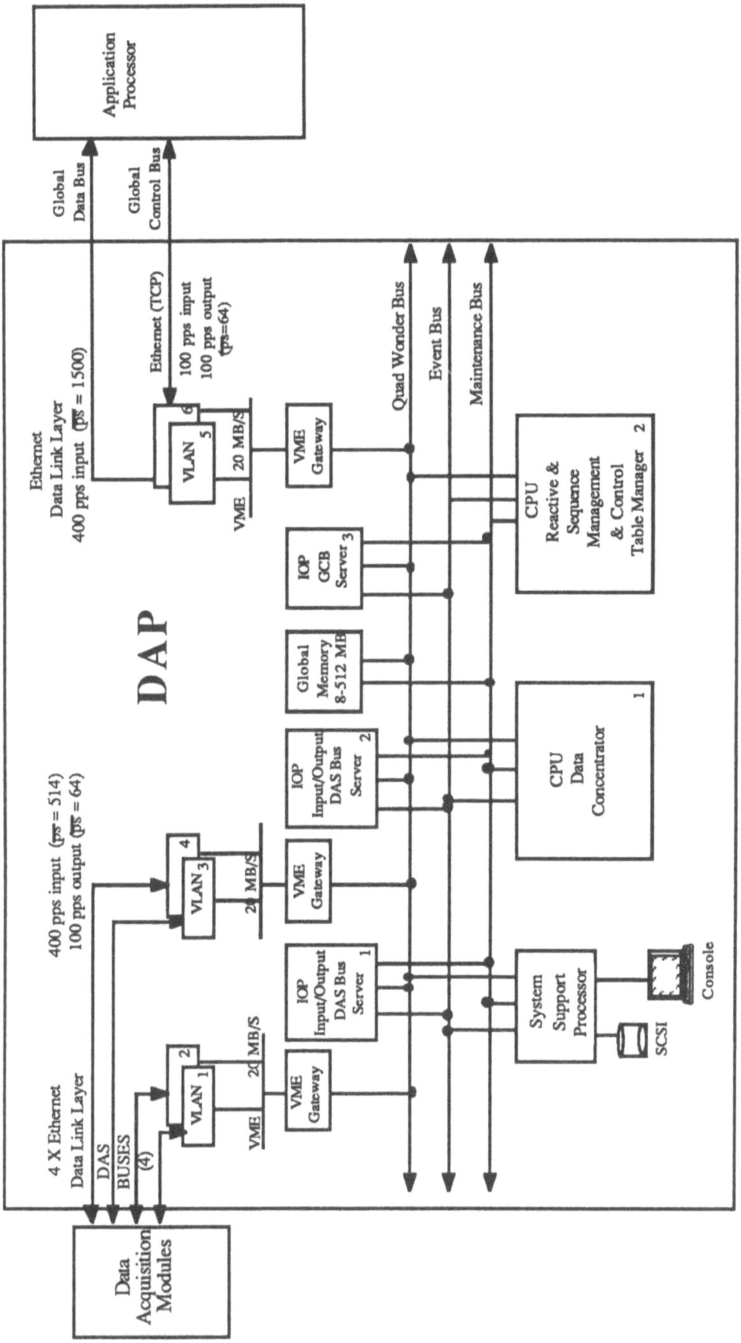

Figure 5.5 - The tightly coupled multiprocessor sy stem configured as the Data Acquisition Processor

Communication Requirements Analysis. The tightly coupled multiprocessor supports the TCP/IP network protocol. These communications functions are provided by the Ethernet controllers connected via the VMEbus™. The maximum transfer rate is 1.2 Mbytes/sec. Performance of the network depends on the layer at which the communication is performed and the packet size. Table 5.3 shows experimental results obtained for the VLAN-E Ethernet controller.

This data was obtained from a dedicated, two-node network. Each node was a MODCOMP model-9730 processor with 8 megabytes of main memory. The model-9730 is based on a Motorola® model-147 CPU board with a Motorola 25 MHz 68030 processor.

Table 5.3
Performance Evaluation of the VLAN-E Ethernet Controller

Layer	Packet size [bytes]	Transfer rate Packets/sec	Kbytes/sec
Data Link Layer	64 512 1024	1937 1486 1169	121 743 1169
UDP	64 512 1024	390 536 497	24 268 497
TCP	64 512 1024 1500	548 361 263 133	34 180 263 195

Front-end Communications. The front-end communications are handled by two I/O processors (#1 and #2) which are used as the I/O DAS bus servers and four related VLAN ethernet controllers (#1 to #4), as shown in Figure 5.5.

The VLAN controllers receive the data from DAMs via DAS buses, form a packet, and when the packet is ready, they send an interrupt to the corresponding I/O DAS bus data server. In response to the interrupt, the I/O DAS bus data server receives the data via the VME bus and stores it in the global memory. The solution proposed here is based on four independent Ethernet lines where communication is performed at the Data Link layer. According to Table 5.3, the transfer rate of the VLAN controller is 1486 packets/sec (or 734 Kbytes/sec), when the packet size is 512 bytes. This meets the DAP requirements, of 400 packets/sec with an average packet size of 514 bytes.

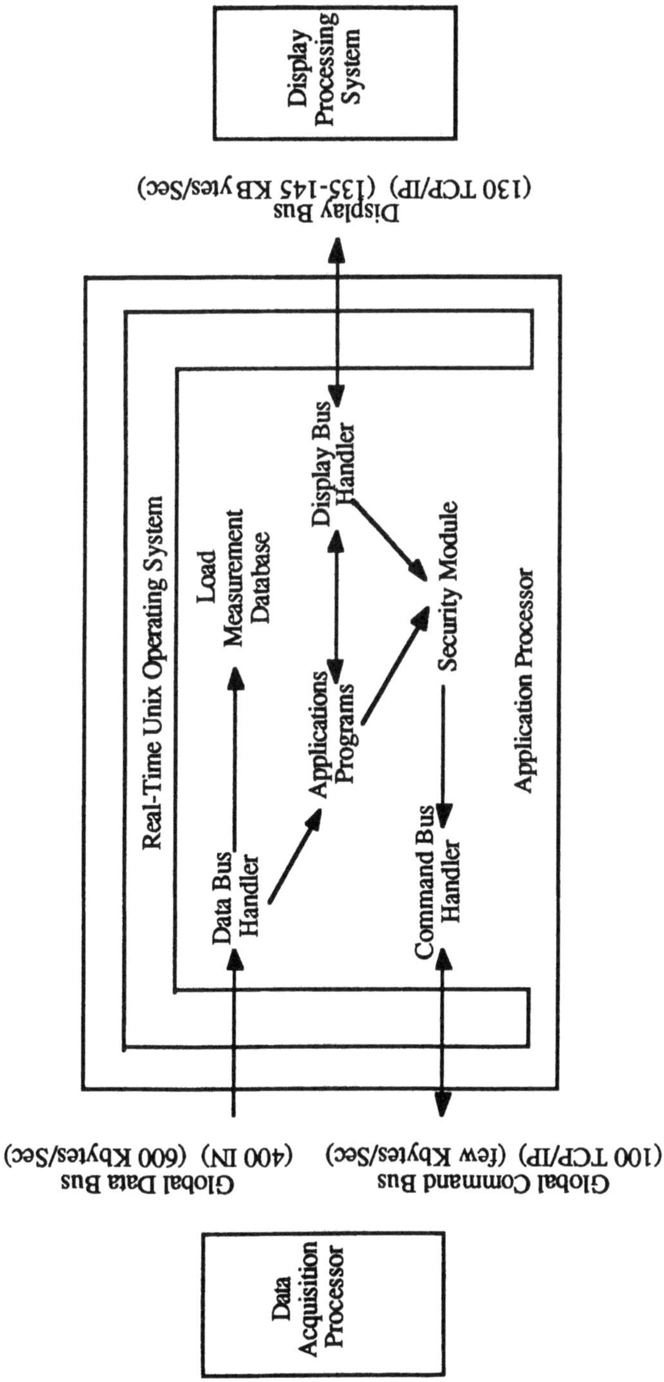

Figure 5.6 - Functional diagram of the Application Processor

The proposed solution to handle the interface to the Application Processor via the General Data Bus consists of another I/O processor (#3), which serves as the GCB Server, and two related VLAN Ethernet controllers (#5 and #6). The VLAN controller (#5) interrupts the GCB Server, whenever it is ready to send the next packet. The GCB Server then passes the packet from the global memory to the VLAN controller, which then sends the packet to the Application Processor. The throughput requirement of 400 pps (ps=1500 bytes), is met at the Data Link layer. As shown in Table 5.3, the transfer rate at the Data Link layer is 1169 pps, with ps=1024 bytes, which exceeds the requirements.

Command Communications. Commands are handled by the I/O processor (#3), the GCB Server, and the VLAN Ethernet controller (#6). The VLAN controller receives the commands from the Application Processor and when the packet is ready, sends an interrupt to the GCB server. This server receives the packet and stores it in global memory. It also sends the corresponding acknowledgement packet, via the VLAN controller, to the Application Processor. The throughput requirements are 100 pps per input and 100 pps per output (average packet size is 64 bytes), which gives a total of 200 pps. The proposed solution is the communication at the TCP level, at which the transfer rate is 548 pps (ps=64 bytes), as indicated in Table 5.3.

5.1.2 The Application Processing System

The Application Processing System, or the Application Processor (AP) acts as a gateway to the rest of the system for the user workstations (DPs). It provides a local copy of every measurement's latest value, which is directly accessible by any application or display program executing in that AP. This allows user programs to dynamically test a measurement without prior setup or overhead and with minimum latency time. The alternative to this would be a mechanism where only those measurements that are currently being looked at by executing programs are updated. The disadvantages to this are the implied system build overhead and much longer latency time for a measurement. Packet traffic could build up considerably and thus reduce overall performance of the system.

The functional diagram of the Application Processor is given in Figure 5.6.

The AP Model. The AP model is derived [Luke89] in order to obtain the worst case computational requirements for the AP. The AP system from Figure 5.6 is partitioned into six processing modules, as shown in Figure 5.7.

The six processing modules have the following functions:

P_1 = Data Bus Handler
P_2 = Command Bus Handler
P_3 = Display Server
P_4 = Application Programs
P_5 = Security Module

P_6 = Display Bus Handler
P_7 = Interrupt Processor

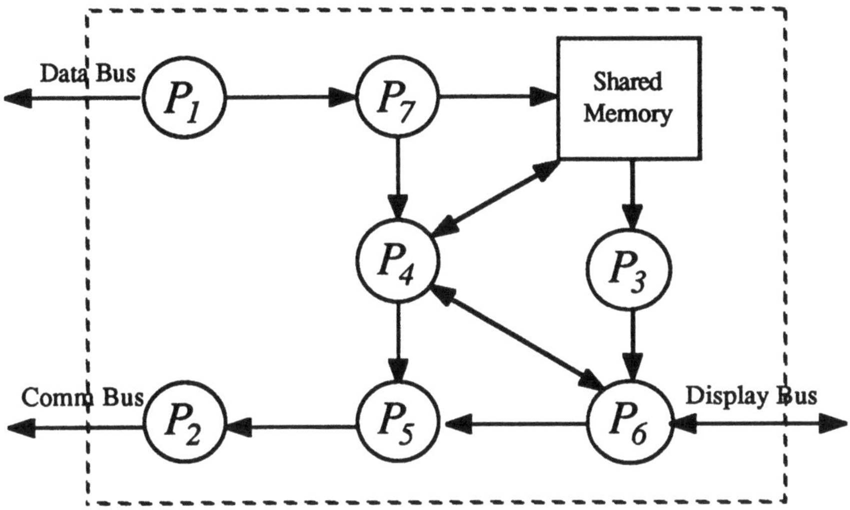

Figure 5.7 - Application Processor Model

In order to handle the worst case data rates, the Application Processor must support the following:

a. Network Interfaces

- 400 packets received per second on the Data Bus
- 400 total packets sent per second on the Display Bus
- 100 packets per second sent on the Display Bus per DP
- 25 packets per second received on the Display Bus
- 25 packets per second sent on the Command Bus

b. Processing Power

As in the case of the Data Acquisition Processor, the required processing power consists of application instruction rate, system call overhead, and context switch overhead.

The application instruction rates (P_i) for seven processing elements and the total application instruction rate (P) are computed as follows:

$$P_1 = \frac{D_{PR}}{M_{length}} \times N_1 = \frac{141{,}719}{8} \times 400 = 5{,}740{,}000\ inst/sec$$

$$P_2 = \frac{D_{PR}}{M_{length}} \times N_2 = \frac{24{,}663}{8} \times 100 = 310{,}000 \; inst/sec$$

$$P_3 = M_3 \text{ X } N_3 = 4000 \text{ X } 100 = 400{,}000 \; inst/sec$$

$$P_4 = M_4 \times 4 = 500{,}000 \times 4 = 2{,}000{,}000 \; inst/sec$$

$$P_5 = \frac{D_{PR}}{M_{length}} \times N_5 = \frac{24{,}663}{8} \times 50 = 310{,}000 \; inst/sec$$

$$P_6 = M_6 \times N_6 = 4000 \times 50 = 200{,}000 \; inst/sec$$

$$P_7 = M_7 \times N_7 = 4000 \times 40 = 160{,}000 \; inst/sec$$

$$P = \sum_{i=1}^{n} P_i = 8{,}960{,}000 \; inst/sec$$

System call overheads (S_i) are calculated as:

$$S_1 = P_R \times I_S = 400 \times 1800 = 720{,}000 \; inst/sec$$

$$S_2 = P_R \times I_S = 50 \times 1200 = 60{,}000 \; inst/sec$$

$$S_6 = P_R \times I_S = 425 \times 1200 = 510{,}000 \; inst/sec$$

$$S_7 = P_R \times I_S + E_R \times I_S = 400 \times 600 + 20 \times 1200 = 264{,}000 \; inst/sec$$

$$S = \sum_{i=1}^{n} S_i = 1{,}554{,}000 \; inst/sec$$

where:

P_R = Packet Rate

D_{PR} = Practical Data Rate

M_{length} = Measurement length

I_S = Number of system instructions

E_R = Exception Rate

The context switch overheads (C_i) are given as:

$$C_1 = P_R \times I_S = 400 \times 4000 = 1{,}600{,}000 \; inst/sec$$

$$C_3 = P_R \times I_S = 50 \times 4000 = 200{,}000 \; inst/sec$$

$$C_6 = P_R \times I_S = 425 \times 4000 = 1{,}700{,}000 \; inst/sec$$

$$C_7 = E_R \times I_S = 20 \times 4000 = 80{,}000 \; inst/sec$$

$$C = \sum_{i=1}^{n} C_i = 3{,}580{,}000 \; inst/sec$$

The total processing power required for the Application Processor is summarized in Table 5.4

Table 5.4
Processing Power Required by the AP

Process	Inst/sec
Application	8,960,000
System Calls	1,554,000
Context Switches	3,580,000
Total	14,094,000

The tightly coupled multiprocessor system as the Application Processor. The AP model from Figure 5.7 is used to map the application processor into the tightly coupled multiprocessor architecture.

Using the data for P_i, S_i, and C_i, the total instruction rate (T_i) for seven processing modules becomes:

$$T_1 = 5{,}740{,}000 + 720{,}000 + 1{,}600{,}000 = 8{,}060{,}000 inst/sec \approx 8.1 \text{ MIPS}$$

$$T_2 = 310{,}000 + 60{,}000 = 370{,}000 inst/sec \approx 0.4 \text{ MIPS}$$

$$T_3 = 400{,}000 + 200{,}000 = 600{,}000 inst/sec \approx 0.6 \text{ MIPS}$$

$$T_4 = 2{,}000{,}000 = 2{,}000{,}000 inst/sec \approx 2 \text{ MIPS}$$

$$T_5 = 150{,}000 = 150{,}000 inst/sec \approx 0.15 \text{ MIPS}$$

$T_6 = 200{,}000 + 510{,}000 + 1{,}700{,}000 \quad = 2{,}410{,}000\,inst/sec \quad \approx 2.5$ MIPS

$T_7 = 160{,}000 + 264{,}000 + 80{,}000 \quad = 504{,}000\,inst/sec \quad \approx 0.5$ MIPS

Total = 14.25 MIPS

Assuming the tightly coupled multiprocessor as the AP system and 33 MHz MC68030 microprocessors as the CPU elements, then each CPU will provide 6.5 to 9.5 native machine instructions/sec and the AP model can be partitioned as shown in Figure 5.8.

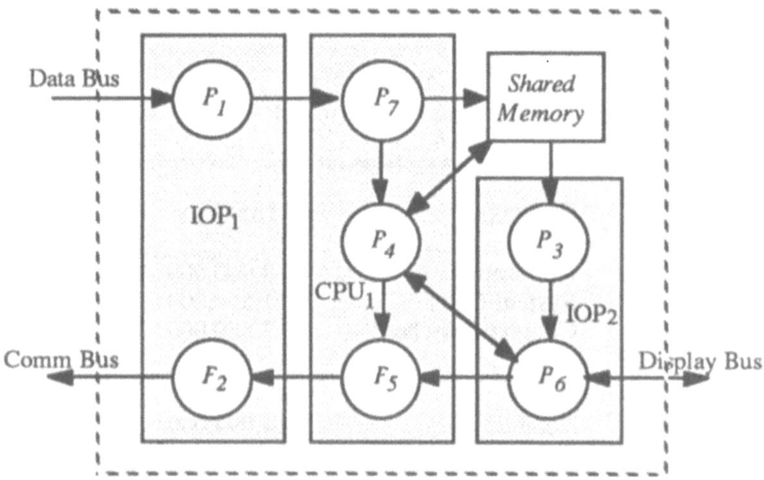

Figure 5.8 - Functional partitioning of the AP system into three processing elements: two I/O processors and one CPU

Thus, the tightly coupled multiprocessor system consists of three processing elements: two for I/O processing and one for application processing. Data and Command Bus Handlers (P_1 and P_2) are partitioned into IOP_1, while Display Server (P_3) and Display Bus Handler (P_6) are partitioned into IOP_2. Application Programs (P_4), Security Module (P_5), and Interrupt Processing Module (P_7) are partitioned into CPU_1.

These three processing elements require the following instruction rate:

$IOP_1 = T_1 + T_2 = 8.1 + 0.4 = 8.5$ Minst/sec

$IOP_2 = T_3 + T_6 = 0.6 + 2.5 = 3.1$ Minst/sec

$CPU_1 = T_4 + T_5 + T_7 = 2 + 0.15 + 0.5 = 2.65$ Minst/sec

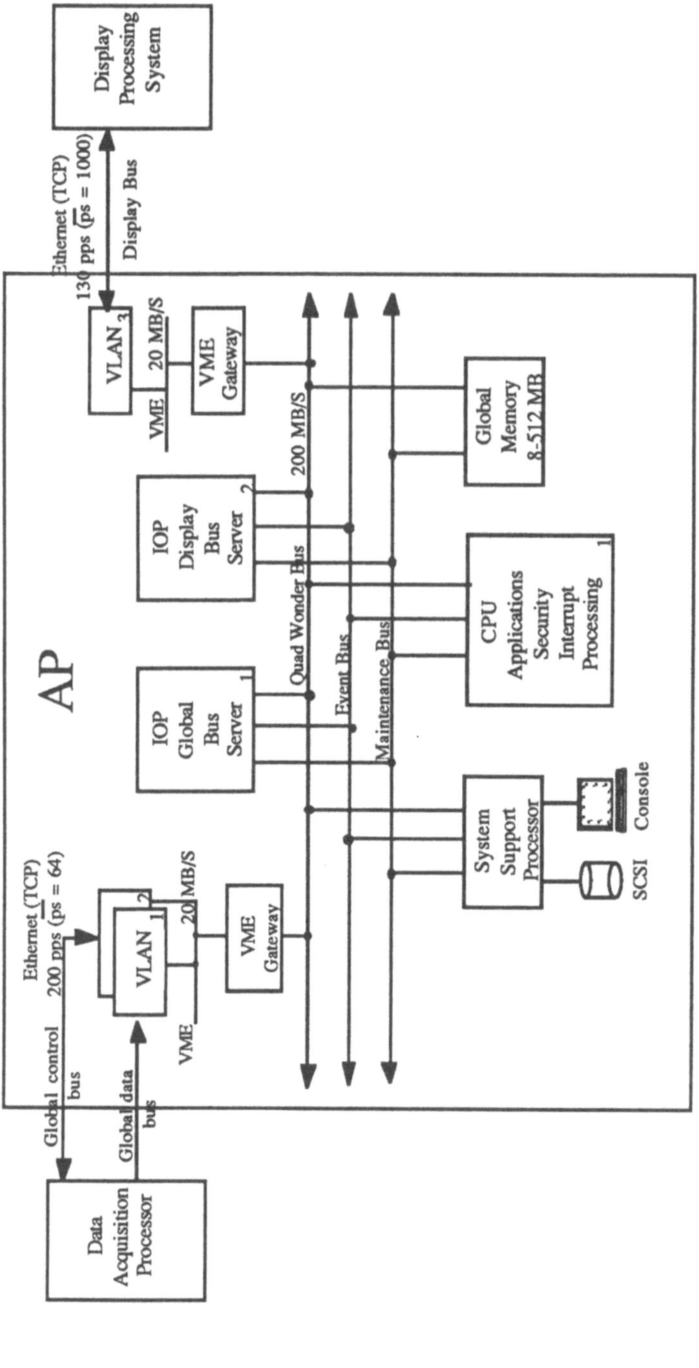

Figure 5.9 - The tightly coupled multiprocessor system configured as the Application Processor

The tightly coupled multiprocessor system, presented in Figure 5.9, consisting of three processing elements meets these instruction processing requirements. Note that functions of IOP_2 and CPU_1 could be combined in one processing element (total required processing power would be 5.75 Minst/sec), however, the proposed solution clearly distinguishes I/O and processing functions, and more readily accommodates future extensions.

The communication requirements of the AP are resolved with the VLAN Ethernet Controllers using an approach similar to that used for the DAP.

In conclusion, this case study has illustrated how a complex application, the Data Acquisition and Space Shuttle Launch Control System at NASA Kennedy Space Center, which requires both intensive communications and high processing power, can be mapped into an open system architecture. This is achieved by employing a tightly-coupled multiprocessor system which includes a high bandwidth common memory bus, an efficient interrupt distribution scheme, and dedicated high-performance I/O processors.

5.2 THE COMMUNICATION PROCESSOR AT JET PROPULSION LABORATORY

This case study represents a demonstration system designed for Jet Propulsion Laboratory in Pasadena, California. The purpose of the demonstration system is to prove that the four most important capabilities required in this JPL application can all be exercised simultaneously. These four elements are (1) the disks, (2) the IEEE-488, (3) the digital I/O interface, and (4) the IEEE-802.3 LAN interface.

The system consists of two MODCOMP Tri-D 9735 machines which are based on 25 MHz MC68030 processors, run the REAL/IX operating system, and include additional components, as shown in Figure 5.10.

The demonstration software system consists of the following tasks:

- Test block generator tasks in both systems which generate data blocks of 600 bytes and pass them to either the protocol software for the IEEE-802.3 LAN interface, the digital I/O interface handler, or to the IEEE-488 handler. Data is generated as one stream at a rate of 2.5 Mbits/second (Mbs) and two streams at 0.5 Mbs, as indicated in Figure 5.10.

  The stream is defined with a unique header portion and a data portion. The header consists of: source address, destination address, serial number of each block, time of day the block was created, and an additive checksum. The data portion consists of a bit pattern.

- The REAL/IX operating system provides the following handlers, indicated in Figure 5.10: (a) disk handler, (b) IEEE-802.3 handler, (c) IEEE-488 handler, (d) line printer handler, and (e) digital I/O handler.

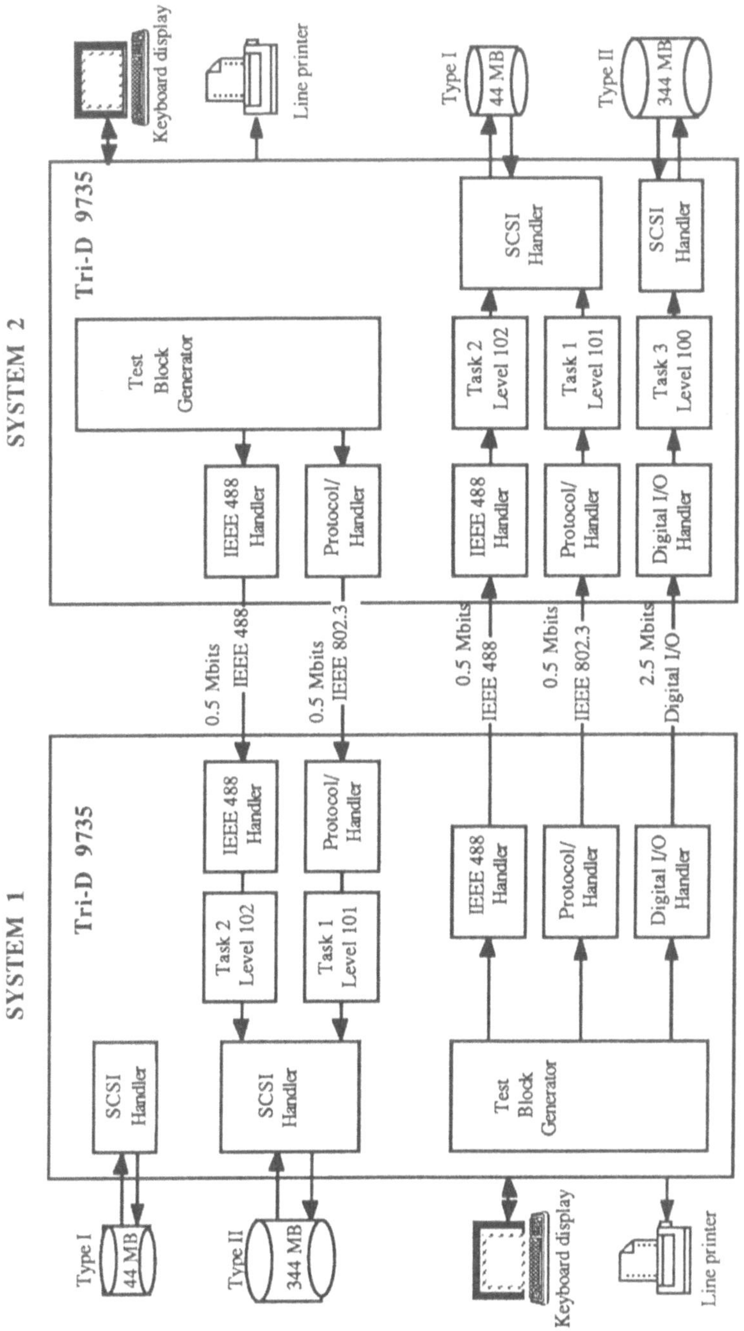

Figure 5.10 - System configuration for the JPL demonstration system

- Task 1 takes data from the IEEE-802.3 handler and writes it to the disk. Two identical tasks 1 run in both systems at priority level 101.
- Task 2 takes data from the IEEE-488 handler and writes it to the disk. Two identical tasks 2 run in both processors at priority level 102.
- Task 3 takes data from the digital I/O handler and writes it to the disk. This task runs only in system 2 at priority level 100.
- A utility task runs after the test and is able to read the disks. The task summarizes the data on the disk, including: number of blocks, source, destination, sequence number, and time. It also reports the number of missing blocks, the number of blocks in error (determined by the checksum), and the sequence numbers of the missing blocks.
- An idle task runs at the lowest priority (254). It runs an infinite loop of fixed known duration and counts iterations through the loop. Every five seconds spent in the idle task is measured as "idle" time, and represents the amount of CPU time left for other applications that are not required to perform data transfers.

The operation of the demonstration system consists of the following steps:

1. Boot each machine and initialize the software.
2. Input the header and data parameters for each test generation.
3. Start up the first two streams in system 1 which run at 0.5 Mbs. The first stream is sent to the IEEE-488 and the other to the IEEE 802.3 interfaces. The two blocks arrive at system 2, and they are recorded on the type 1 disk. These streams run at least 2 minutes and the CPU utilization of both machines is measured.
4. Start up the third stream in system 1 which runs at 2.5 Mbs. This stream is sent over the digital I/O to system 2, where task 3 receives the data and writes it to the type II disk. The CPU utilization of both machines is measured.
5. Two 0.5 Mbs streams are started in system 2. The first stream is sent to the IEEE-488, and the second to the IEEE-802.3 interface. The data is recorded on the type II disk on system 1.
6. The data flow continues until all the disks are full.

The test verification consists of measuring and continuously displaying the CPU idle time. In addition, upon completion of the test, the utility program runs to verify the contents of the disks.

JPL's requirements for the CPU idle time were: 35% for system 1 and 18% for system 2.

The demonstration system consisting of two 9735 machines, which were running the REAL/IX operating system, achieved the following CPU idle times: 45% for system 1, and 31% for system 2 [Hell90].

For illustration, Figures 5.11, 5.12, and 5.13 show C programs for tasks 1, 2, and 3, respectively.

Note that all three tasks have the same structure. They all consist of (a) an initialization part in which the task requests real-time privileges in order to set up its priority, to connect to shared memory, and to initialize the interface and the disk transfer; and (b) the main loop, in which the task receives the data from the handler, packs the data, and transfers the data to the disk.

```
/*
        Task12 reads from Ethernet and writes to /TYPE1/stream1
        Runs in CPU2
*/

#include <sys/types.h>
#include "common.h"
#include <fcntl.h>
#include <stdio.h>
#include <errno.h>
#include <signal.h>
#include <sys/ipc.h>
#include <sys/shm.h>

extern int errno;
char *getmem();

int chksum();
void alldone();

static int nread = 0;
static struct testblock buf;

main(argc,argv)
int argc;
char **argv;
{
        register int i;
        register struct common *cmn;
        int err;
        int shmid;
/*
 *      request real-time privileges
 */
        if (setrt() == -1) {
                fprintf(stderr,"task12: cannot setrt()\n");
                exit(-1);
        }
/*
 *      set priority  to 101
 */
        if (setpri(0,101) == -1) {
                fprintf(stderr,"task12: cannot setpri()\n");
                exit(-2);
        }

/*
 *      connect to shared memory
 */
        if ((cmn = (struct common *)getmem(TBGETBUFFERS, 1)) ==
                        (struct common *)-1) {
                fprintf(stderr,"task12: cannot shmget(), errno = %d\n", errno);
                exit(-1);
        }

        cmn->taskpid[0] = getpid();
/*
 *      initialize TCP/IP
 */
        tcprinit();
/*
 *      initialize disk write subroutine
 */
        if ((err = wdinit("/TYPE1/stream1")) != 0) {
```

Figure 5.11 - Task 1: Reads data from the IEEE-802.3 and writes to the disk

```
                fprintf(stderr,
                        "task12: cannot open output device, error = %d, errno = \
%d\n", err, errno);
                exit(-4);
        }
/*
 *      set up to catch stop signal
 */
        sigset(SIGQUIT, alldone);
/*
 *      MAIN LOOP
 */
        for (nread = 0; ; nread++) {
/*
 *      read TCP/IP
 */
                if ((i = tcpread((char *)&buf, BLOCKSIZE)) != BLOCKSIZE) {
                        fprintf(stderr,"task12: TCP/IP read %d characters\n", i)\
;
                        if (i == 0)
                                alldone();
                }
/*
 *      pack input data for transfer to disk
 */
                pack(&buf, i);
        }
}

void
alldone()
{
        int i;
        long buf[BLOCKSIZE / 4];

        for (i = 0; i < (BLOCKSIZE / 4); i++)
                buf[i] = 0;
        pack((struct testblock *)buf, BLOCKSIZE);
        flush();
        fprintf(stderr,"Number of blocks read from Ethernet = %d\n",nread);
        exit(0);
}
```

Figure 5.11 cont'd

```
/*
        Task21 reads from IEEE 488 and writes to /TYPE2/stream2
        Runs in CPU 1
*/
#include "common.h"
#include <sys/types.h>
#include <fcntl.h>
#include <stdio.h>
#include <errno.h>
#include <signal.h>
#include <sys/evt.h>
#include <sys/aio.h>
#include <sys/cintrio.h>
#include <sys/gpib.h>
#include <sys/ipc.h>
#include <sys/shm.h>

#define TRUE 1
#define FALSE 0

extern int errno;
extern int ready[];
int chksum();
char *getmem();
void alldone();

static int nread = 0;

static event_t evnt;
static int eid1, eid3;
static struct cintrio intr;
static int stat;
static struct aiocb aio[4];
static int data[4];


main(argc,argv)
int argc;
char **argv;
{
        register struct common *cmn;
        register char *buf;
        int shmid;
        int i;
        register int fd;
        int err;
        register int one = TRUE;
/*
 *      request real-time privileges
 */
        if (setrt() == -1) {
               fprintf(stderr,"task21: cannot setrt()\n");
               exit(-1);
        }
/*
 *      set priority to 102
 */
        if (setpri(0,102) == -1) {
               fprintf(stderr,"task21: cannot setpri()\n");
               exit(-2);
        }
/*
 *      allocate I/O buffer space in A24 memory
 */
        if ((buf = (char *)getmem(TASK2BUFFERS, 1)) == (char *)-1) {
               fprintf(stderr,"task21: cannot shmget(), errno = %d\n", errno);
```

Figure 5.12 - Task 2: Reads data from the IEEE-488 and writes to the disk

```
                exit(-1);
        }
/*
 *      connect to shared memory
 */
        if ((cmn = (struct common *)getmem(TBGENBUFFERS, 1)) ==
                        (struct common *)-1) {
                fprintf(stderr,"task21: cannot shmget(), errno = %d\n", errno);
                exit(-1);
        }
        cmn->taskpid[1] = getpid();
/*
 *      open IEEE 488 device
 */
        if ((fd = open("/dev/gpib1_list", O_RDONLY)) == -1) {
                fprintf(stderr,"task21: cannot open /dev/gpib1_list, errno = %d\\
n", errno);
                exit(-3);
        }
/*
 *      input will be queued in two bursts of two asynchronous reads.
 *      the second read in each burst will have an event associated
 *      with its completion.
 *
 *      get two events from the OS
 */
        if (( eid1 = evget(EVT_QUEUE,0,0,0)) == -1 ) {
                fprintf(stderr,"task21: evget failed!, %d",errno);
                exit(-101);
        }
        if (( eid3 = evget(EVT_QUEUE,0,0,0)) == -1 ) {
                fprintf(stderr,"task21: evget failed!, %d",errno);
                exit(-101);
        }
/*
 *      initialize buffers for transfer to disk
 */
        if ((err = wdinit("/TYPE2/stream2")) != 0) {
                fprintf(stderr,"task21: cannot open output device, error = %d, e\
rrno = %d\n", err, errno);
                exit(-4);
        }

/*
 *      initialize four asynchronous I/O contrlo blocks
 */
        for (i = 0; i < 4; i++) {
                aio[i].rt_errno = 0;
                aio[i].whence = 0;
                aio[i].aioflag = 0;
                aio[i].offset = 0;
                aio[i].nobytes = 0;
                aio[i].eid = 0;
        }
        aio[1].aioflag = EVT_POST;
        aio[1].eid = eid1;
        aio[3].aioflag = EVT_POST;
        aio[3].eid = eid3;

/*
 *      start all four reads
 */
        for (i =0; i < 4; i++)
                if (aread(fd, &buf[i * BLOCKSIZE], BLOCKSIZE, &aio[i]) == -1)
                        fprintf(stderr,"task21(%d): cannot queue aread, errno = \
%d\n",
```

Figure 5.12 - cont'd

```
                                        i, errno);

/*
 *      set up to catch stop signal
 */
        sigset(SIGQUIT, alldone);

/*
 *      MAIN LOOP
 */
        for (;;) {
/*
 *      wait for an event
 *      if the event identifier > 1 (in this case 2 or 3), the event
 *      belongs to the pack subroutine, so pass it on to pack, via ready[]
 */
                evrcv(1,&evnt);
                if (evnt.ev_eid > 1) {
                        ready[evnt.ev_eid - 2] = TRUE;
                        continue;
                }
/*
 *      find out which of the two burst completed.
 *      do error checking and report errors unless timeout, in which
 *      case ignore the error.
 *      if no error, pack the block for transfer to disc.
 *      in either case, fire off the two reads again
 */
                i = 0;
                if (evnt.ev_eid == eid3)
                        i = 2;
                if (aio[i].rt_errno) {
                        if (aio[i].rt_errno == EINPROG)
                                fprintf(stderr,"task21(%d):ouch!\n", i);
                        if (aio[i].rt_errno != ETIME)
                                fprintf(stderr,"task21(%d): could not read from \
IEEE, %d\n",
                                        i, aio[0].rt_errno);
                } else {
                        pack((struct testblock *) &buf[i * BLOCKSIZE], BLOCKSIZE\
);
                        nread++;
                }
                if (aread(fd, &buf[i * BLOCKSIZE], BLOCKSIZE, &aio[i]) == -1)
                        fprintf(stderr,"task21(%d): cannot queue aread, errno = \
%d\n",
                                i, errno);
                i++;
                if (aio[i].rt_errno) {
                        if (aio[i].rt_errno == EINPROG)
                                fprintf(stderr,"task21(%d):ouch!\n", i);
                        if (aio[i].rt_errno != ETIME)
                                fprintf(stderr,"task21(%d): could not read from \
IEEE, %d\n",
                                        i, aio[0].rt_errno);
                } else {
                        pack((struct testblock *) &buf[i * BLOCKSIZE], BLOCKSIZE\
);
                        nread++;
                }
                if (aread(fd, &buf[i * BLOCKSIZE], BLOCKSIZE, &aio[i]) == -1)
                        fprintf(stderr,"task21(%d): cannot queue aread, errno = \
%d\n",
                                i, errno);
        }
}
```

Figure 5.12 - cont'd

```
void
alldone()
{
        int i;
        long buf[BLOCKSIZE / 4];

        for (i = 0; i < (BLOCKSIZE / 4); i++)
                buf[i] = 0;
        pack((struct testblock *)buf, BLOCKSIZE);
        flush();
        fprintf(stderr,"Number of blocks read from IEEE 488 = %d\n",nread);
        exit(0);
}
```

Figure 5.12 - cont'd

```
/*
        Task3 reads from DR11W and writes to /TYPE2/stream3
        Runs in CPU2
*/

#include <sys/types.h>
#include "common.h"
#include <fcntl.h>
#include <stdio.h>
#include <errno.h>
#include <signal.h>
#include <sys/drw_ioctl.h>
#include <sys/aio.h>
#include <sys/evt.h>
#include <sys/ipc.h>
#include <sys/shm.h>

char *getmem();
extern int errno;
extern int ready[];
int chksum();
void alldone();

static int nread = 0;
static struct aiocb aio[5];
static int eid[5];
static event_t ev;

#define TRUE 1

main(argc,argv)
int argc;
char **argv;
{
        register int fd;
        register int i;
        int err;
        int shmid;
        register struct common *cmn;
        register char *buf;
/*
 *      request real-time privileges
 */
        if (setrt() == -1) {
                fprintf(stderr,"task3: cannot setrt()\n");
                exit(-1);
        }
/*
 *      set priority to 100
 */
        if (setpri(0,100) == -1) {
                fprintf(stderr,"task3: cannot setpri()\n");
                exit(-2);
        }
/*
 *      allocate I/O buffer space in A24 memory
 */
        if ((buf = (char *)getmem(TASK3BUFFERS, 1)) == (char *)-1) {
                fprintf(stderr,"task3: cannot shmget(), errno = %d\n", errno);
                exit(-1);
        }
/*
 *      connect to shared memory
 */
        if ((cmn = (struct common *)getmem(TBGENBUFFERS, 1)) ==
                        (struct common *)-1) {
```

Figure 5.13 - Task 3: Reads data from the digital I/O (DRIIW) and writes to the disk

```
                fprintf(stderr,"task3: cannot shmget(), errno = %d\n", errno);
                exit(-1);
        }
        cmn->taskpid[2] = getpid();

/*
 *      open DR11W device
 */
        if ((fd = open("/dev/vdr0", O_RDONLY)) == -1) {
                fprintf(stderr,"task3: cannot open input device, errno = %d\n", \
errno);
                exit(-3);
        }
/*
 *      initialize DR11W to use attention with a 5 second timeout
 */
        ioctl(fd, DR11WSET_ATTN, 0);
        ioctl(fd, DR11W_TIMEOUT, 5);
/*
 *      set up to catch stop signal
 */
        sigset(SIGQUIT, alldone);
/*
 *      input will be queued in two bursts of two asynchronous reads.
 *      the second read in each burst will have an event associated
 *      with its completion.
 *      the following code sets up four asynchronous I/O control blocks
 *      obtains two events from the OS and starts all four reads
 */
        aio[0].offset = 0;
        aio[0].whence = 0;
        aio[0].rt_errno = 0;
        aio[0].nobytes = 0;
        aio[0].aioflag = 0;
        aio[0].eid = 0;
        if (aread(fd, buf, BLOCKSIZE, &aio[0]) == -1) {
                fprintf(stderr,"task3: cannot queue aread, errno = %d\n",errno);
                exit(-6);
        }
        aio[1].offset = 0;
        aio[1].whence = 0;
        aio[1].rt_errno = 0;
        aio[1].nobytes = 0;
        aio[1].aioflag = EVT_POST;
        if ((eid[1] = evget(EVT_QUEUE, 0, 0, 0)) == -1) {
                fprintf(stderr,"task3: cannot evget(), errno = %d\n", errno);
                exit(-5);
        }
        aio[1].eid = eid[0];
        if (aread(fd, buf + BLOCKSIZE, BLOCKSIZE, &aio[1]) == -1) {
                fprintf(stderr,"task3: cannot queue aread, errno = %d\n",errno);
                exit(-6);
        }
        aio[2].offset = 0;
        aio[2].whence = 0;
        aio[2].rt_errno = 0;
        aio[2].nobytes = 0;
        aio[2].aioflag = 0;
        aio[2].eid = 0;
        if (aread(fd, buf + (2 * BLOCKSIZE), BLOCKSIZE, &aio[2]) == -1) {
                fprintf(stderr,"task3: cannot queue aread, errno = %d\n",errno);
                exit(-6);
        }
        aio[3].offset = 0;
        aio[3].whence = 0;
        aio[3].rt_errno = 0;
```

Figure 5.13 - cont'd

```
        aio[3].nobytes = 0;
        aio[3].aioflag = EVT_POST;
        if ((eid[1] = evget(EVT_QUEUE, 0, 0, 0)) == -1) {
                fprintf(stderr,"task3: cannot evget(), errno = %d\n", errno);
                exit(-5);
        }
        aio[3].eid = eid[1];
        if (aread(fd, buf + (3 * BLOCKSIZE), BLOCKSIZE, &aio[3]) == -1) {
                fprintf(stderr,"task3: cannot queue aread, errno = %d\n",errno);
                exit(-6);
        }
/*
 *      initialize disk buffers for transfer
 */
        if ((err = wdinit("/TYPE2/stream3")) != 0) {
                fprintf(stderr,"task3: cannot open output device, error = %d, er\
rno = %d\n",
                        err, errno);
                exit(-4);
        }
/*
 *      MAIN LOOP
 */
        for (;;) {
/*
 *      wait for an event
 *      if the evnt identifier > 1 (in this case 2 or 3), the event belongs
 *      to the disk pack subroutine, so pass it on using ready[]
 */
                if (evrcv(1, &ev) == -1) {
                        fprintf(stderr,"task3: evrcv failed, errno = %d\n", errn\
o);
                        exit(-5);
                }
                if ((i = ev.ev_eid) > 1) {
                        ready[i - 2] = TRUE;
                        continue;
                }
/*
 *      find out which burst of I/O completed
 *      if error, report it, otherwise pack it for transfer to disk
 */
                if ( i == 0 ) {                                         \
/* 1st set of aio's is done */
                        if (aio[0].rt_errno)
                                fprintf(stderr,"task3: aread returned rt_errno =\
 %d\n",
                                        aio[0].rt_errno);
                        else {
                                nread++;
                                pack(buf, BLOCKSIZE);
                        }
                        if (aread(fd, buf, BLOCKSIZE, &aio[0]) == -1) {
                                fprintf(stderr,"task3: cannot queue aread, errno\
 = %d\n",errno);
                                exit(-6);
                        }
                        if (aio[1].rt_errno)
                                fprintf(stderr,"task3: aread returned rt_errno =\
 %d\n",
                                        aio[1].rt_errno);
                        else {
                                nread++;
                                pack(buf + BLOCKSIZE, BLOCKSIZE);
                        }
                        if (aread(fd, buf + BLOCKSIZE, BLOCKSIZE, &aio[1]) == -1\
```

Figure 5.13 - cont'd

```
) {
                                        fprintf(stderr,"task3: cannot queue aread, errno\
 = %d\n",errno);
                                        exit(-6);
                                }
                        }
                        else {                                                  /* 2nd s\
et of aio's is done */
                                if (aio[2].rt_errno)
                                        fprintf(stderr,"task3: aread returned rt_errno =\
 %d\n",
                                                aio[2].rt_errno);
                                else {
                                        nread++;
                                        pack(buf + (2 * BLOCKSIZE), BLOCKSIZE);
                                }
                                if (aread(fd, buf + (2 * BLOCKSIZE), BLOCKSIZE, &aio[2])\
 == -1) {
                                        fprintf(stderr,"task3: cannot queue aread, errno\
 = %d\n",errno);
                                        exit(-6);
                                }
                                if (aio[3].rt_errno)
                                        fprintf(stderr,"task3: aread returned rt_errno =\
 %d\n",
                                                aio[3].rt_errno);
                                else {
                                        nread++;
                                        pack(buf + (3 * BLOCKSIZE), BLOCKSIZE);
                                }
                                if (aread(fd, buf + (3 * BLOCKSIZE), BLOCKSIZE, &aio[3])\
 == -1) {
                                        fprintf(stderr,"task3: cannot queue aread, errno\
 = %d\n",errno);
                                        exit(-6);
                                }
                        }
                }
}

void
alldone()
{
        int i;
        long buf[BLOCKSIZE / 4];

        for (i = 0; i < (BLOCKSIZE / 4); i++)
                buf[i] = 0;
        pack((struct testblock *)buf, BLOCKSIZE);
        flush();
        fprintf(stderr,"Number of blocks read from DR11W = %d\n",nread);
        exit(-6);
}
```

Figure 5.13 - cont'd

Bibliography

[Aho88] A. V. Aho, B. W. Kermigham, and P. J. Weinberger, "The AWK Programming Language", Prentice-Hall, Englewood Cliffs, NJ, 1988.

[Arth86] J. Arthur, "Programmer Productivity and the UNIX System", *UNIX World*, July 1986, pp. 26-33.

[Bach84] M. J. Bach and S. J. Buroff, "Multiprocessor UNIX Operating Systems", *The Bell System Technical Journal*, Vol. 63, No. 8, October 1984, pp. 151-167.

[Bach86] M. J. Bach, "The Design of the UNIX Operating System", Prentice-Hall, Englewood, Cliffs, NJ, 1986.

[Bode84] D. E. Bodenstab, T. F. Houghton, K. A. Kellerman, G. Roukin, and E. P. Schau, "UNIX Operating System Porting Experiences", *AT&T Bell Laboratories Technical Journal*, Vol. 63, No. 8, October 1984, pp. 1769-1790.

[Bour78] S. R. Bourne, "The UNIX Shell", *The Bell System Technical Journal*, Vol. 57, No. 6, July-August 1978, Part 2, pp. 1971-1990.

[Bour83] S. R. Bourne, "The UNIX System", Addison-Wesley, Reading, MA, 1983.

[Bunt76] R. B. Bunt, "Scheduling Techniques for Operating Systems", *Computer*, Vol. 9, No. 10, October 1976, pp. 10-17.

[Carr89] L. Carr, R. Kibler, S. Hippen, and T. Gargrave, "G32: A High Performance VLSI 3D Computer", *Proceedings of the 22nd IEEE Hawaii Conference on System Sciences*, Kona, Hawaii, January 1989.

[Chen88] S. C. Cheng, J. A. Stankovic, and K. Ramamrithan, "Scheduling Algorithms for Hard Real-Time Systems", *IEEE Tutorial on Hard Real-Time Systems*, IEEE Computer Society, 1988, pp. 150-173.

[Cole85] C. T. Cole and J. Sundman, "UNIX in Real-Time", *UNIX Review*, November 1985, pp. 61.

[Cook84] B. Cook, G. Ho, "Real-Time Extensions to the UNIX Operating System", *Proceedings of the UniForum*, Washington, D.C., January 1984, pp. 293-299.

[Cool83] E. Coolahan, and N. Roussopoulus, "Timing Requirements for Time-Driven Systems Using Augmented Petri Nets", *IEEE Trans. on Software Engineering*, Vol. 9, No. 5, September 1983, pp. 603-616.

[Dasa85] B. Dasarathy, "Timing Constraints of Real-Time Systems: Constructs for Expressing Them, Methods for Validating Them", *IEEE Trans. on Software Engineering*, Vol. 11, No. 1, January 1985, pp. 80-86.

[Deit90] H. M. Deitel, "An Introduction to Operating Systems", Second Edition, Addison-Wesley Publishing Company, 1990.

[Dema78] T. DeMarco, "Structured Analysis and System Specification", Yourdon Press, New York, 1978.

[Dija68] E. W. Dijakstra, "Cooperating Sequential Processes", in F. Gennys ed., "Programming Languages", Academic Press, New York, 1968, pp. 43-112.

[Dough87] S. M. Doughty, S. F. Kary, S. R. Kusmer, and D. V. Larson, "UNIX for Real Time", *Proceedings of the UniForum 1987*, Washington D. C., January 1987, pp. 219-230.

[Egan88] J. I. Egan and T. J. Teixeira, "Writing a UNIX Device Driver", John Wiley and Sons, New York, 1988.

[Emer89] "Real-Time UNIX in Critical Real-Time and Transaction Processing", Vol. 1, 1989, Emerging Technologies Group, Inc., 1989.

[Falk88] H. Falk, "Developers Target UNIX and ADA with Real-Time Kernels", *Computer Design*, April 1, 1988, pp. 55-70.

[Furh89a] B. Furht, G. Rabbat, R. Kibler, J. Parker, and D. Gluch, "The Design of Tri-D Real-Time Computer Systems", *Proceedings of the Euromicro Workshop in Real-Time*", Como, Italy, June 1989, pp. 84-92.

[Furh89b] B. Furht, J. Parker D. Grostick, H. Ohel, T. Kapish, T. Zuccarelli, and O. Perdomo, "Performance of REAL/IX - A Fully Preemptive Real-Time UNIX", *ACM Operating Systems Review* Vol. 23, No. 4, October 1989, pp. 45-52.

[Furh89c] B. Furht, O. Perdomo, and P. Shironoshita, "MODCOMP's Tri-Dimensional Analyzer", *Real Times*, Vol, 1, No. 2, Fall 1989, pp. 6-7.

[Furh90a] B. Furht, D. Grostick, D. Gluch, J. Parker, and W. Pastucha, "Issues in the Design of an Industry Standard Operating System for Time-Critical Applications", *Proceedings of the Real-Time 90*, Stuttgart, W. Germany, June 1990.

[Furh90b] B. Furht, D. Joseph, D. Gluch, and J. Parker "Open Systems for Time-Critical Applications in Telemetry", *Proceedings of the International Telemetry Conference*, Las Vegas, Nevada, October, 1990.

[Furh90c] B. Furht, D. Gluch, and D. Joseph, "Performance Measurements of Real-Time Comptuer Systems", *Proceedings of the International Telemetry Conference*, Las Vegas, Nevada, October, 1990.

[Gajs87] D. Gajski, V. M. Milutinovic, H. J. Segel, and B. Furht, eds., "Computer Architecture", *IEEE Tutorial*, Computer Society Press, 1987.

[Gluc89] D. P. Gluch, and B. Furht, "Fault Tolerance Strategies for High-Performance Real-Time Computers", *International Journal of Mini and Microcomputers*, Vol. 11, No. 2, June 1989, pp. 24-30.

[Gros90] D. Grostick, D. Gluch, and B. Furht, "REAL/IX: A Real-Time UNIX Operating System", *Presented at the International Conference on Accelerator and Large Equipment Physics Control Systems*, Vancouver, Canada, October 1989, and published in *Nuclear Instruments and Methods in Physics Research*, A293, 1990, pp. 271-275.

[Hell90] M. Hellstrom, L. Skipper, "JPL Test Results", Report, MODCOMP, Fort Lauderdale, Florida, May 1990.

[Hotl88] D. J. Hotley, and I. A. Pribhai, "Strategies for Real-Time System Specification", Dorset House Publishing, New York, NY, 1988.

[John78] S. C. Johnson, and D. M. Ritchie, "Portability of C Programs and the UNIX System", *The Bell System Technical Journal*, Vol. 57, No. 6, Part 2, July-August 1978, pp. 2021-2048.

[Kar89] P. Kar and K. Porter, "Rhealstone - A Real-Time Benchmarking Proposal", *Dr. Dobb's Journal*, February, 1989, pp. 14-24.

[Kern84] B. W. Kernighan and R. Pike, "The UNIX Programming Environment", Prentice-Hall, Englewood Cliffs, NJ, 1984.

[Kuro84] J. F. Kurose, M. Schwartz, and Y. Yemini, "Multiple-Access Protocols and Time-Constrained Communication", *Computing Surveys*, Vol. 16, No. 1, March 1984, pp. 43-70.

[Lapi87] J. E. Lapia, "Portable C and UNIX Programming", Prentice-Hall, Englewood Cliffs, NJ, 1987.

[Levi90] S. T. Levi, A. K. Agrawala, "Real-Time System Design", McGraw-Hill Publishing Company, 1990.

[Luke89] D. Luken, "GCS Performance Study", Report, NASA Kennedy Space Center, August 1989.

[McKu84] M. K. McKusick, W. N. Joy, S. J. Leffler, and R. S. Fabry, "A Fast File System for UNIX" *ACM Transactions on Computer Systems*, Vol. 2, No. 3, August 1984, pp. 2103-2114.

[Moor85] R. F. Moore, "Programming in C with a Bit of UNIX", Prentice-Hall, Englewood Cliffs, NJ, 1985.

[Peac84] D. R. Peachey, R. B. Bunt, C. L. Williamson, and T. B. Brecht, "An Experimental Investigation of Scheduling Strategies for UNIX", *Performance Evaluation Review*, 1984 SIGMETRICS Conference on Measurement and Evaluation of Computer Systems, Vol. 12, No. 3, August 1984, pp. 158-166.

[Pusc89] P. Puschner and C. Koza, "Calculating the Maximum Execution Time of Real-Time Programs", *Real Time Systems Journal*, Vol. 1, No. 2, September 1989, pp. 159-176.

[Rabb88a] G. Rabbat, B. Furht, R. Kibler, "Three-Dimensional Computers and Measuring Their Performance", *ACM Computer Architecture News*, Vol. 16, No. 3, June 1988, pp. 9-16.

[Rabb88b] G. Rabbat, B. Furht, R. Kibler, "Three-Dimensional Computer Performance", *Computer*, Vol. 21, No. 7, July 1988, pp. 59-60.

[Ripp89] D. L. Ripps, "An Implementation Guide to Real-Time Programming", Yourdon Press, Englewood Cliffs, NJ, 1989.

[Ritc81] D. M. Ritchie and K. Thompson, "Some Further Aspects of the UNIX Time-Sharing System", *Mini-Macro Software*, Vol. 6, No. 3, 1981, pp. 9-12.

[Ritc84a] D. M. Ritchie, "The Evolution of the UNIX Time-Sharing System", *AT&T Bell Laboratories Technical Journal*, Vol. 63, No. 8, Part 2, October 1984, pp. 1577-1594.

[Ritc84b] D. M. Ritchie, "A Stream Input Output System", *AT&T Bell Laboratories Technical Journal*, Vol. 63, No. 8, Part 2, October 1984, pp. 1897-1910.

[Sha86] L. Sha, J. D. Lehoczky, and P. Rajkumar, "Solutions for Some Practical Problems in Prioritized Preemtpvie Scheduling", *Proceedings of the IEEE Real-Time System Symposium*, New Orleans, LA, December 1986, pp. 181-191.

[Simp89] D. Simpson, "Will the Real-Time UNIX Please Stand-Up", *System Integration*, December 1989, pp. 46-52.

[Stan88a] J. A. Stankovic, and K. Ramamrithan, "Tutorial on Hard Real-Time Systems", *IEEE Computer Society*, 1988.

[Stan88b] J. A. Stankovic, "Misconceptions About Real-Time Computing", *Computer*, Vol. 21, No. 10, October 1988, pp. 10-19.

[SVID85] "System V Interface Definition", Issue 1, AT&T Customer Information Center, Indianapolis, IN, Spring, 1985.

[Tane85] A. Tanenbaum and R. Von Rennesse, "Distributed Operating Systems", *ACM Computing Surveys*, Vol. 17, No. 4., December 1985, pp. 419-470.

[Thom74] K. Thompson and D. M. Ritchie, "The UNIX Time-Sharing System" *Communications of the ACM*, Vol. 17, No. 7, July 1974, pp. 365-375.

[Thom78] K. Thompson, "UNIX Implementation", *The Bell System Technical Journal*, Vol. 57, No. 6, Part 2, July - August 1978, pp. 1931-1946.

[Unif89] UniForum, "Your Guide to POSIX", Santa Clara, California, 1989.

[Vana84] J. Vanada, "Vanada Benchmark", Sampson Computer Consulting, Inc., Pleasant Valley, Iowa, 1984.

Index

accessing files, 82
aeronautical engineering and space transportation systems, 11
Application Processing System, 274, 275, 286
archival and data base system, 274
asynchronous I/O, 39, 41, 43, 50, 55, 75, 84, 85, 106, 107, 110, 229, 232, 233, 234, 235, 236, 237, 271

batch control applications, 7
binary semaphores, 73, 113, 151, 152, 154, 156, 201, 202, 203, 204, 206
binary standards, 42
block, 33
block I/O, 85
block size, 85, 87, 89, 91, 92, 114, 120, 230, 263
buffer cache, 50, 55, 82, 84, 85, 102, 104, 105, 106, 230, 232, 259
bypassing the buffer cache, 86, 229, 231, 233, 204

cache memory, 18
centralized system, 4, 34
child process, 57, 58, 60, 61, 82, 84, 87, 115, 124, 144
common event notification, 73, 75, 85, 109, 233
common event notification mechanism, 50, 84, 140, 146, 232, 239, 259
communication processor, 11, 273, 292
connected interrupts, 50, 75, 109, 111, 114, 116, 146, 236, 239, 247
context switch, 26, 38, 39, 60, 65, 68, 114, 120, 125, 127, 238, 278, 281, 287, 289
contiguous files, 50, 229
continuous performance systems, 19
creating files, 230

Data Acquisition Modules, 275
data caching, 86
data region, 57, 63, 64, 137, 138, 141, 142
data storage blocks, 88, 91, 92, 93, 94, 96
datagram throughput, 21, 24, 25
deadline scheduling, 2, 3
deadlock breaking time, 21, 24
descriptor table, 82, 96, 99, 100, 101, 229
device driver, 91, 101, 102, 109, 236, 237, 251
device files, 54, 78, 101, 102, 144
device I/O, 101
device interrupts, 107
device switch tables, 102
digital I/O, 294, 302
digital I/O handler, 292, 294
digital I/O interface, 292
direct I/O, 50, 103, 109, 111, 114, 236, 249
directories, 77, 78, 80, 81, 88, 100, 263, 265
directory files, 77
directory organization, 265
directory tree, 78, 96
disk handler, 292
display processing system, 274
distributed system, 4, 34
driver entry point routines, 102, 106
drivers, 39, 41, 52, 55, 56, 68, 85, 102, 109, 110, 111, 116, 146, 151, 239

electric utility monitoring, 8
energy management system, 10, 11
energy management system, 10
ethernet controller, 284, 286, 292
event, 1, 13, 38, 39, 70, 71, 72, 75, 76, 114, 142, 144, 150, 238, 239

event bus, 18
event identifier, 142
event mechanism, 76, 129, 144, 146, 147, 240
event notification, 75, 109, 146, 147, 240
event structure, 148, 149
extent list, 90, 93, 231
extents, 229
external interfaces system, 274

F5, 229, 231, 263
  architecture, 82
  file system architecture, 230, 231
  file systems, 114, 120
fast file system, 229
file
  access tables, 99
  descriptors, 82
  extents, 96
  listings, 78
  names, 77, 81, 87
  permissions, 79
  subsystems, 49, 50, 53, 54, 77, 78, 83, 101, 229, 235
  systems, 41, 50, 78, 80, 81, 82, 85, 87, 88, 90, 91, 92, 93, 94, 96, 97, 101, 113, 114, 120, 229, 230, 231, 235, 236, 261, 262, 263, 266
  system access tables, 96
  system organization, 265
  system requirements, 4
  system structure, 87, 263
  types, 77
fixed-priority scheduler, 66
fixed-priority scheduling, 2
flags, 90

General Language System, 34
graceful degradation, 19, 20

handling events asynchronously, 149
handling events synchronously, 150
hard real-time (HRT) systems, 2, 12, 13
header files, 158, 163, 182, 258, 260
high availability systems, 19

I/O
  operations, 106
  subsystem, 20, 49, 50, 53, 54, 78, 82, 101, 229
  transfer methods, 104
IEEE POSIX, 34, 46
IEEE-488 handler, 292, 294
IEEE-802.3 handler, 292, 294
inodes, 81, 87, 88, 90, 91, 92, 93, 94, 96, 229, 231, 235, 266
instrumentation systems, 7, 12
interfacing devices, 236
interprocess communication mechanisms, 113
interprocess communications, 13, 38, 39, 40, 49, 50, 113, 144, 151, 154, 177, 201, 208
interrupt, 26, 38, 238, 239, 268, 286
  handler, 238
  handling, 1, 14, 26, 27, 40, 103, 108, 109
  handling routine, 238, 239
  latency, 26
  latency time, 21, 22, 23
  level, 102, 105
  notification, 240
  vector, 107, 108
IPC mechanisms, 144, 151

Jet Propulsion Laboratory, 273, 292

kernel
  function, 109, 121, 252
  kernel preemption, 33, 46, 68, 120
  kernel preemption and scheduling, 121
  kernel semaphores, 56, 68, 69
  level
    semaphores, 69
    driver, 116
    processes, 147

library routines, 53

line printer handler, 292
locking pages into memory, 139

memory
  allocation, 39, 63, 64, 113, 137, 138
  management, 13, 15, 50, 53, 59, 60, 61, 137, 138
  memory violations, 75, 139, 140, 143
messages, 21, 40, 50, 51, 73, 111, 113, 144, 151, 152, 156, 208
metal industry applications, 7
Motif, 34
multiple host access systems, 11

NASA Kennedy Space Center, 273, 292

object standards, 42
on-line transaction processing, 12
open system call, 53, 99, 100
open systems, 3, 33, 41, 42

packet switched networks, 11
page fault handler, 63
page faults, 62, 238
paging, 62, 63, 64, 71, 86, 140, 264
paging areas, 262
path name, 78, 79, 80, 99, 100
path name conversion, 101
petrochemical applications, 7
pipes, 40, 144, 151
pipes and named pipes, 73, 144
planetary exploration applications, 11
portability, 86
porting applications, 46, 257
porting SVID-compatible applications, 258
POSIX standards, 43
posting an event, 147
preallocating file space, 116, 230
preallocating memory, 140
preemption points 33, 46, 47, 48
preemption time, 21, 22, 25
preemptive kernel, 48, 49, 65, 68
preemptive scheduler, 47
preemptive scheduling, 38
priority queuing, 104
privileges, 54, 55, 66, 76, 79, 114, 123, 295
process
  concept, 55
  creation and termination, 57,26, 44, 269
  environment, 56, 57
  priorities, 40, 65, 71, 122, 125
  region, 60
  scheduling, 64
  states, 58, 59
  subsystem, 49, 55
process dispatch latency time, 21
program overhead, 29
proprietary systems, 3, 15, 41
proprietary UNIX, 46

Quad Wonder Bus, 17, 18

real-time
  communications, 1, 11, 12, 20, 35
  computing, 1, 3, 34, 50
  measures, 1, 21, 29, 33
  operating systems, 12
  privileges, 55, 123, 124, 125
  system architectures, 12
  systems 3, 12, 20, 21, 33, 39
  timers, 39, 44, 71, 72, 128
  UNIX standards, 37, 41
Real/Stone, 32
Real/Stone benchmark, 21, 30, 31
region table, 60, 154, 264
resident system call, 64
Rhealstone Metric, 21, 25
root directory, 80, 99
run queue, 46, 64, 67, 127

S5, 229, 263
S5 architecture, 82, 87, 229, 230
S5 file systems, 120
SCADA, 9
SCADA/EMS systems, 9
scheduler, 40, 44, 46, 49, 64, 66, 104, 123, 127

scheduling processes, 113, 120
SCSI interface, 51
semaphores 15, 39, 43, 48, 50, 51, 69, 73, 77, 144, 151, 152, 156, 177, 180, 186
semaphore processor, 19
semaphore shuffling time, 21, 23
shared memory, 4, 39, 40, 43, 50, 60, 61, 63, 64, 73, 76, 113, 118, 137, 138, 139, 147, 151, 154, 156, 160, 162, 295
shared memory identifier, 157
shared memory region, 156, 157
shared memory segment, 155, 157, 168
shared memory system calls, 155
sharing files, 87
shell 43, 52, 57, 84, 116, 123, 127, 260
shell programming, 120
signal mechanism, 50, 73, 75, 146, 149
soft real-time (SRT) systems, 2
source standards, 42
space transportation systems, 11
spin locks, 48, 56, 68, 70
stack region, 55, 57, 137, 138, 139
synchronization, 13, 48, 68, 70, 177, 235
synchronization mechanism, 77
synchronous, 236
synchronous file systems, 90, 235
synchronous I/O, 236
system calls, 53
system clock, 70
system overhead, 29, 76, 103, 249
system performance, 86

task scheduling, 2
task switching time, 21, 22
TCP/IP, 35, 45, 284
time-sharing scheduling, 66
timers, 70
timing functions, 71
trainers and simulators, 12
tri-dimensional analyzer, 269
tri-dimensional measure, 21, 27

virtual address, 43, 77, 118, 202
VME standard, 35
VMEbus, 284
Volume, 11, 28, 29, 272

water plant monitoring, 10

X-Window 34

MIX
Papier aus verantwortungsvollen Quellen
Paper from responsible sources
FSC® C105338

If you have any concerns about our products,
you can contact us on
ProductSafety@springernature.com

In case Publisher is established outside the EU,
the EU authorized representative is:
Springer Nature Customer Service Center GmbH
Europaplatz 3, 69115 Heidelberg, Germany

Printed by Libri Plureos GmbH
in Hamburg, Germany